THE FABLES OF LA FONTAINE

ALSO BY MARIANNE MOORE

Collected Poems

LA FONTAINE BY JEAN ANTOINE HOUDON

The Fables of
LA FONTAINE

Translated by
MARIANNE MOORE

New York
THE VIKING PRESS · MCMLIV

Thanks are due to E. McKnight Kauffer for the design of the monogram which appears on the binding
of this book.

Of the fables in this volume, certain appeared originally in *Perspectives USA, Harper's Magazine, Yale
French Studies, New Republic, Poetry, The Hudson
Review, The Kenyon Review, Harper's Bazaar, Coun-
terpoint, Accent, Chicago Review, Partisan Review,*
and *Encounter.*

Library of Congress catalog card number: 54-6427

PRINTED IN THE U.S.A. BY THE VAIL-BALLOU PRESS, INC.

To

John Warner Moore

CONTENTS

CONTENTS

PART FIVE

APPENDIX

INDEXES

FOREWORD

Acknowledgments other than performance are artless, besides running the risk of incriminating rather than honoring. I should like to say, however, that W. H. Auden—consulted by a publisher in 1945 —is responsible for this undertaking, and is to be thanked in so far as the result is an asset, forgiven if a detriment; he has not seen it— subsequently attempted for The Viking Press on condition that Professor Harry Levin examine the work to ensure a sound equivalent for the French. Possible "refreshment against chores of the term" became what must have seemed to him a verbal counterpart of the Laocoön; and if "revision is its own reward," the reviser rather than the adviser should be the one to say so. Remuneration—one's instinctive expedient to offset the maiming endlessness of preceptorial altruism—was summarily declined by Professor Levin on the ground that "it would make him professional and seem to know more than" he did—modesty thus lending luster to virtuosity; if this rendering of the fables is not "neat," it is not the fault of the preceptor. Titanic patience and commensurate linguistic tenacities, necessitated by disparity in education, merit a better protégée; acknowledgment is a travesty.

After scholastic intensities of supervision such as the twelve books of fables involve, they were at intervals, as completed, submitted to The Viking Press—to Pascal Covici and Monroe Engel. Persisting ungainlinesses were then ameliorated by Mr. Engel. As consulting editor at the Press, Malcolm Cowley pronounced portions of the text "rather far from the French"; he has contributed lines in addition to pedagogy, and but for the disservice of being credited with what he might repudiate, should be denominated Supervisor Extraordinary of the present version. My first endeavors were supervised by Walter Pistole and Elizabeth Ford, and I have been aided by Mrs. M. K. Chamberlain, Miss Kathrine Jones, Glenway Wescott, Monroe Wheeler, Mrs. Henry Church, Miss Malvina Hoffman, Pierre Schneider, and Donald Gallup. The rectifying for me by Kathrine Jones of an erroneous concept of accent constituted for me not mere timely assistance but a veritable rescue, as may be inferred from my effort to approximate the original rhythms of the fables. And in this regard the reading aloud by Wallace Fowlie and Robert Franc, of certain typical fables, obviated purblindnesses of indecision.

The influence here of Ezra Pound as translator may not be apparent, but for rhythm and syntax, unsatisfactory though the result may be to him, I reiterate with the immodesty of the amateur that the practice of Ezra Pound has been for me a governing principle—as deduced from his "Guido Cavalcanti," his "Seafarer," and certain French songs: the natural order of words, subject, predicate, object; the active voice where possible; a ban on dead words, rhymes synonymous with gusto.

Verbal decorum on the part of my mother, and impatience with imprecision, have influenced me to dislike, if not avoid, contractions and the wish for the deed. Perceptible progression toward climax in certain fables is the result of drastic if brief insistence on the part of my brother that the English should embody the equivalent in emphasis of emphasis in the French. Fixed confidence on his part in the auspiciousness of my efforts—an understatement indeed—has been a main factor in my perseverance.

By presenting me with significant scarce versions of the fables, Lester Littlefield has afforded me aid so indispensable, its importance for me could not so much as be suggested. He, Mrs. Chamberlain, Mrs. W. Murray Crane, Lincoln Kirstein, William McCarthy, Wallace Stevens, W. Bryher, Miss Elizabeth Bishop, and Howard Griffin have made possible for me a comparison of rarities with trade editions. And, worthy or flat, these fables constitute a gratitude to the John Simon Guggenheim Memorial Foundation and to the Bollingen Foundation, Inc., for what is to me the epitome of liberality—assurance that if the translation should fall short of its possibilities, even so, it would have been an attempt justifying support.

Mrs. John Schmidt's typing and retypings of the text have not merely facilitated publication but have contributed permanently to my morale.

MARIANNE MOORE

June 1953

PARTS ONE AND TWO

To
HIS ROYAL HIGHNESS
THE DAUPHIN

REVERED PRINCE,

Could there be anything in the whole of literature more ingenious than Aesop's manner of teaching? Would that a hand more accomplished than mine were lending it the enticement of poetry—considered not inappropriate by the wisest of ancient philosophers. I am venturing, revered Prince, to provide you with certain tales. They are indeed the very thing for one of tender years. At an age when recreation and pastimes are permitted a prince, you will be thinking now and again of what is serious; all of which we find in Aesop. And his simplicities, though of a juvenile aspect, I admit, are simplicities cloaking what in truth is profound.

Need one ask if OUR YOUNG LORDSHIP could look other than favorably upon ingenuities so profitable and at the same time delightful! What more could one desire? such preoccupations having been responsible for the growth of science. Aesop surely devised a unique means of attaining two objectives at once: the unsuspecting reader, implanted with the seeds of virtue, acquires self-knowledge without realizing that he does, believing the while that he pursues other ends. This method, so happily employed by the instructor His Majesty has chosen to direct your education, should enable you to learn painlessly, or rather, with enjoyment, whatever a prince ought to know. We look for great things from such a program. But assuredly, MONSEIGNEUR, there are grounds upon which to base yet brighter hopes—the qualities with which our invincible king has endowed you and the example set you by him each day. When you see the noble projects he entertains, and how he contemplates, unmoved, the turmoil in Europe and the forces marshaled to deflect him from his purposes; when he advances at a stride to the heart of a province though hampered at each step by insurmountable obstacles, subduing another in a week, at a time of year unpropitious to war, when he not only masters men but the elements, and upon returning from an expedition in which he has been a victorious Alexander, you find him governing his subjects like an Augustus, are you not, MONSEIGNEUR, despite your youthful years, moved by pride in illustriousness and impatient for the day when you will vie with him in paying court to it, celestial influence that it is? You do not, MONSEIGNEUR, await this glamour but presage it. I need no other proof than your regal impetuosities, your ardent and lively temper, the intelligence, courage, and magnanimity which are your unfailing characteristics. To observe the growth of a young plant that will some day afford shade to numberless peoples and lands, must rejoice not only our supreme ruler, the king, but all mankind.

I might well expand this theme, but being constitutionally better fitted to amuse than to praise, I hasten on to the fables; and to the verities I have presented, MONSEIGNEUR, would merely add that I am in all homage

Your very humble, very obedient,
and very faithful servant,
DE LA FONTAINE

LA FONTAINE'S PREFACE

That some of my fables have met with indulgence encourages me to hope favor for these—not that putting them into verse has not been questioned by one of our masters of composition who thinks their chief ornament is to have none and that the restrictions of meter, together with the rules to which our language must conform, would often embarrass me and in most instances make impossible that conciseness which is the very life of a story, without which interest is sure to flag. This opinion naturally could only have been voiced by a man of taste.[1] I would merely ask that he modify it a trifle and concede that spartan graces and the French muses are not too incompatible to be persuaded at times to walk hand in hand.

After all, I have—I shall not say the ancients' example, which is irrelevant to my purpose—but the sanction of contemporary usage. Whatever the period or nation, verse is, for fables, an accepted expedient. Aesop's fables, as they were called, had no sooner appeared than Socrates perceived that they bespoke the garments of the Muses. Plato's observations in this connection are so charming, I cannot refrain from including them. He said that after Socrates had been condemned to death, the execution was put off because of certain festivities. Cebes went to see him the morning of the day he was to die and Socrates told him that the gods had apprised him in dreams a number of times that he ought to devote himself to the study of music before he died. He had not at first perceived the point of the dream, since if music makes one no better, why study it? Here was a mystery; the stranger, that the gods were continually reminding him of it. He had the dream again at the time of a certain festival; so clearly that while dreaming about this obligation of his to the gods, it came to him that, music and poetry being interrelated, it might possibly be the latter with which he was to concern himself. There is no real poetry without

[1] Patru, the lawyer, friend of Boileau and La Fontaine.

[5]

harmony, any more than without play of fancy, and Socrates never strayed from the truth. Finally he hit upon a compromise; to choose certain fables which contained an element of truth, like Aesop's, and the last moments of life were employed by him in putting them into verse.

Socrates is not the only one who considered poetry and fables akin; Phaedrus testified to the same belief, and thanks to the excellence of his work we may infer how well Socrates, the prince of philosophers, wrote. Then came Avienus, and later, the moderns, not only here but abroad. It is true that when our countrymen wrote fables, the language was so different from ours, we must treat them as foreigners. This, however, by no means deterred me from my undertaking; on the contrary, I flattered myself that if I did not acquit myself well, I at least may be credited with having opened a way to others.

Nor is it impossible that my work should stimulate others to carry the thing further. Far from exhausting the material, I have left more fables in their original form than I have put into verse. I have, to be sure, chosen the best—or should I say those I thought the best; but of course I might be mistaken in my choices; and again, it would not be difficult to give a different turn even to the ones I have chosen; and the new version, if shorter, would be almost certain to be preferred. In any case the world will always be indebted to me, either because my temerity resulted happily and I have not been too wide of the mark, or for encouraging others to do better.

I have perhaps justified my project sufficiently: with what degree of success the reader must judge. He will find nothing like the elegance and concision which set the work of Phaedrus apart—qualities quite beyond me. Since I could not match him there, I felt I must even things by imparting an added liveliness to the work. Not that I find fault with him for acceding to his limitations: Latin admits of only so much; and in this instance, if one is sufficiently analytical, one discovers in him both the quality and spirit of Terence. The simplicity of these masters is dazzling; I, who command nothing like their niceties of speech, cannot even approach it. Yet one must manage to offset insufficiency, and this I have somewhat venturesomely endeavored to do, inasmuch as Quintilian said a story cannot be too vivacious. Need I substantiate the statement? That it is Quintilian's is enough. However, since the fables are familiar to all, I realize that I am contributing nothing if I do not lend them a certain piquancy—the desideratum nowadays—originality, humor. When I say humor I do not mean jocosity, but an alluring, irresistible something that can be imparted to any subject however serious.

It is not by the form I have given it, let me say, that the worth of what I have done should be judged, so much as by its profitableness and content: for what do you find in any works of intellectual ardor foreign to fables? They seem so inspired that many of the ancients attributed most of them to Socrates, the mortal we think of as closest in sympathy with the Divine. I do not know why these particular fables were not supposed to have descended from heaven or why people should not put them under the protection of a god as they did poetry and rhetoric. Nor is what I am saying fantastic, since if what we hold most sacred can be mentioned in the same breath with the errors of paganism, we find that truth herself has spoken in parables, and what is a parable but a fable? that is to say, an imaginary episode used as an illustration; all the more penetrating and effective because familiar and usual. Anyone who offered us none but master minds to imitate would be affording us an excuse for falling short; there is no such excuse when ants and bees are capable of performing the tasks we are set.

So one understands why Plato excluded Homer from his Republic and gave Aesop a place of honor, hoping that the young would absorb fables along with their mothers' milk—advising that nurses teach them to children—since one cannot at too early an age acquire a love for wisdom and virtue. Rather than have to mend bad habits, instill good ones in the young while they are still strangers to virtue or vice. And what better means to this end than fables? Tell a child how, when warring on the Parthians, Crassus invaded the country without having provided a strategy of withdrawal, and thus perished, he and his army, though doing his best to retreat. Tell the same child how the fox and the goat sprang into a well to quench their thirst and how the fox got out by using the goat's shoulders and horns as a ladder, whereas the goat had to stay down, through lack of similar foresight—implying that we should always look before we leap. Now might I ask, which of these expositions would make the deeper impression on a child?

Would it not be the second, which is simpler and better adapted to youthful minds than the other? No need of telling me that children's thoughts are childish enough as it is, better not fill their heads with yet further nonsensical stories—so in appearance only, for fables in reality have plenty of depth. And, as by determining a point, drawing a line, defining an area, and other equally familiar procedures, we arrive at science which measures the sky and earth, in the same way, inferences and conclusions drawn from fables affect habit and insight, fostering ability of a high order.

Nor are the fables just a good influence; they also extend our knowledge of the modes of behavior of animals and thus of ourselves, since we epitomize both the good and the bad in creatures of restricted understanding. Prometheus, when creating man, took the predominant characteristic of every animal, and from contradictory elements formed mankind, instituting what is known as our little universe. So the fables are a panorama in which we see ourselves. What they set forth confirms in persons of riper years truths which experience has affirmed, and teaches children what it is well they should know. Since these last, as little newcomers to the world, do not understand people or themselves, they should not be left in ignorance if we can help it. We should teach them what a lion is, a fox, and so on, and why a person is sometimes compared to a fox or a lion. Fables undertake to do this, providing first impressions of things.

Although I have already exceeded the usual length of a preface, I have not yet touched upon technicalities.

A fable consists of two parts, which might be termed body and soul; the story being the body, and the moral the soul. Aristotle would have nothing but animals in fables, to the exclusion of persons and plants, but this is merely a matter of taste, not a fundamental principle, since neither Aesop, Phaedrus, nor any other fable-writer adheres to it; whereas no one has dispensed with the moral. I have sometimes done so, but only when I could not include it appropriately, or where the reader could supply it himself. In France we consider only what pleases: the one requisite, and, so to speak, the only one. It has never seemed to me a crime to ignore the ancient conventions if one could not adhere to them gracefully. In Aesop's day the fable was told simply, with the moral separate and always at the end. Phaedrus did not confine himself to this arrangement but elaborated the fable proper and sometimes transferred the moral to the beginning. In trying to find a place for it, I may have left it out where it was needed but only as observing a principle no less important—in deference to Horace, who said a writer should not stubbornly go against his limitations or those of the subject. He says a man who wants to write well never does that, but abandons themes with which he knows he can do nothing.

> If you cannot expect a happy result,
> Don't attempt it.

So with me when doubtful about including a moral.

Now in closing a word or two concerning the life of Aesop. I find hardly anyone who does not think Planudes's account of him ficti-tious. Critics are given to saying that it attempts to create a personality and experiences that would correspond with the fables, and the notion impressed me as plausible at first, but is a theory that in the end failed to satisfy me. It is partly based on the account of Xanthus and Aesop. They say it is too full of absurdities. Though what wise man has not been similarly victimized? Even the life of Socrates has its farcical side. Confirming my impression, Aesop's personality as presented by Planudes is identical with the one given him by Plutarch in his Ban-quet of the Seven Sages; that is to say, a subtle fellow who allows nothing to escape him. I shall be told by someone inclined to doubt the whole thing that the "Banquet" also is feigned. For my own part, I can scarcely see how Plutarch—a man who made a point of relia-bility and fidelity to his subject—could have wished posterity to be misled by his work.

Suppose he did, I should merely mislead on the strength of another's deception. Would I seem more trustworthy if I devised something my-self, since all I can offer is conjecture, which I shall call "The Life of Aesop"? However plausible I made my account, nobody could take it for certainty, and fable for fable the reader would always prefer Planudes's version to mine.

[9]

FABLES

À MONSEIGNEUR

LE DAUPHIN

Je chante les héros dont Ésope est le père,
Troupe de qui l'histoire, encor que mensongère,
Contient des vérités qui servent de leçons.
Tout parle en mon ouvrage, et même les poissons.
Ce qu'ils disent s'adresse à tous tant que nous sommes.
Je me sers d'animaux pour instruire les hommes.
ILLUSTRE REJETON D'UN PRINCE aimé des Cieux,
Sur qui le monde entier a maintenant les yeux,
Et qui, faisant fléchir les plus superbes têtes,
Comptera désormais ses jours par ses conquêtes,
Quelque autre te dira d'une plus forte voix
Les faits de tes aïeux et les vertus des rois.
Je vais t'entretenir de moindres aventures,
Te tracer en ces vers de légères peintures,
Et, si de t'agréer je n'emporte le prix,
J'aurai du moins l'honneur de l'avoir entrepris.

FABLES

I sing when Aesop's wand animates my lyre.
Make-believe is here in its antique attire—
Insight confirmed by direct observation;
Even fish speak. As each finds expression,
Animals enact my universal theme,
Educating man, fantasist though I seem.
DAZZLING CHILD OF A PRINCE whom the gods have made their care,
All eyes converge upon what you may be and are.
With the noblest minds acknowledging your sway,
You'll count your days by conquests in glittering array.
Resonance deeper than mine must sing
What it was and is to have been born a king.
These verses sketch on unassuming textures,
The byplay of inconsequential creatures;
And if I have failed to give you real delight,
My reward must be that I had hoped I might.

BOOK ONE

THE GRASSHOPPER AND THE ANT

Until fall, a grasshopper
      Chose to chirr;
With starvation as foe
When northeasters would blow,
And not even a gnat's residue
Or caterpillar's to chew,
She chirred a recurrent chant
Of want beside an ant,
Begging it to rescue her
With some seeds it could spare
Till the following year's fell.
"By August you shall have them all,
Interest and principal."
Share one's seeds? Now what is worse
For any ant to do?
Ours asked, "When fair, what brought you through?"
—"I sang for those who might pass by chance—
Night and day, an't you please."
—"Sang, you say? You have put me at ease.
A singer! Excellent. Now dance."

THE FOX AND THE CROW

On his airy perch among the branches
    Master Crow was holding cheese in his beak.
Master Fox, whose pose suggested fragrances,
    Said in language which of course I cannot speak,

"Aha, superb Sir Ebony, well met.
How black! who else boasts your metallic jet!
If your warbling were unique,
Rest assured, as you are sleek,
One would say that our wood had hatched nightingales."
All aglow, Master Crow tried to run a few scales,
Risking trills and intervals,
Dropping the prize as his huge beak sang false.
The fox pounced on the cheese and remarked, "My dear sir,
Learn that every flatterer
Lives at the flattered listener's cost:
A lesson worth more than the cheese that you lost."
The tardy learner, smarting under ridicule,
Swore he'd learned his last lesson as somebody's fool.

III

THE FROG WHO WOULD BE AN OX

That great ox, built just right!
Eying the beast, although at best
A mere egg's height or less, the frog mustered might
And spread out and swelled and expanded his chest
To approximate the ox, his despair;
Then said to another frog, "Compare:
I'm his size. See, now I need not defer."
"Still small."—"Now?"—"By no means."—"Now I am
not outclassed."
"Not nearly large enough." The poor envier
Burst; overtested at last.

Our world is full of mentalities quite as crude:
The man of trade must house himself so kings would stare;
Each small prince's deputies are everywhere.
Each marquis has pages—a multitude.

IV

THE TWO MULES

As two mules were journeying, one had oats as a load;
    The other, silver for the king from salt on which a tax fell.
The latter gloried in bearing a burden so notable
And would not have changed it for millions bestowed.
        Prancing along with head in a cloud,
        Jingling his bells as he'd nod in duet,
        He was held up by highwaymen
        In search of funds his pack might contain;
Whereupon they compelled him to almost sit
        As they jerked up the rein that held the bit.
        The mule in trying to work free again,
Was dealt blows till he bled and groaned and gasped in fear,
"It's this, is it, that my reward was to be?
A mule who sees his boon companion keeping clear,
        Is left in mortal jeopardy!"
        —"Now comrade," the other mule said,
"High office may be good, but there are exceptions to the rule.
If you'd been like me, no more than a miller's mule,
        Your plight would not now be so sad."

V

THE WOLF AND THE DOG

The poorest barebones wolf you ever knew
        (Watchdogs had made his life so hard)
When on the prowl met a mastiff matched by few—
Each hair in position as he foraged, off guard.
        Jaws agape, on fire to start a fray,
        Sir Wolf feared to bring him to bay,
        Knowing that it is do or die
        Against such a brute, so did not try
        Attacking the phenomenon

[15]

Who could have torn up anyone;
And all propitiation,
Flattered the beast as a joy to look upon,
A great dog any would revere.
"My lord, if you set store by good cheer
As I do," the dog said, "and crave a glossy skin,
Forsake the woods and be as I've been:
Your pinched pack of underfed wolves
Literally bring themselves
To death's door they are so dangerously thin.
You have no free bones to gnaw, nothing stowed away;
Food only as fruit of some mad fray.
Come with me; escape the fortunes of your wretched kin."
The wolf inquired, "And what tasks need I share?"
The dog said, "Almost none; rush out when beggars are seen,
Fasten on a cudgel or shin,
Fan conceit and trail your master everywhere:
You would enjoy dainty fare,
Every sort of tidbit a pet dog is thrown—
Now a chicken, now a squab bone,
With pats from all you address."
The enraptured wolf almost fainted away,
While tears said what he could not express.
As they trotted, a scar on the dog's neck was a giveaway.
"What's that?" the wolf asked.—"Nothing."—"Nothing?"
—"Nothing about which to make a fuss."
—"But what?"—"My neck's chafed where my chain hasn't play—
To explain what is making you curious."
—"You're chained?" said the wolf. "You can't investigate
Or range at will?"—"Not always. What have I lost?"
—"It's so vast," was the retort, "no matter what I ate,
I don't want comfort at such cost—
Would abhor even empires of your bestowing."
This said, Master Barebones fled and is still going.

VI

THE HEIFER, THE GOAT, AND THE SHEEP
IN PARTNERSHIP WITH A LION

Ewe, goat, and heifer, fond sisters all three,
Were in partnership with an overlord to dread—
A lion, if one may trust mythology.
Any gains or loss must be shared, he said,
And the goat, when a stag was mired on her property,
Assembled her partners without delay;
Whereupon the lion, counting on his claws,
Observed, "There are four of us to share the prey,"
Then apportioned as many parts as there were jaws;
But it would seem that the king had the first and largest share:
"The reason is clear," he said, "to everyone,
      From the term leonine."
      They had nothing to say; it seemed fair.
"To the second portion I should of course fall heir,
As share of the strongest—the most powerful's share.
And the third is for the hardiest, me alone.
If any of you looks upon the fourth as her own—
      I shall strangle her then and there."

VII

THE BEGGAR'S WALLET

Jupiter said one day, "Come, all who breathe heaven's air;
Everyone is now summoned, so let him appear;
If any has a blemish he feels is unfair,
      He may confess it without fear
      And he shall have speedy redress.
Come, monkey, you be first to confess.
Say, when you have seen the fine points of each one
      And his physique, how yours compares.

[17]

Satisfied?" The monkey asked, "I? How am I outshone?
Have you not given me four feet like theirs?
My face so far has not been hard for me to endure.
But look at poor bear, a mere caricature;
Not, if I'm a judge, what anybody would paint."
The bear approached, you would think with a complaint.
Not at all: was just right, he rejoiced to declare,
But was sure the elephant must be in despair.
He ought to grow more tail and shear away some ear;
How had this monstrosity dared to appear?
      The elephant was then as severe.
Wise though he is, one would have blushed to hear:
      He confessed that for him personally
      The whale's girth offended taste.
Dame Ant deemed a mite an absurdity
      And thought her own skeleton, vast.
The beasts were dismissed by Jupiter in disgust—
Each self-complacent. But of all the obsessed
None equaled mankind, whose folly takes the palm:
A mole toward myself, and a lynx toward the rest,
I forgive others naught and condone all I am.
Who sees oneself as one sees the next man?
      Ordained in accord with God's plan,
We are all alike and have a kind of begging-gear
Divided into parts as it was formerly:
We put our own defects in pockets at the rear
And others' at the front, for everyone to see.

VIII

THE SWALLOW AND THE LITTLE BIRDS

A swallow made flight after flight
And had become a seer. Naturally such a bird,
　　　Who recollected what occurred,
Had learned the ways of the wind until her trained sight
　　　Was sufficient before storms broke,
　　　To predict them to sailor-folk.
She had come home at the season when hemp is sown
And, seeing a sower who was industrious,
Observed to the little birds, "Nothing more ominous:
I am sad, although after the hemp is full-grown
I can fly south and live in some cleft.
What more persistent than that hand with the grain?
　　　In the end, and not much time is left,
　　　Hemp-seed sown is certain to cause you pain,
　　　Providing snares in which you will be abducted
　　　And springs to which birds are attracted;
　　　In fact, means to murder one,
　　　Which will leave you as time goes on,
　　　Dead or battened upon;
　　　Caged or put with some soup bone!"
　　　The swallow said, "I've warned you well;
　　　Pick that seed out, for I am right."
　　　The birds thought her laughable:
　　　Eat all the seed that lay in sight?
　　　When the hemp-field became green,
The swift said, "Chew it till chaff and do it oft,
　　　Pick the stuff off till none is left
　　　Or no other birds will glean."
—"Prophetess of doom; rigmarole," they laughed.
　　　"You'd turn us into major thieves.
　　　If millions plucked, there'd still be sheaves,
Though each bird worked and all were deft!"
　　　The hemp harvest now was assured:
"This is very bad," reiterated the swift.

[19]

"Evil seed is soon matured.
You who have felt all along that I was daft,
    Will find that I was not absurd,
    When what you see is harvested.
    Reapers work that they may be fed,
    So will wage war on every bird.
    Nets and traps set where you go,
    Will have become your mortal foe.
    None should dare to be out of doors;
Remain in your retreats or emigrate,
Following the wild duck's or snipe's or crane's course.
    You are handicapped by fate,
And cannot skim waves, then skirt leagues of sand
    In searching out some other land.
There is just one expedient which need not be feared;
Seek cracks in the wall where no mortar's been smeared."
    The little birds were deaf to more,
And all together chattered and cheeped their scorn,
Like Trojans whom their one faithful counselor,
    Cassandra, tried to warn.
    They fell like Trojans into the snare,
    Which then made slaves of many a little bird.

Egotism discounts advice as doctrinaire
And disaster would seem, till it smites us, absurd.

IX

THE TOWN RAT AND THE COUNTRY RAT

    In this ancient parable,
    Town rat proffered country rat
    A fashionable meal
    As a change from this and that,

    Where on a rug from Turkey,
    A feast for two was ready.
    Fond fancy alone could see
    The pair's joint ecstasy.

Fine food made each's plate replete—
More dainties there than greed could paint,
But as they were about to eat,
Noises were heard; the pair felt faint.

At the door, sniff and smell.
What was scratching steadily?
Both frightened ill, half fell,
Then fled confusedly.

When they had dared to reappear,
In seclusion with relief,
The city rat resumed, "My dear,
Come now, divide the beef."

—"I have dined," the field rat said;
"Be my guest, pray, a day hence,
Though you'll not find, I am afraid,
Similar magnificence.

Yet I'm never in danger: I've supped,
Carefree from year to year;
And so farewell. What is good cheer
Which death threats can disrupt?"

X

THE WOLF AND THE LAMB

Force has the best of any argument:
    Soon proved by the story which I present.

    A thirsty lamb was drinking where
    A brook ran crystal clear.
Up came a wolf who had been lured there
    By hunger, since it was a spot where prey might be.
"Soiling it, intrepid transgressor?" the wolf growled,
    "Leaving me to drink what you fouled?
Such impropriety involves a penalty."

[21]

—"Bear with me," the lamb said, "your Majesty.
    I've not trespassed anywhere.
    I'm twenty feet from where you were;
    Am here, where what you can't drink went
        In its descent;
    And to be mathematical,
How have I possibly by what I have done
    Polluted water of your own?"
—"You stirred the mud." Bloodthirsty minds are small.
"And the past year as well, I know you slandered me."
—"How?" the lamb asked. "I, unweaned, born recently—
    This very year? I still require home care."
      —"Your brother then, you've one somewhere."
—"But I have none."—"It was some relative then;
    All of you sheep are unfair;
    You, your shepherds, and the dogs they train.
I have a debt to myself to discharge."
    Dragged down a wooded gully,
    The small was eaten by the large
    Unconditionally.

XI

THE MAN AND HIS REFLECTION

For Monsieur le Duc de la Rochefoucauld

Thinking himself one with whom none could compare,
A man supposed himself the handsomest of mankind
And found fault with every mirror anywhere,
So that in time he had become morally blind.
To cure him, obliging fate made mirrors a commonplace,
    Holding up to him anywhere he chanced to gaze
Those silent counselors to which the Graces incline;
Mirrors in houses, and where merchandise is shown
    Mirrors of the sort a dandy would own,
    Mirrors dangling in the folds that belts confine.
What could our Narcissus do but stay away,
In the kind of place in which he would be safe all day

From any mirror that might catch him unaware?
Then a stream fed by a spring somewhere,
      Ran near the retreat he had found for the day
And once more he resented what would give him away,
Distorting his face and causing him pain.
Yet how turn from such crystal clearness as he saw?
      Now that clear stream without a flaw,
      Was too attractive to disdain.

      You will have seen what I have done here—
    Described a fool, but folk are much the same
And alike the prey of their folly, it would appear.
The man is the mind in terror of self-blame;
Others' faults are the mirrors he feared to see,
Which would picture to him how his faults must seem.
      The canal? is a celebrity
Whose *Maxims*[1] we hold in high esteem.

XII

THE DRAGON WITH MANY HEADS
AND THE DRAGON WITH MANY TAILS

      I've read how the ambassador
From the sultanate to a German Emperor
Remarked that his master's troops were those men most fear.
      "Well, well!" said a German standing near.
      "We have a sovereign
      Whose tributaries could each maintain
An army and do it without a subsidy."
      The shrewd Turk said then,
      "I have heard unofficially
How large an army each Elector could lend the Emperor.
      This reminds me, furthermore,
Of a thing as strange as true, which I happened to see—
Hid by a hedge where a hydra's filamentary
Of five-score serpent heads darted at me,

[1] Of La Rochefoucauld, published 1664.

[23]

Congealing my blood instantly
Since threatening mortal jeopardy!
However, but for fear, I was not hurt at all
Because what had seemed terrible
Could come no nearer, nor get through anywhere.
I was thinking back to the affair
When another dragon, with a single head though supplied
With more tails than one, nearly caused me to faint—
Instantaneously stupefied—
In terror of unfair intent.
Head and trunk slid along; then tails in their train,
Each making a path for the rest—not one thrown
Out of line. It is so, I maintain,
With your Emperor and my own."

XIII

THE THIEVES AND THE ASS

Quarreling over an ass they'd dared to waylay,
One of two thieves said keep it and one, let it be sold.
As each was giving his fists free play
And imagining he had got the better hold,
A third surprised the erring men
And the ass was stolen again.

Now the ass could mean a province which all despise
And two kings victimize—
Turkish, Hungarian, or Transylvanian.
Instead of two, a third sees chance of gain—
No dearth of gentry primed for robberies.
Often among thieves none gets what he would seize.
Thief four appears without consulting the three
And the ass is his property.

XIV

SIMONIDES AND THE GODS

Praise of three objects can not be overdone:
      God, the king, and her whom you love best—
Sentiments of mine which Malherbe once expressed,
      Sound to the core, every one.
All love encomiums, as we shall see,
And gratitude is a law which even gods obey.

      Having an athlete's eulogy
To phrase, Simonides found to his dismay
That anything he could find to say seemed stupid;
The relatives so obscure, who knew what they did!
This honest philistine was trivial as trite—
      A mere bore, honor him as one might.
First the poet extolled the athlete's prowess—
In fact dwelt upon it with conscientious care;
Then abandoned the theme and praised with minuteness
Castor and Pollux—known, he said, everywhere
For feats which other wrestlers deem illustrious;
Each of their performances had been glorious,
He declared, and then specified year and place,
      His praise being so generous,
      The pair took two-thirds of the space.
Though the athlete had agreed to pay a talent,
      The wretch viewed his predicament
And paid a third, observing with detachment,
"Athletes do not compete with deities yet;
Let Castor and Pollux meet the unpaid debt.
      But dine with us all. Be present
When we celebrate; join in the gaiety.
      It will be just my family
      And a few we know intimately;
      Afford us your society."
The poet complied, distrusting the bore
Lest nothing be paid and there be no *réclame;*

[25]

Found all in high spirits when he came;
The gourmets made the whole room roar.
Then a servant said two men had something to report,
Must see the bard and were importunate.
He left the others to their sport
And food—intent on what they ate.
The eulogized gods had themselves come to call.
They thanked him and praised the art in which he was versed,
Then said that the house would fall
And that he must flee a place that was accursed—
Word fulfilled that very day.
The ceiling sagged when a pillar bent
And came down for want of its mainstay
On feast and food and wine; in its descent
Harmed servants too, though innocent.
But what was worse, to punish a shameless cheat
And make the poet's revenge complete,
A beam lamed the legs of the athlete;
Thus guests who had been at ease and gay,
Were limping when they went away.
Ah! the hum spread as wonder grew; the dazed conversed.
Uncanny! All marveled, and doubly reimbursed
For his verse, a man the gods cared to empower.
There were none in families regarded as first
Who weren't vying to pour out gold in a shower
To have their forebears' fame rehearsed.

In returning to our theme, as my first comment
I would say that praise is a thing of moment—
To gods and to their like. Melpomene for her part
May accept a fee without reproach, I'd assert.
Lastly, there is no disparity between other arts and poetry.
The lord who lauds an artist scarcely seems a dunce.
Olympus and Parnassus once,
Were brothers and dwelt in amity.

XV

DEATH AND THE POOR WRETCH

XVI

DEATH AND THE WOODMAN

Once Death spared a wretched sufferer,
    Who called her each time he must stir
And murmured, "O Death, where is there one so beautiful?
Shorten a life in which cruelty has been the rule!"
Thinking him sincere, Death came to take him away
And stood there all bones, hollow-eyed and gaunt.
"A ghoul heeds my call. Don't stay," he pled, "don't stay.
    Foul and hideous Death, avaunt.
    How can I bear such a sight!
Back, Death, I implore you, dire blight!"

    'Twas Maecenas, friend of mankind,
Who once said somewhere, "Maim me time and again,
Cut off hands and feet, send gout; if left my mind,
I've life in a way; it would be worth the pain."
O Death, stay away from me, is the whole world's refrain.

*Aesop has treated this theme in a different way, as we see in the next fable. In composing this one I was constrained to present it in general terms. But it has been suggested that I should keep to the original; that I was slighting one of Aesop's best ingenuities. So I was obliged to reconsider. We can't outdo the ancients or lay claim to more luster than that of succeeding them worthily. At all events, I conjoin my fable to Aesop's; not that it deserves the place, but that I may include Maecenas's observation as appropriate—so choice in fact, that I felt it should on no account be omitted.—*LA FONTAINE.

A poor woodman with faggots to be charred,
Burdened by the weight of years and wood cut down,
Groaning and bent awry, came home as he had gone,
Though in the dusk how find his hut the soot had blurred?
In helpless misery, unable to do more,
He set his burden down, exhausted and heartsore.
"Of what pursuit since birth have I, poor man, been fond?
Has any soul on earth had more cause to despond?
Never a real night's rest, the larder always low."
For whom could it be home where soldiers come and go!
　　　　State labor, debts, taxes one can't retard—
He was dejection's portrait; existence was too hard.
So he called his mortal foe, and Death appeared
　　　　To ask why he had sent for her.
　　　　He said, "Just this; the wood I've cleared.
Kindly cheer me by lifting the load I laid there."

　　　　Heir to no ill that Death cannot cure,
　　　　We dare not look her in the eyes.
　　　　"Nothing too hard to endure
　　　　But Death," is every man's device.

XVII

MIDDLE AGE AND TWO POSSIBLE WIVES

　　　　A man a trifle gray
　　　　Though not an aged person,
　　　　Felt it an obligation
　　　　To wed without more delay;
　　　　　　And men of position,
　　　　　　It's certain,
　　　　Are popular. Pursued everywhere,
Our fought-for conqueror risked procrastination—
　　　　Courtship involves considerable care—
Then braved two widows in particular;
　　　　One sprightly, the other a touch mature—
　　　　　　But ripened charms, matured too far,

Can copy effects that are demure.
The widows were lovers of fun,
Implying that it was a treat
To be dressing hair as it should be done.
The elderly began, and plucked their swain's dark hair—
His final trifle of which to take care—
For in view of her years he had not felt at ease.
Whereupon the younger pulled the gray hairs out.
Both were denuding him by degrees
Till the maltreated man was no longer in doubt.
"Ladies dear," he said, "I am grateful indeed;
Since good sense has been substituted
For hair, I am compensated;
Marriage is not what I need.
Choose either and bear with her inclination;
But then how do as I incline?
My own shorn head had best be mine.
Dear ladies, thank you for your admonition."

XVIII

THE FOX AND THE STORK

Shrewd Master Fox had been such a courtier
That stately Miss Stork had said she'd dine with him;
But his preparations involved no great flutter,
It being the rascal's whim
To provide consommé; thrift seemed important.
The broth was offered the stork upon a dinner plate:
Her long beak caught so little, the creature scarcely ate,
Yet the rogue lapped all of his up in an instant.
Later, to requite his perfidy,
The stork offered him hospitality.
"I'm charmed," he said, "and to those I know intimately
Come enthusiastically."
On the hour he was punctually
At his hostess's address,
Blessing her for her thoughtfulness;

[29]

That the meal was not quite done
Gave him an appetite; foxes are famed for one.
Oh, the scent of meat; it made his whole being expand!
Cut fine, he inferred, and turned by a careful hand.
Yet what had he not to endure,
Since it was served in a tall, very small-mouthed ewer.
The stork's bill was so long, the vase was scarcely taller,
But what fox-nose can probe a mere aperture!
The embarrassed guest was soon trotting home hungry,
Looking as if caught robbing a hennery—
Ears and tail limp, not caring how they were.

My words here are particularly
Addressed to foxes without fur.

XIX

THE CHILD AND THE SCHOOLMASTER

That fools' preaching is devoid of power
Is what I am trying to explain.

A child all but drowned in an idle hour
When frolicking on a bank of the Seine.
Yet fairly near the little fellow
Providence had placed an enormous willow.
Well, as the child clutched some branches that trailed,
A teacher approached and his ears were assailed
By cries of, "Help! I'm drowning. Rescue me."
The schoolmaster, pausing impersonally
As though reproving iniquities,
Said, "The little blockhead has fallen in!
See? Punishment for stupidities!
Think of undertaking the rogues. Imagine.
Unlucky parents who must keep a watchful eye
On the renegades, alert for tricks they may try.
Pitiful. I am pained for them to the core!"
He ranted, and then drew the child ashore.

[30]

Many more types are implied than I include—
The loose-tongued, carpers, prigs who cannot unbend;
Self-evident, those to whom I allude;
A whole tribe represented by a single trend.
The Creator blessed the seed of each brood.
They find, whatever their occupation,
  A pretext for talking all day.
Ah, friend, first effect my salvation,
  Then tell me what you have to say.

XX

THE COCK AND THE PEARL

 A scratching cock struck back
 A pearl, which he took
 With a cluck to a jeweler,
 Saying, "Exceptional—
 But no grain is too small
 To be treasure that I would prefer."

 A blockhead was bequeathed a book
 In manuscript, which he took
 To a nearby connoisseur,
 Remarking, "A rarity—
 But a mere ha'penny
 Would afford me what I would prefer."

XXI

THE HORNETS AND THE HONEY BEES

The expert is known by what he has done.

There were some honeycombs with no proprietor.
        "Ours," said some hornets, laying claim to the store.
        "Ours," said the bees in unison,
And the case was referred to a certain wasp to decide.
Of the verdicts which he could render, none applied:
When asked to testify, the witnesses as one
Said they'd seen winged insects of a peculiar dun
With bodies rather long—like a bee's in a way—
Who were always about. Hornets also, not bees alone,
        Had been described, one would say.
The wasp was bewildered by contradiction
And called from their hill, ants whose words he might compare
        And thereby make his verdict fair.
        The darkness became no brighter.
        "Heaven tell, has it made things better?"
        Asked a bee of experience.
"For nearly six months we have been in suspense,
        No further on now than we were.
        Meanwhile the honey will go to waste.
It is time the magistrate made haste:
        Why tongue the fur until the cub is bare?
Enough. No more hard words from interlocutors
        And rigmarole behind closed doors;
        Hornets, aid if work is what you seek,
And store our nectar in cells that cannot leak,
        To find who can make wax durably."
        That not a single hornet would take part
        Proved none possessed cell-building art,
And the Judge's verdict was in favor of the bee.

Gods above, if we could but do things in this way,
Administer the law as a Turkish judge would,

And good sense take the place of some legal code,
We would not have so much to pay,
Or be mere marrow bones to crunch—
Bled pale by a suit that lasts for years,
Downed in the end like an oyster, by the bench—
The shells left for the arguers.

XXII

THE OAK AND THE REED

The oak said to the reed, "You grow
Too unprotectedly. Nature has been unfair;
A tiny wren alights, and you are bending low;
If a fitful breath of air
Should freshen till ripples show,
You heed her and lower your head;
Whereas my parasol makes welcome shade each day
And like the Caucasus need never sway,
However it is buffeted.
Your so-called hurricanes are too faint to fear.
Would that you'd been born beneath this towering
tent I've made,
Which could afford you ample shade;
Your hazards would not be severe:
I'd shield you when the lightning played;
But grow you will, time and again,
On the misty fringe of the wind's domain.
I perceive that you are grievously oppressed."
The rush said, "Bless you for fearing that I might be
distressed;
It is you alone whom the winds should alarm.
I bend and do not break. You've seemed consistently
Impervious to harm—
Erect when blasts rushed to and fro;
As for the end, who can foresee how things will go?"
Relentless wind was on them instantly—
A fury of destruction
Which the North had nursed in some haunt known to none.

[33]

The bulrush bent, but not the tree.
Confusion rose to a roar,
Until the hurricane threw prone
That thing of kingly height whose head had all but touched
God's throne—
Who had shot his root to the threshold of Death's door.

BOOK TWO

FOR THOSE IMPOSSIBLE TO PLEASE

Might I have begged at birth something magical to keep
Of gifts bestowed upon us by Calliope,
I would have asked the gift that made old Aesop deep—
Of make-believe and verse, twined indivisibly.
But don't think I think myself one in the Muses' eyes,
Able to rarefy a tale as he has done;
One can polish a thing that has already shone;
Meanwhile, I've attempted what I think rather new,
Had a wolf speak and lamb reply as never hitherto;
Not merely this; my plants and trees are eloquent
As well as the animals you hear descant.
Now who is to say that it does not enchant?
       "Ah, true," authorities concede.
       "Five or six tales in a juvenile strain,
        You expound with magniloquent pen."
—"If it is valor, critics, of which you care to read,
In heightened style, consider this: After ten
Years of war, the Trojans behind their barricades,
Attacked by the Greeks time and time again—
       Tested by thousands of ruses and raids—
Stood firm beneath the battering; proud Troy still stood,
And then Minerva intervened and made a horse of wood.
       The flanks of this odd masterpiece
Hid wise Ulysses and his accomplices,
Brave Diomedes and Ajax the impetuous:
       The huge device of which they made use
With their auxiliaries to obtain ingress to Troy.
Deeming its very gods not too sacred to destroy—
Since resentful of all they had borne year by year,
       They invented their great decoy of pine."

—"Enough," a ruthless voice breaks in upon me here:
"You've made your readers pant; you have too long a line;
      Your wooden horse and choice
    Of heroes forming phalanxes are labored to excess,
      Surpassing a fox's unnaturalness
When he flatters a crow about his voice."
—"Very well, my style shall be lowered for Amaryllis, a tale
Of how dreaming about Alcippus had made her lily pale,
Entrusting her secret for fear harm be done,
To the flock which she tended and sheep dog alone.
While thinking willows hid him, Thyrsis dared to crawl
Near enough his delectable lass to overhear it all
      And her prayer that Zephyr bear her tune
      To the then distant favored one."
      —"Stop; an impossible type of rhyme,"
      The critic objects in captious tone.
      "Not rich enough by far, this time,
      And the content is not good.
Put it into the melting pot—recast that tiresome chant."
      —"Harsh sir, pray spare your bearish mood
      Though a last word's something you'll not grant.
      No critical endeavor thrives
      Where one would try to suit your sort."

      The difficult lead fretful lives.
      To please them, stop before you start.

II

THE RATS IN COUNCIL

      Puss Rodilard's name cast a spell
    Like death upon all the rats there were;
      Indeed but few were visible,
Relentless slaughter having been his ardent care.
Such as were not caught did not dare venture out
And lived on a fourth of what any of them sought,
Till Rodilard was to those whose blood he seemed to freeze,
      No mortal cat but Mephistopheles.

[36]

Now as he climbed, or creeps lengthened his loin
In his renegade quest for some tabby he'd court,
Through the witches' sabbath in which they'd consort,
Surviving rats had seen fit to convene
In a corner to discuss their lot.
Then a doyen, known as a diplomat,
Said that without delay they must master their fear
And tie to Rodilard's neck a bell which they could hear,
So that any he'd hoped to devour
Might dart down holes and circumvent the wretch's power.
Agreed, that the tying must be done.
The good rat's arguments had satisfied everyone
But how and when find a favorable hour?
The problem was, which pair of paws should tie?
"This much is sure," said one. "I'm not the fool to try."
Another said, "Nor I." And since everyone seemed to cower,
All withdrew. I have seen monastics too
Confer and arrive at nothing new—
Not on stairs, but with a dean in a canon's close
Or cloister; I've seen some of those.

Concerned with points none need decide,
The courtroom swarms since all attend;
But when the cat's bell must be tied,
All flee on whom one might depend.

III

WOLF VERSUS *FOX BEFORE JUDGE MONKEY*

A wolf had been robbed, or so he pretended,
And named as beast to pay the penalty
A fox who lived near, who might well be suspected.
The judge was a monkey before whom the pair pleaded—
In person—and neither was aided legally.
Themis had never heard justice so twisted
In a monkey's age of cases contested.
The bench sweat under the torrent of fallacies—
With points on each side exhaustively stated,

[37]

Bared, shrilled out, and debated.
The judge, aware of their propensities,
Said, "Friends, I am familiar with your history
And both of you will have to be fined;
Since you, wolf, weren't robbed and haven't brought suit legitimately;
And you, fox, are a thief and stole something of some kind."
The judge maintained that whatever the facts were,
When you punish a rogue, you have not been too severe.

IV

TWO BULLS AND A FROG

Two bulls locked horns about a herd each wished to head
And a heifer in the herd.
A frog sighed till another said,
"You are panting, friend. What has occurred?"
—"Alas," said the lugubrious one,
"You'll see; it's inevitable;
For undoubtedly the downfall
Of either bull means that the other, banned from his estate—
Those magnificent flower-dotted meadows we see—
Will leave the grass upon which he fed formerly,
Nourish upon marsh grass, since outlawed by his foe,
And maim us with clumsy feet however deep we go;
We shall one, then another, know helpless distress
In the feud for her ladyship, this heifer they'd possess."
The frogs underwent that very fate:
One of the bulls retired to the shore
Where the frogs were mangled by his weight
As hourly he trod on twenty or more.

From the first it has been so—how unfortunate!
The weak must suffer for the follies of the great.

V

THE BAT AND THE TWO WEASELS

A bat when descending on a curve
Entered a weasel's nest, and as it lay there flat
The foe, whom opportunity seemed to serve,
      Rushed forward to devour the bat.
"Look! Well!" the weasel said. "Effrontery to the core.
Mice a constant pest and one darkens my very door!
Now no subterfuge; you're a mouse, surely one;
It's what you are or I'm no weasel," she said.
      —"Forgive me," the poor morsel pled,
      "A race quite different from my own.
Mouse! Enemies have invented the tale.
      Thank God, who made every creature here,
      I'm a bird with wings on which I sail:
      Long live lords of the atmosphere!"
      Such words leave one favorably inclined:
      Skill she'd commanded had intervened
      To ward off the use of force.
      Two days from then, since she could not see,
      Our legless mouse did even worse—
Disturbed a weasel who looked on birds with enmity—
A deed for which she might have answered mortally.
The long-nosed lady of the house
Would have eaten the specimen of a hated race
When the entrant met injustice with these words:
"I? You did not look or you could not think me that;
      For what but feathers have made birds, birds?
      I am a mouse: long live the rat!
      Jupiter confute the cat!"
      She'd saved herself twice in the selfsame way,
      Since she had known just what to say.

Scores have found it wise to reverse the argument
To escape extinction which they saw threatening:
      Wisdom finds it best sometimes to assent
      To both "Long live the League! Long live the King!"

VI

THE BIRD WOUNDED BY AN ARROW

Pierced by a feathered shaft that brought her to the ground,
Mourning injury for which no cure could be found,
A bird crushed by mounting distress exclaimed, "Forlorn
To play a part in one's own doom when overborne!
   Hardhearted man, to pluck from me a plume
Which hastens to its end the instrument of doom!
Ruthlessness, do not shrug. Heartless humanity, take heed.
Your fate may have been symbolized by my feather,
Since Iapetus peopled this earth with a brood
   Intent on harming one another."

VII

BITCH AND FRIEND

   A bitch who approached each hutch with a frown,
Since a-shiver to shelter an imminent litter,
Crouched perplexed till she'd coaxed from a vexed benefactor
A lean-to as a loan and in it lay down.
The benefactor returned but the barefaced borrower
Begged a fortnight's extension and still she lingered—
Must stay till her puppies no longer lumbered.
   Well, least said the better.
When that term had lapsed too, the friend made a plea
   For her house, her room, and bed;
The coaxer bared her teeth and said,
"I'm prepared to depart and with my family
   If you will turn us out of doors."
   The puppies were by then tall curs.

One certainly rues aid to the malevolent.
   If you'd recover what you lent,
   A physical blow is all they feel.

You have to beg and then to beat.
Yield but a foot to their appeal
And find they have usurped four feet.

VIII

THE EAGLE AND THE BEETLE

Harried by an eagle, Jack Rabbit had to bound
In so mad a zigzag he scarcely seemed to light
By a dimple-sized tumblebug-nest in the ground.
   Conjecture its worth in his plight,
Though best hope as he crouched inconspicuously.
Notwithstanding, the eagle's talons sank into his wool.
   Then the beetle as intermediary
Begged, "Princess of birds, it would be trivial
To carry away an unfortunate guest.
Be so kind as to spare my friend discourtesy,
Jack Rabbit begs his life in all humility.
In Heaven's name spare him or bear both to your nest—
   My gentle neighbor. I hold him dear."
Jove's bird without rejoinder struck the little thing,
   And struck him hard with a strong wing,
   So hard he dared not speak for fear,
And bore Master Rabbit away. Blood boiling because foiled,
The beetle broke the bird's eggs when she'd flown off for
          sustenance—
Her eggs, her tender eggs, hope of continuance.
   He did not leave an egg unspoiled.
In hoping to hatch a brood that year the mother had failed.
The next season she nested higher still and then
The beetle chose his time and spoiled the eggs again.
Jack Rabbit's murder was a deed that had recoiled.
Harsh cries throughout the wood expressed a grief so deep
   That for six months no animal could sleep.
   Then she whose wing bore Ganymede
Appealed to the god of all the gods for aid,
Laid her eggs on his own lap and was content—
Insured against such harm as might be imminent.

Jupiter would care for them—do so for his sake—
  Eggs which only the bold would take;
  Too high for theft, true enough,
  But the -bug had a neater trap to be sprung;
He dropped on the god's royal robe a ball of dung.
Jove ruffled his robe and the eggs were shaken off.
  Apprised of the accident,
  The bird hectored Jupiter;
She might renounce his court for desert provender
  And not be his constituent;
  Her plaints were so extravagant
  That poor Jupiter was mute.
The beetle now approached the judgment seat with his suit—
  His plea and his version of what occurred.
The eagle was rebuked—had been a wrongdoer.
But since neither, when he heard the foe's charge, would concur,
The monarch of the gods, that peace might be insured,
Set the mating season for eagles at another time of year—
Winter—when beetles are in a torpid state
And, like marmots, go underground to hibernate,
  Hiding from the sunshine when they disappear.

IX

THE LION AND THE GNAT

"Begone, objectionable gnat; you pollute the air!"
  The lion affected this tone
  In addressing the little one,
  Who himself shrilled a challenge to war.
"Do you think the name king," he said to the great cat,
  "Has sovereign power to terrify?
  An ox though harder to combat,
  Behaves as fancy dictates to me."
  He had scarcely expressed the thought
  That he'd taken charge of the campaign,
  When his gnat note rang out.
  He circled the enemy's mane,
  Took his time and bit the great cat

On the neck. Almost crazed by the gnat,
The quadruped foamed. Lightning shot from his eyeball.
He roared. The neighbors trembled and rushed underground,
    Cowering from what had disorganized all.
    A mere gnat held them terrorbound.
The minute pest was intolerable;
A hundred times stung the spine, forced the mouth to close,
    Then ventured up into the nose.
Whereupon the victim really lost his head.
The invisible foe laughed at the great beast's despair,
Whose own teeth and claws were drawing blood—
Defeat costing the cause of it not a care.
The miserable cat tore grooves in his own frame,
His whirling tail lashed his flanks with a smiting sound.
He beat the blameless air, self-tormented till tame—
And with muscles slack, sank exhausted upon the ground.
Mars' insect withdrew in a halo of fire.
As he'd bugled the charge, he announced he'd retire—
His last taunt to the tamed; then encountered a skein
    He'd not seen, of a web which some spider had spread.
    He would never tame lions again.

And what is the moral that has been conveyed?
A double one: don't underrate an enemy;
The direst enemy may be too small to see;
The other: we may surmount what few could bear;
    Then something minute end our earthly career.

X

THE DONKEY WITH SPONGES
AND THE DONKEY WITH SALT

    The pair were led by a donkey-man
    Of imperial mien breathing Roman disdain—
    Each gray long-legged, long-eared steed.
The donkey with sponges suggested a courier's speed;
    The other one seemed of opposite breed,
    Walking on eggs as if loath to proceed:

[43]

He had been laden with salt. Down dale and up again,
        Our conquerors of hill and plain
Persevered to a ford where they stood stock-still to stare
        With a suddenly bewildered air.
The donkey-man year after year had crossed with a careless splash,
        Now mounted on Sponges, and as rash,
        Drove the other donkey ahead.
        Stumbling since no longer led,
The ass lunged, hoof in hole, went down with a crash,
        Came up, and gained the bank with a dash
        For the salt sank as the river flowed,
        Washing away what weighed him down.
        He could struggle out on being thrown,
        Since relieved of his heavy load:
Brother Sponges copied him faithfully
As sheep follow sheep automatically.
Aha, water-donkey is taking a plunge,
        Neck deep with master and every sponge!
All three—donkey, sponges, and donkey-man—
        Drinking as much as any sponge can;
        These last gaining weight as they drank
        From the current, absorbing more and more
Till the drowning donkey could not make shore.
        The donkey-man clung, convinced as they sank
        That death was certain that very hour.
Someone saved them—no need to name their rescuer.
It is enough if I have managed to explain
        That we can't all act in the same way; it's said there—
        At least I hope I have made it plain.

XI

THE LION AND THE RAT

XII

THE DOVE AND THE ANT

When we show friendliness, we find that friends abound;
One might need aid from one much smaller than one is,
And there are a pair of fables illustrating this,
     Though scores could have proved the statement sound.

     When a rat darted from its den
Into a lion's paws, it thought death a certainty.
That the king of beasts was a true king, he made plain
By sparing the rat and granting him his liberty—
     A kind deed that did not go for naught.
     And yet could anyone have thought
     That cats' and rats' enmity could be reversed?
Then, wandering the woods, the lion was beset
     By toils and, lying in the net,
Roared to no purpose as it would seem at first.
Master Rat sped forth, gnawed fast, and the frayed net ran
As a parted stitch runs the goods' whole length.
     Time for what patience first began,
     Is better than embattled strength.

And here, a tiny form of life lends me authority.

Near a pure rivulet a dove came down and drank;
Then a thirsty ant fell forward, almost sank,
And one might have seen the midget struggling helplessly,
Too frustrated each time, to reach what it desired.
The dove's quick action proved that mercy was not dead
When she bore and loosed a straw from overhead
To act as an earthwork whenever her friend tired.

[45]

It was a successful ruse.
But a churl by chance had crept up without his shoes,
And carried a crossbow to bag birds for his pot.
      Venus' bird then tempted its use;
His eye grew bright at thought of the dainty dove he'd caught
And he was about to bring it down—hardhearted sot—
      When the ant pinched his heel; whereupon
      The lout turned his head before he shot;
The pigeon had heard and then was gone,
So no supper for churl as a result of his toil.
      "No penny, no pigeon possible."

XIII

THE ASTROLOGER WHO FELL INTO A WELL

    Once an obstacle tripped an astrologer
    Who fell into a well. The neighbors said,
    "Poor fool! You can't see what's underfoot, and you a seer.
    How read the stars above your head?"

This incident speaks for itself; without comment
Can serve as a lesson to the most of mankind.
Among earthlings there are not many you could find
      Who are not of a temperament
      To imagine they should let a seer
Act as the book of fate's interpreter—
That book put into verse by Homer and others we've read—
A thought which I am sure you have anticipated.
      What was it in ancient times? chance; in ours,
                        Providence.
      But supposing there were a science of chance,
      It surely would be wrong if there were,
To call it chance, fortune, or luck any longer, since an affair
      Too uncertain. And how discern
      God's intentions? Who could learn
What none knows but Himself? How read the design
Hid in the heart of Him who created all by his dictates alone?
Would He have entrusted to stars to reveal

What the night of eternity wraps in its veil?
To what purpose? Prompt wit to volubility
Concerning the heavenly sphere? or globe as it may be,
Help us avoid the unavoidable
And forestall our good fortune by foretelling it all?
Disgusting us in advance with cause for eagerness
Till blessings anticipated become a bitterness.
That kind of thing is wrong, I would make clear.
The starry heavens change, the stars themselves stay there,
   The sun is bound to appear.
Succeeding shades of night, it will be day, we infer;
Without constituting a lesson we ought to have read
Except that the sun illumines and has light to shed,
To usher in the seasons, nurse yield from incipience,
And shed on bodies its fruitful influence.
Besides, how can our universe's unvarying course
Be what it is and look on luck as a vital resource?
   Charlatans and casters of the horoscope,
  Forsake princely courts of Europe as outside your scope.
Take the alchemists with you to the last man.
Only such frauds as they and you should combine.

But I digress. Back to what I was saying at first
About the star-gazer constrained to quench his thirst.
Not to mention art—with him, bogus instead;
Gaping at the stars and feeding on gossamer
   While danger looms ahead
   To land, limb, or whatever he should hold most dear.

XIV

THE HARE AND THE FROGS

  In his form a hare would meditate;
For what can a hare do in his form but dream?
Devoured by apprehension, his fear was so great:
The creature was sad—a-shiver in every nerve it would seem.
   "When persons are born timorous,"
  He said, "it makes them dolorous.

[47]

Every morsel tastes queer which they attempt to eat;
Joy is not joy because of quivers everywhere.
I don't exaggerate; not even sleep is sweet.
Since focused on thin air, my two eyes stare and stare.
Curb your fears, moralists say, and all will be well.
  Fear cure itself? But when has that been possible?
  Perhaps these strong fears stabbing me,
  Stab human beings equally."
  So he mused, and quivered in his fright
  While he maintained a sharp lookout—
  Shivering and glancing about:
Some shadow or sound shot his fever to a height.
  The melancholy animal,
  Musing on his despair,
Took a slight rustle as a sign that the blow must fall
  And darted away to his lair,
Skirting a pond by which a footpath chanced to run.
Frogs at once sprang from wherever they hid.
Frogs sprang into the grottoes they had in the mud.
  "Ah," he said, "I'm not the only one
  In whom fear is stirred, since by chance
I find I've caused it, creating panic as others have done!
  I too have broken a lance!
How so! I induce timidity? I stun!
  A cannonading thunderer?
There is, I see, no coward anywhere
  So craven he can't find a greater one."

XV

THE COCK AND THE FOX

An old cock perched on a branch which made all visible.
  He was ingenious, indeed profound.
"Dear fowl," said a fox as he made a purring sound,
  "The war is ended that has been mutual.
  The truce declared is far-reaching and sound.
I'm announcing it; hop down and be embraced.
  Dear cock, come down; I am in haste,

[48]

Should be twenty places at once, have no time to squander.
　　　You and your flock may cluster or wander—
　　　In either case free of care.
　　　Feathers and fur are now a pair.
　　　Bonfires tonight should end our war,
　　　But first, let salutes seal the oath we swore
　　　To make it indissoluble."
The cock replied, "Dear friend, nothing I've ever heard
Could seem more sweet, indeed delectable,
　　　　　　Than that fowl
　　　　　And fox be paired;
　　　It really makes the heart bound
To hear the news from you! Two greyhounds yonder I conjecture,
　　　Are couriers sent—I'm quite sure—
　　　With the tidings of peace attained,
Like the wind, so the pair should arrive rather soon.
I'll descend and exchange salutes all around."
—"Farewell," said the fox, "I've far to go, have pledged my word,
And felicitations must be deferred—
　　Be postponed." The rascal spun about
　　　To seek safety in a lookout—
　　　Chagrined that he was forced to run.
　　　Our old cock chuckled at what he had done
　　　And at the frightened frightener.
The pleasure is doubled, of taking a snarer in his snare.

XVI

THE CROW APING THE EAGLE

Jupiter's eagle seized a sheep on which to dine.
　　　Admiring his exciting power,
A crow, though feebler, was so greedy as to pine
　　　To do as much that same hour as the greater would dare,
　　　So circled a hundred, taking stock,
Then selected the fattest, fairest of the flock,
　　　Truly a sheep for sacrifice.
It had been reserved as fit for deity's use.
Greedy-eyed young caw, since envious and ravenous,

[49]

Remarked, "Reared on whatever nurse's advice,
Your proportions mean you'd afford me the choicest meat—
Truly tempting provender"—
And lighted on the beast, which merely dared to bleat.
His woolly masterpiece in fur
Weighed more than a cheese: its caparison
Was matted as firm as its frame—
A curly coat with which nothing could be done—
A true Polyphemus' beard to tame.
The tangled curls so detained the claws of the crow
That the arch-trespasser could not get them out.
The shepherd caught him, refused to let him go,
And the children had a toy to tease and drag about.

We should estimate our strength. Of this there can be no doubt:
Weak thieves come to grief in daring what strong ones dare.
Another's gain should not make envy stir.
Not every despoiler is lord of earth and air.
Wasps break from webs in which a gnat dies prisoner.

XVII

THE PEACOCK'S COMPLAINT TO JUNO

The peacock sought out Juno to complain
And said, "No wonder, Goddess, that I experience pain,
Mourn, and exhibit righteous ire:
My harsh voice grates on everyone—
Pitched so that any ear must tire.
Though the nightingale, puny thing, seems specked with mire,
The notes she trills are dazzling as the sun,
Announcing to all that fair spring has begun."
Incensed by the attack on her,
Then Juno retorted angrily, "You who should hold
your tongue—jealous envier—
You have dared to envy the song of the nightingale?
Though your sapphire necklace grows dark by turns and pale—
With a thousand rainbow tints that nearly fade, then stay;
You flaunt or fold your fan away,

[50]

With whose colors and glinting elegance
>A jeweler's shop cannot compare.
>What other bird beneath the sky's expanse
>Enchains attention everywhere?
Though none, great or small, claims each proficiency,
Each has its distinguishing rare quality:
Some have magnificence and some, a leader's blood:
Hawks are swift; eagles, fearless in hardihood.
>The crow warns from the wood
Of present ills; the raven forebodes despair.
>All are content with plumage I thought good.
No more complaints, or be stripped of feathers folk revere
>And go naked for daring to be rude.

XVIII

THE CAT CHANGED TO A WOMAN

A man one time became dementedly fond of his cat—
The silkiest, daintiest, most exquisite, he thought.
>Indeed the mere sound of her miaow
>Thrilled him until he had somehow,
By tears and prayers of a touched brain,
>Forged potent forces of a chain,
>As only sorcery could have done,
>And transformed his cat, when the links were one,
>To an actual woman, at dawn, in the room!
>Our Merlin wed her that very day
>And ecstatic folly reversed the gloom
>Of ill-starred love—sickness, I'd say.
>No temptress really beautiful
>Charmed a man so easily
>As this strange wife her marital fool
>Who had been brooding constantly.
>He saw no trace of cat to regret,
But while gnawing a mat that night, mice were a threat
To the peaceful sleep of the newly wed.
>The enchanted cat by a dart from bed
>Missed the mice she inferred were near,

[51]

Crouched forward since certain that they would reappear,
 And the next time took them by surprise;
   For having discerned no form to fear,
   They had not avoided her disguise.
   Her weakness remained a curse of course;
   Such is Nature's interior force.
Instinct scorns rebukes when one has reached maturity.
The fold is in the goods; a scent haunts the vase persistently.
   Deflecting nature is absurd
   From whatever course it has pursued.
   Bring pressure to bear but rest assured
   Matters will stand just where they stood.
   Prod habit with pitchforks however hard,
   It behaves as if nothing had occurred.
   Or beat with leather till it's a shred.
   You've tried to reform what will not learn.
   Shut doors on traits that you wish were dead;
   They will open a window and return.

XIX

LION AND ASS A-HUNTING GO

On his birthday once, the beast whom all propitiate
  Thought of a hunt by which to celebrate.
Now lions' prey is not such game as a tomtit bags,
But ferocious boars, fleet hinds, and old belligerent stags.
   As part of his hunting gear,
   The lion had the ass appear
   Since his bray was spectacular.
As Master Lion's horn, Mister Ass's voice would reach far.
So the ass was shown where to lie and on him leaves were laid;
The lion commanded him to bray, sure his fearsome refrain
Would frighten the boldest from dens where they'd lain.
Nothing they had ever heard or known had ever made
   Noise so like an equinox.
The terrific shudder seemed interminable,
Extending terror from the treetops to the rocks.
All fled—all caught in a trap that was infallible.

The lion seized them one by one.
—"Was I not indispensable in what you've done?"
The ass asked as if he had actually dealt blows.
The lion said, "You aided; I admit that you brayed:
If I'd not known the source from which the sound arose
      I might myself have been afraid."

The ass would have resented the slur but did not dare,
Even though the point of the jest was a sound one.
For who would want an ass to boast of what he'd done?
      It would not be in character.

XX

AESOP EXPLAINS A WILL

    Believe what has been said, and we conclude
      That Aesop was the sage of Greece.
      In fact, this one man's sagacities
Outdid the Areopagus—a multitude.
      And now some curious history,
      Parts of which will please you, I am sure.

    A man had daughters, in fact had three—
      Each with a different vice to cure;
      One loved wine and one was a flirt;
      The third had hoarding most at heart.
      Now this man had had his will drawn
      As local law required that one shall—
The heirs being left all in equal parts, with one payable
      To the mother as soon
      As each daughter possessed none at all—
Till each daughter had exhausted her share.
      When the father died as was natural,
The three sped to see what was left to each heir
      And read the will; it was too profound
      To be fathomed by an amateur.
      Not one discovered upon what ground
      Each of the daughters must spend her share—

Each sister spend funds apportioned her
      Before the mother become an heir!
      Indeed, the provision is scarcely plain
      That payment wait till no funds remain.
      How lay the will's dark purpose bare?
Attorneys consulted—scores working away,
      Ferreting out what the will did not say,
      Taking a thousand kinds of care.
They threw up their hands then and said they were through—
      Assign each legatee her share;
Better divide it—the thing to do,
      And "as for the widow, each daughter owes
A third to the mother as everyone knows—
A third, that is, from each sister to the mother—
      Unless the mother wishes, rather,
Some sort of stipend or yearly competence,
      As retroactive maintenance."
The assets were listed accordingly, by group:
      First, the wineshops and stocks of wines,
      And tables underneath the vines;
Any kind of tankard or beaker or cup,
      Whatever malmsey there might be,
And the kitchen staffs; a word sums it up—
      Such things as pertain to gourmandry;
In portion two, accessories to gallantry:
Town house and furniture with marquetry,
      Eunuchs and embroiderers;
        The heirs' coiffeurs;
      Gorgeous gowns and jewelry;
With farms to comprise group three—along with the hired
                              hands,
      Flocks and herds and grazing lands,
      Plows and horses and men for hire:
If they drew lots, no sister would like what fell to her—
      Perhaps not a sister
      Be pleased with her share;
So each named that to which she inclined,
      Evaluating what she wished assigned.
      And they were Athenian
      Who had this trouble with a will.

High and low, all found acceptable
   The division and choice; Aesop alone
   Said despite the trouble to which they had gone,
   They'd defeated what the testator wished done.
"If the dead," he exclaimed, "were alive to speak,
   He'd deal with Athenians scathingly
   As people who think themselves unique—
Regarding themselves as a synonym of subtlety—
Thus grossly misunderstanding the aim
   Of the testator." Having said this, he showed how they
            had erred,
   Himself assigned what each hoped to claim,
Appointing to each a lot she abhorred.
   He gave each the things she considered dull,
   In fact inimical to her role:
   The coquette received what is suited to sots—
   Perhaps say, to a drinker's needs;
   And the sot, the agrarian one of the lots,
   While the miser got gauds to which smart life leads.
   Such was the advice of the Phrygian,
   Who said no other plan would mean
   Compelling these girls, these legatees,
   To rid themselves of their goods and then
Find husbands—sons of good families
   When the fact that they had funds was plain;
   Pay their mother cash as their father meant—
Since the property was no longer a care—
   And carry out the will's intent.
The people wondered. The ablest there were—
   A multitude—outdone by one shrewd man
   And he not an Athenian!

BOOK THREE

I

THE MILLER, HIS SON, AND THE ASS

To Monsieur de Maucrois [1]

An aptitude for art, birthright of ancient Greece,
Made fables possible, bequeathing us some of these;
Even so, irrespective of what we have read,
A few gleanings may still be harvested.
Given the wilderness of fancy anywhere,
Every author finds himself a discoverer.
Now here is a tale ingeniously constructed
For young Racan whom Malherbe as it were adopted—
Both heirs as well as rivals of Horace's lyre,
Apollo's sons, each a master whom we admire.
Exchanging inmost thoughts and queries when alone,
Since sure they would not be disturbed by anyone,
Racan began, "Might I ask if not a liberty,
That you tell me, for you have seen life thoroughly
And by now have come to know its every turning
As well as all I shall eventually be learning,
What course to pursue, now that I must choose at once.
You have known me well and my every circumstance.
Shall I live in the country, perhaps become a squire?
Try the army? Might court life be what I require?
Life has its bitterness and its beatitudes:
Marriage can drive you mad; war has its interludes.
If I did as I please, I'd know how to proceed.
But to friends, court, and the public, one must concede."
"You would please them all!" said Malherbe. "Quite unsound.
Consider this story in which my answer is found.

[1] A canon of Reims.

[56]

"In what book I can't say—I was reading casually—
A miller and his son just short of maturity,
Not more than fifteen if I'm trustworthy there,
Had a donkey to sell and were going to the fair.
That the beast might seem fresh and show agility,
They cat-cradled his legs to a limb from a tree
And carried him suspended as though a chandelier:
Pathos personified, the poor pair were so queer!
The first person met, laughed until his sides ached
And asked, 'What is the farce they are going to act?
It's not the ass this time, who really is the dunce.'
The miller saw the point of the insult at once,
Set longears on his feet and bade the beast proceed.
It complained in its dialect. Contented on that score,
The miller, with son riding, was plodding as before,
Passed by three rich merchants they seemed to annoy.
The oldest of them called out as loud as he could to the boy,
'My, oh my, get down, my fine youth, it is not just
That your old gray lackey follow in the dust!
Ride and have him walking? This must be corrected.'
The miller said, 'Good sirs, I'll do as you've directed.'
The younger bade the elder mount to meet the plaint,
Till three girls came along. One said, ' 'Twould try a saint;
A monster of injustice up there if you ask me—
Grizzled Bishop Bones with an air of majesty
At ease while his son walks! You'd think he'd have some pride.'
—'At ease,' said the miller. 'And why should years not ride?
The back's the best part of a goose. Be off. You heard.'
After more cross-firing and flinging back of a word,
Old age took heed and had the younger riding too—
Scarcely thirty steps till a third three came in view,
Who taunted the pair thus: 'Uneducated boors!
Beating an ass to death however much he endures:
Thin him down till he's merely a starved drudge's skin,
Goading an old friend who has served year out, year in;
Perhaps sell his drubbed hide at the fair when he drops.'
—'Bless me,' said the miller, 'there's a point at which one stops
Exhausting oneself trying to do as folk desire;
Accommodate oneself to the world and his sire?

[57]

Even patience gives out.' For fear the ass collapse,
The two then dismounted and walked some yards perhaps
When they met someone else who said, 'Is it the mode
For the ass to take his ease and master tramp the road?
Ought it to be the ass or man whom toil abases?
Asses, since such rarities, merit crystal cases;
Conserving donkey bones although their shoes wear thin.
Not Nicholas when he journeyed to Jeanne, whom he hoped to win,
On his donkey as in the song, handed down from antiquity.
A trio of donkeys.' The miller said, 'I agree.
On my soul you are right for once, and I say so:
Hereafter accord me a blessing or a blow,
Be content or be rasped, till your patience is gone;
I shall do as I please,' and he did from then on.

"As for you, go to war; court kings' or Love's bans;
Live agog and a-flutter; be a squire who will not dance;
Politician, functionary; monk; have wife or none;
The world will be carping, no matter what you've done."

II

BELLY AND MEMBERS

One ought to honor royalty
When introducing what is said:
Yet depict Messire Gaster discerningly
And a kind of king has been portrayed.
Starve him and you find the whole animal undone.

Having tired of work, that Gaster need do none,
The members resolved that they'd live as gentlemen,
Lay down their tasks and cite Gaster as justifier.
"Were it not for us," they said, "he would have to live on air.
We sweat, we toil, like beasts by whom heaped carts are drawn.
Why toil that Gaster swell, just he? We do not feast
On what we've earned for him by straining like a beast.
Shirk. Idling is a trade he is qualified to teach."

[58]

They did as said. The hands refused to grasp, as in their
                               dissident speech.
        The arms did not lift; the legs were not walking
And told Gaster, "Go hang; your slave crew is revolting."
'Twas soon clear that their error was costing them dear,
These fine folk before long had grown very spare
Since the heart could no longer send blood anywhere.
The fact that the members felt their strength disappear,
        Demonstrated to each mutineer
That the very one charged with weak unprofitable ways
Deserved to be the object of everyone's praise.

This is like monarchy in its benefits to all,
Calling upon all and aiding all as well.
Its subjects must be loyal and it maintains them then—
        Affording them each some source of gain;
Rewarding craftsmen for what they have designed,
Maintaining the Bench, making merchants' profits vast,
Paying laborers, keeping the sentry at his post,
Disbursing everywhere, benefits as inclined,
        Preserving the state from holocaust—
        As Menenius [1] of old had made clear:
The plebs were seceding from the Senate in disgust,
Saying it usurped authority which all should share—
The power, the wealth, the honor, the dignity;
While evils were their lot, imposed in totality—
Taxes and levies and the weariness of war;
The people had poured forth, resolved on mutiny,
The majority vowing to emigrate somewhere.
        But shown by Menenius that they'd dared to shirk
        As the members had shirked in his tale,
They saw that they'd been indispensable,
        Grew docile, and went back to work.

---

[1] Menenius Agrippa, in persuading the plebs to come back from Mount Sacer, ended his discourse with the fable of the Belly and the Members.

III

THE WOLF PLAYS SHEPHERD

A wolf who had not got his share, it would appear,
      Of sheep pastured near his wood,
Said to himself, "I'll play the fox and make guile my care."
      Assuming a novel attitude,
Putting on a shepherd's smock, he then took a cane
      Or crook, to make the inference plain,
      And shepherd's pipes to aid the ruse.
      Glad of any touch that might appear of use,
He was all but tempted to print upon his headgear,
"This is Giles, the shepherd, whose sheep are grazing near."
      Demureness concealing his wolfish look,
Apart from furred paws crossed on his shepherd's crook,
Hairy Hypocrisy crept up in his false gown.
Good Giles, the real Giles, lying prone as if sunstruck,
      Was lost in a dream on the down,
His dog muter than the Pan pipes he kept with his flock,
And the sheep fast asleep—or say nearly every one.
      Hypocrite of course took care
To lead sheep into his snare imperceptibly
And thought that his voice ought to lend his garb verity—
      Essential to his pseudo-character.
      But he miscalculated there.
He could not counterfeit a shepherd's gentle voice;
His kind words, which filled the woods with a raucous noise,
      Served to involve him in despair.
      All woke as if he had fired a gun—
      Sheep, dog, shepherd, everyone.
      The poor wolf was in a fine plight,
      Impeded by his shepherd's gown,
      Neither able to run away nor fight.

A counterfeit's sure to be exposed to the light.
      A wolf is a wolf in every pulse;
      No use pretending something else.

[60]

IV

THE FROGS ASKED FOR A KING

Although democratic then,
The frogs begged a royal yoke,
Croaking again and again
Till Jupiter sent a king to calm the constant croak.
He sent one who fell from the sky and never spoke
Though the noise of his fall was itself a source of pain
Since amphibians in those bogs
Were shallow-brained timorous frogs
So perturbed when they heard a thud,
They'd sprung among reeds in the mud,
Into holes where cattails stood—
Not even looking at the king they'd hoped would be good,
Some of them supposing that he must be a giant frog,
Whereas he was a forest log
That had hurtled from the sky and filled them with fear.
Curiosity counseled, Begin:
A brave one dared to reappear,
Though with throat skin going out and in.
Another hopped up upon the monarch's skin—
Millions of them and then more,
As where ants swarm from hills on land one tries to clear—
Till all were hopping up on King Log
Who had not made a sound or even threatened a frog.
But again the malcontents were making Jupiter ill,
And said, "Grant us a king who will not lie so still."
The king of the gods sent a crane with a long bill,
Who crushed, pained them at will,
Devouring anything there—
Gulped large and small till all complained
And Jove replied, "Give ear! You'd dare direct your arbiter?
You'd have divinity constrained!
You should have managed to get on
With the government of your own;
But no. Your first king was one whom any frog could bear—

Benign, gracious, in every way desirable.
　　Accept this one as suitable
　　Or endure a harsher with whom he can't compare."

V

THE FOX AND THE GOAT

Captain Fox was padding along sociably
With Master Goat whose horns none would care to oppose,
Though he could not see farther than the end of his nose;
Whereas the fox was practiced in chicanery.
Thirst led them to a well and they simultaneously
　　Leaped in to look for water there.
After each had drunk what seemed a sufficiency,
The fox said to the goat, "Well, friend, and from here where?
We can't be always drinking, Master Goat, can we?
Put your feet up; your horns will rise to that degree,
Push against the wall until your rump is snugged in;
　　I'll climb you like a ladder then,
　　Up the back, up the horns again.
　　In that way, as you have seen,
　　Before long I'll be where we first stood
　　And can draw you up if you think good."
—"Genius," said the goat. "By my beard, what finesse!
　　Nothing like a fox's wit;
　　A ruse on which I could not have hit;
　　A superlative mind, I confess."
The fox leaped out of the well; the goat had to stay down—
　　Harangued as by a sage in a gown
　　About patience and experience;
Yes; told: "If Heaven had only given you as good sense
As the beard on your chin's an exceptional one,
　　You'd not be an adventurer
Into wells, as you have been. Therefore good-by, I must depart.
Strain up high; each leap can be a new start.
　　As for me, I'm due far from here;
I can't stand about as if at an inn."

Better think of the outcome before you begin.

[62]

VI

THE EAGLE, THE SOW, AND THE CAT

At the top of a hollow tree eaglets stared mute;
 Kittens mewed halfway; a sow grunted at the root—
Separate certainly, but in a sense one brood—
Some young, some old, enjoyed the old tree's quietude
Till the mother cat lied and that changed the atmosphere.
She climbed to the eagle's nest and said, "We're doomed, I fear—
At least our little ones, and nothing hurts mothers more;
 Inevitable furthermore.
Look where that destructive sow rolls, roots, and will remain,
Constantly rooting. Why is that done?
To obliterate our broods—kill every little one;
 For of course when the tree has given way,
 They will be devoured as I say;
I'd hold my tongue if she gave even one a chance."
Having suggested a fictitious circumstance,
 Ill will slipped down from the eagle's bough
  To perturb the sow—
 Big mother and pigs with no room between—
 Saying, "Friend and neighbor on whom I lean"
(She whispered it all), "you'll go off innocently
And that bird up there will prey upon your progeny.
 Don't breathe what I've whispered in your ear,
 For vengeance might be my overthrow."
She exerted herself to deal blow upon blow,
 Then sought her hole, pleased to disappear.
Fear so unnerved the eagle that she could not hunt
 Or feed her young. The sow could scarcely grunt—
Fools not to know that they must not die of want,
That survival should be the one object to attain;
But the eagle and sow were obsessed to remain
To succor a brood that disaster might wreck—
 The royal bird in case the tree went down;
 The sow in case of an attack.
Starvation effaced them; it did not leave one.

[63]

Every pig there'd been, every eaglet was gone.
All had vanished. Death had decreed
For milords the cats, decisive aid.

Nothing can do more harm than false tongues, I confess—
The apex of perniciousness—
Of the miscellany set free
When Pandora's box burst,
Deceit was the worst pest with which mankind was cursed—
At least most abhorrent to me.

VII

THE DRUNKARD AND HIS WIFE

Each has some vice which he has never overcome
Despite fear or obloquy.
I recall a tale which brings the matter home—
Would say that almost invariably
An illustration's good. A votary of wine, by its misuse,
Had impaired health, mind, funds, and under Bacchus' curse,
Like all renegades, had gone from bad to worse,
So was bankrupt and without an excuse.
One day the man with his wits in the bottle instead of his head,
Was as helpless, really, as though dead,
And his wife incarcerated him in a tomb.
Effects of the alcohol, we may assume,
Wore off in the course of time, for when he could move,
The man perceived mortuary arrangements and bier,
Winding sheet, torch, and similar gear.
"Oh," he wailed, "what have I done? Widowed her I love?"
Whereupon his wife, dressed as Alecto might have been,
Speaking with a disguised voice in a sepulchral tone,
As if serving him she had wished to inter,
Approached the bier with a broth fit for Lucifer,
Confirming the man's suspicion of where they were—
Hell, as he was obliged to infer.
"Tell me who you are," he then asked of the ghost.
She said, "Stewardess of the kingdom where Satan is host.

When food is served the inmates, I convey it
To them in the gloom in which they are immersed."
The husband replied—by mere force of habit seemed
to say it—
"Do you not bring them something to quench their thirst?"

VIII

GOUT AND THE SPIDER

After making gout and the spider benighted,
Hell said, "My daughters, you should be elated
For mankind has been spited;
You should be scourges to dread—
Accommodated of course with a roof and a bed.
There are huts huddling at our feet;
Or select a palace sumptuously gilded.
You must have some sort of suitable retreat;
Look; draw straws if you can't decide yet,
And accept what you get, unconsulted."
The spider said, "Don't assign me a mere interstice."
On the contrary, seeing the palaces full of folk known
As physicians, gout said, "If thrown
Among them, life could not be a success,"
Chose a cottage, and having alighted
Was at ease on a poor man's toe through which she could roam,
Saying, "Disease has found an ideal home,
Since it is not likely to be combated;
Hippocrates will never come."
Meanwhile the spider spun industriously
A silken ceiling web and spun it exquisitely
As though lifetimes could not destroy her artistry;
Hasty fly after fly could agree.
But bridget with a broom wrecked webs as soon as made,
In fact the moment the spider found a spot to start;
The creature could not spin a web that was not frayed.
After endless waste of her art,
She was on the march to the place where gout might be found.
Embittered by all she had stood,

[65]

Gout had borne more than the spider's stiff round.
Her poor master had kept her outdoors splitting wood,
Digging, grubbing, hoeing, since told, bear down on gout
And literally drive the thing out.
"Oh!" she said, "I'll endure no more of it, sister.
Let us change places, good spider." And therefore the latter,
Taking her at her word, stole without a sound
To the cottage where no whisking broom made her scamper.
Gout on the other hand, went straight, as lodger,
To the palace of a bishop, who was bedbound
Thereafter, her helpless prisoner.
A poultice? God knows doctors are conscienceless.
Disease goes from bad to worse under their therapy.
Both, as they viewed their respective advantages,
Felt that they had exchanged homes auspiciously.

IX

THE WOLF AND THE STORK

Wolves can outeat anyone;
Indeed at a festivity,
Such gluttony second to none
Almost ended fatally
When a bone choked a wolf as he gulped what he ate;
But happily since he was inarticulate,
A stork chanced to hear him groan,
Was besought by frowns to run and peer,
And ah, had soon relieved the beast of the bone;
Then, having done him a service, had no fear,
So asked him how compensate her.
"Compensate?" he inquired with bared teeth,
"A humorist, I infer!
You should be glad that you draw breath.
Thrust your beak down my throat and you somehow
escaped death?
Be off. You are unappreciative;
Shun my paws if you care to live."

X

THE VANQUISHED LION

In this painting persons came to view,
A mere man was putting pressure
On a fine lion he overthrew—
To the lion's discomfiture—
And observers were filled with pride, of course,
Till a passing lion silenced the pointless chatter
By remarking, "Nothing could be easier
Where vanity knows no remorse;
Poetic license there, overpowered
One who would not exercise restraint.
My confreres would have been conqueror, rest assured,
If lions had the power to paint."

XI

THE FOX AND THE GRAPES

A fox of Gascon, though some say of Norman descent,
When starved till faint gazed up at a trellis to which grapes were
tied—
Matured till they glowed with a purplish tint
As though there were gems inside.
Now grapes were what our adventurer on strained haunches
chanced to crave,
But because he could not reach the vine
He said, "These grapes are sour; I'll leave them for some knave."

Better, I think, than an embittered whine.

XII

THE SWAN AND THE COOK

Of the miscellany
In a man's aviary,
A swan swam, and a goose waddled:
One a sublime sight that made the garden complete;
Or so the owner thought; and one, a bird to eat.
One enhanced the flowers; one stayed near the house and puddled.
They would ornament the moat simultaneously,
Now and then side by side or were seen converging;
At times merely drifting, again were submerging,
Apparently looking for something illusory.
One day the cook, who had had an extra drop,
Took the swan for the goose, held it up
By the neck, would have cut its throat and had it simmering;
But at the point of death it burst into song so ravishing,
The astonished cook perceived
That his dulled eyes had been deceived
And said, "What! make so sweet a singer into soup!
Dear, dear; God forbid murder to which my hand could stoop.
Close a throat whose uses are delectable!"

So when the horseman is hovered by perils too dire to outleap,
Sweet speech does no harm—none at all.

XIII

THE WOLVES AND THE SHEEP

Though for ten thousand years they had quarreled and fought,
The wolves and sheep vowed to live peaceably—
A resolve which affected both advantageously,
Since if wolves devoured sheep that wandered about,
There was a wolfskin on any shepherd one might see.
Neither had liberty; the sheep weren't free to feed;

[68]

Wolves dared not stalk the prey they need,
And trepidation impaired contentment for everyone.
So a peace was signed, with hostages as agreed;
The wolves gave cubs; the sheep, dogs; and all was done
Formally with commissioners there.
Presently their lordships the cubs had reached wolf's estate,
And with all of them ravening for butchery,
Bloodthirstily watching for what they might seize,
Struck when their absent lordships the shepherds
could not retaliate,
Slaughtered half the lambs—the ones already fat—
In gory jaws carried them toward the woods and disappeared,
Having secretly notified their folk what would be done.
The trustful dogs were asleep and strangled to the last one
Before they could wake and run:
It all was too sudden for them to be prepared.
Not one escaped, since they were torn to pieces where caught.

We might take to heart this thought:
Our war on the wicked must be continual.
Peace is best as everyone knows.
I agree—in case it is possible;
When is it, with dishonorable foes?

XIV

THE LION GROWN OLD

A lion who had made his world tremble,
Mourning lost youth and succumbing to distress,
Was attacked by those formerly servile,
Who dared to profit by his feebleness.
The horse came up and let him feel the force of a heel;
The wolf tore off some skin, the ox gave a prod with his horn.
The unfortunate lion, languid, depressed, and forlorn,
Was without strength to roar; age had made him a cripple.
Lying mute, without a moan, he could scarcely draw breath.
When he saw even the ass come running to the lair,
He said, "Die, yes, but ah! this is too much to bear.
To suffer blows from you is die a double death."

[69]

XV

PHILOMEL AND PROCNE

The swallow, Procne, fables tell,
Once went darting from her dwelling,
Following celestial trilling,
Toward the nightingale's note in a shadowy dell,
And said, "How have you fared, sweet sister I have lost?
It seems a thousand years that you've been tempest-tossed,
Your absence from our coast has given me no rest;
All Thrace has mourned your loss, these many months distressed.
How overcome despair?
Is there no other spot a singer might prefer?"
The nightingale said, "Where? I like a forest best."
Procne continued, "Ah, the seraphic music you make—
For mere wild animals it might please,
Or some dazed farmer with a rake.
Why choose a desert for your brilliant ecstasies?
Come where townsfolk are. Sing to ears thrilled by surprise.
Then in looking upon trees continually,
You must recall each day how formerly,
With a scene like this before your eyes,
Tereus, assaulting your heavenly charms, was your undoing."
—"I'm held here by that deed of which I almost died,"
Her sister said. "If I should see men as I sing
Each, alas, would seem that same foul king!
My thoughts of him would be intensified."

XVI

THE DROWNED WOMAN

No, I am not the man to say—"Oh well, it's done;
Too bad that she should drown"—
Of awesome tragedy. You'll be told by anyone,
With a sigh, that woman is man's chief crown.

What I shall now relate is not irrelevant,
    Since this is a tale attempting to tell
    Of a woman who met with a death we don't want—
In the water—an end to life, that was terrible.
    Her husband scanned the river for her
    To do at that juncture what lay in his power—
    Honor her with burial. It happened at an hour
    When people were strolling here and there
    On the banks of the stream that made him aghast;
They'd not noticed that someone had fallen in
    And when he asked if his wife had been seen,
If any had seen a form floating past,
One said, no, they'd not, "but you might search below;
    Better follow the river's course."
Another said, "No, not the way the water would flow.
    Your course should be the reverse.
The victim would surely incline
    To resist the water's natural force.
    By the fact of being feminine,
    She would take the opposite course."

The man's jest was scarcely wit on this occasion:
    Perversity's quite complex;
    There might have been justification.
    By no means convinced, I for one
    Don't confine it to the fair sex;
    For anyone born contrary
    Will die contradictory—
    Be even afterward probably
    An unwearying adversary.

XVII

THE WEASEL IN THE STOREROOM

Adroit Miss Weasel, with a body to suit,
Found ingress to a storeroom, although it was minute.
   She'd ailed, but no longer an invalid
   Made up for having been lean
   By eating with gluttonous speed,
   Gnawing and gulping with evident greed,
Nibbling stored-up flitches. Devastation marked the scene!
   Thus the form that had been thin
   Was becoming sleek—spheroid indeed.
At the end of a week when she'd feasted till stout,
She heard a noise and tried to get out,
But somehow could not, thought she had been deceived,
   And was running to chinks here and there,
Saying, "Yes, the place; a thing I'd not have believed.
No more than five or six days ago I entered here."
   A rat saw her perplexity
And said, "Your little waist had a little less convexity.
Thin come in, thin go out, if you would use the same door."

It's been said to many as applying to their affairs,
But let the analogy rest without saying anything more,
   Or confusing our problems with theirs.[1]

---

[1] An allusion to financiers and King's farmers as venturers into storerooms,
who in 1660 had surrendered their wealth to the King's treasury. As a former
protégé of Fouquet—no longer in power—La Fontaine stops and becomes deli-
cately vague.

XVIII

THE CAT AND THE OLD RAT

I read one time in a fairy tale
Of a Rodilard, or cat Alexander-the-Great—
    An Attila like the hand of fate,
    A synonym of fear to all.
    As just said, in this tale he was a scourge,
    A beast whose name rang like a dirge—
A Cerberus of the classical kind;
Ridding the earth of rodents was foremost in his mind.
Even the slat propped on a slat with nicety,
    Rat bane or trap which folk prepare,
    Were surpassed by puss continually.
    Since he kept each a prisoner
    In its hole, not a mouse dared appear;
And with none stirring forth, lest he find himself spindling,
The rapscallion strung himself up with head dangling—
Pretending to be dead. The reprobate
Caught some cords from which he suspended himself by the feet
And the mice accordingly inferred a punishment
For audacious inroads on cheese or joints of beef;
Thought he'd scratched someone—been a pest, must have, in
                                     brief,
Brought on this appropriate predicament.
    All, as said, joined in the merriment,
Keen for the burial which now seemed imminent.
Noses debonair, with rounded ears thrust out,
    They saw that their nests were circumspect,
    Danced a quadrille, advanced and backed
    And then were off to the rout—
    Or funeral as it turned out.
Dropping upon light feet, the pendant puss was pouncing
    And catching mice as he chose.
"Tom knows more than one," he said as he was crunching,
"Of these old tricks, my dears. Playing the mouse recluse
Won't save you, let me say, and I say it openly;

[73]

You'll all be coming back to me."
Master Puss was right. Our sweet Tom's ingenuity
Deceived and trapped them once again.
Floured till no hair of him was seen,
That is to say, completely hid,
With paws curled under, he crouched in an open kneading trough,
Bound to succeed in what he did:
Then waited for the twinkling toes he would bear off.
One veteran rat would not so much as sniff it from afar.
A genuine old stager, he knew the art of war—
In a battle had sacrificed even his tail.
"That's a mound of meal," he said, "that it does not pay to smell."
From a distance he called to General Cat, "I think I suspect
The kind of flour you've sacked. You feign
To be flour. What you are is quite plain.
Say you were the sack itself, I'd be leaving you intact."

He spoke to the point, with a prudence which has my
acquiescence.
From experience he had come to see
That caution is but common sense,
The mother of security.

BOOK FOUR

THE LION IN LOVE

To Mademoiselle de Sévigné [1]

Mademoiselle—goddess instead—
In whom the Graces find a school
Although you are more beautiful,
Even if with averted head,
Might you not be entertained
By a tale that is unadorned—
Hearing with no more than a quiver
Of a lion whom Love knew how to conquer.
Love is a curious mastery,
In name alone a felicity.
Better know of than know the thing.
If too personal and thus trespassing,
I'm saying what may seem to you an offense,
A fable could not offend your ear.
This one, assured of your lenience,
Attests its devotion embodied here,
And kneels in sworn obedience.

Before their speech was obstructed,
Lions or such as were attracted
To young girls, sought an alliance.
Why not? since as paragons of puissance,
They were at that time knightly fellows
Of mettle and intelligence
Adorned by manes like haloes.

---

[1] Mlle. de Sévigné, later Mme. Grignan, daughter of Mme. de Sévigné. Many of Mme. de Sévigné's letters were addressed to her.

[75]

The point of the preamble follows.
A lion—one in a multitude—
Met in a meadow as he fared,
A shepherdess for whom he cared.
He sought to win her if he could,
Though the father would have preferred
A less ferocious son-in-law.
To consent undoubtedly was hard;
Fear meant that the alternate was barred.
Moreover, refuse and he foresaw
That some fine day the two might explain
Clandestine marriage as the chain
That fettered the lass, bewitched beyond cure,
By fashions conducive to hauteur,
And a fancy that shaggy shoulder fur
Made her willful lover handsomer.
The father with despair choked down,
Said though at heart constrained to frown,
"The child is a dainty one; better wait;
You might let your claw points scratch her
When your heavy forepaws touch her.
You could if not too importunate,
Have your claws clipped. And there in front,
See that your teeth are filed blunt,
Because a kiss might be enjoyed
By you the more, I should think,
If my daughter were not forced to shrink
Because improvidently annoyed."
The enthralled animal mellowed,
His mind's eye having been shuttered.
Without teeth or claws it followed
That the fortress was shattered.
Dogs were loosed; defenses were gone:
The consequence was slight resistance.

Love, ah Love, when your slipknot's drawn,
We can but say, "Farewell, good sense."

[76]

II

THE SHEPHERD AND THE SEA

As carefree as his flock, it seems there was a man
Who lived by the sea and life was a delight.
   At shearing time his gains were slight
   But at least there would be gain.
Then, sad; he saw a trader's gorgeousness displayed,
Was thus lured to part with his one and only flock
And invest what he'd earned in a ship; but ah, the shock—
   Wrecked in return for all he'd paid.
He was hired to tend sheep that had been his property—
As merely a herd of course with no authority,
Since he had financed the sea with his cavalcade.
Thyrsis or Corydon as he had been formerly,
   Was now Hodge whom none but sheep obeyed.
But he had saved money presently,
   Bought back a few sheep of his own,
And then one morning when the wind had died down
And boats crept in so gently they did not even rock,
He said, "Ladies of the sea, find someone else to mock,
Might I suggest? since it's money you expect.
Bless me! no more ships of mine shall be wrecked!"

This is no whimsy it has amused me to expand.
   It should help us to understand
   What one learns by experience—
   That you've more with a single sou in hand
   Than with promise of five some days hence.
That we be content with our situation has been shown:
To temptations which ambition and the sea intone,
   We must be deaf—our ears, citadels.
For one who gains from the sea [1] she makes ten thousand groan—
   Promising mountains and miracles,
Providing storms and piracy. Stand stiff if you'd not be undone.

[1] The sea—a reference to The East India Company.

III

THE FLY AND THE ANT

A fly and an ant each claimed superiority
   Till the fly burst forth, "O Jupiter!
That one should see self-esteem blind modesty
   So shockingly as in her.
   Vile groveling animal,
Daring to consider herself my airy equal!
Frequenting mansions, I take my place with the royal
And am first to taste the gods' sacrificial roast
Whereas that poor thing, good for nothing but toil,
Needs three days to devour a straw the farmer lost.
   My precious pest,
Do you find a king's head a perch of which to boast?
   Emperor's or belle's whose gems dazzle?
Watch me touch a girl's hair if I fancy its sheen,
   Or print a kiss below her chin.
Fly-freckle patches make pallor more beautiful.
Before a charmer decks herself that hearts may bleed,
   A hand skilled in beauty's rite
Adjusts the artificial flyspecks she will need.
   Fiend take you, you thimble full of spite,
   You and your storerooms." —"Your answer to me?
   Is that it?" the economist sparred;
"My haughty palace fly! scourge loathed by royalty!
   As for rare morsels you have marred,
   Which were to be the gods' own food,
   Could fly footmarks have made them good?
You dart in where you will, and so do the most crass;
Pre-empting the head of a king or an ass,
Alighting and flitting, I don't dispute the fact;
   And you die by as swift an act,
Since malapertness operates suicidally.
Her patch or mouche makes her pretty, you tell me.
I agree that it is black as you or I.
I admit that it's called 'fly'; does that justify

[78]

Emphasis on the merits you advertise?
Are not parasites also known as flies?
Then stop making these boasts that are inane.
      Don't harbor notions so lofty.
      Flies—*mouches de cour*—are expelled without
                                                    mercy;
In wartime such flies are hung; you'll starve in the cold rain,
      Freeze, faint, and die of despair,
When the sun is reigning in another hemisphere—
Whereas I'll thrive as one by whom life's understood,
      Who does not scour the neighborhood
      In rain that whirls tempestuously,
      In fact I'll live delightfully.
My painstaking toil will have guaranteed calm,
      A formula for true heart's balm.
Learn to tell what is gold from what is base ore.
Farewell: I'm hard-pressed; deferred duties counsel speed.
      Mere words do not dispose of a chore
      Or swell my bins with food ants need."

IV

THE GARDENER AND THE SQUIRE

      A devoted gardener—
      A not quite rustic, not quite citified one—
      Possessed in a village somewhere
A trim well-cared-for garden, by tillage he'd sown.
A snug hedge framed what he was growing with green.
Sorrel and lettuce grew at will within,
Flowers enough to make Betsey a bouquet should she wed,
A touch of Spanish jasmine and mats of thyme that spread;
Then a hare was found nibbling the greens in each bed.
Our man informed the squire of the indignity.
"This demon devours every seed I've sown," he said.
"Morning, noon, and night, he laughs at any strategy.
The sticks and stones I hurl fall innocuously;
He's a sorcerer." —"Sorcerer? Leave him to me,"
The squire said. "Though the devil lends him a coat,

[79]

And he doubles, my Miraut will be at his throat.
I'll deal with him, my man, I guarantee."
—"But when?" —"By tomorrow noon you shall have the
                                        vermin's skin."
He appeared, and with friends who were soon swarming in.
"Aha! breakfast!" he said. "Tender pullets you've browned?
You've a daughter somewhere. Tell her she has callers.
Wedding bells for—let me see. Who can find the lucky hound?
Give in, my man; scrape up and rain the dollars.
            You'll have to yield; you know it all too well,"
He said, then accosted the lass—over-affable—
            And seated her by him, almost on his chair—
Hand on arm, on hand; even turned up her fichu to stare—
            Acts so unpermissible
            She could but ignore the attack,
Till her father was squirming like one on the rack.
Meanwhile the fricassee; the cook's frown summed up the scene.
"Hams you've cured this season? Ideal fat and lean."
—"Have them, Squire; accept them. Do." —"That I shall.
                                        Upon my word!"
            The squire said. "Treated like a lord."
He ate, was helped again—each friend as heartily.
Dogs and horses were fed; grooms; the horde was regaled
As at inns where hired waiters are there to be hailed;
            He drank and fawned on the lass loutishly.
Huntsmen tramped in and out when refection had staled.
            Breathless excitement was charging the air
As post-horns and trumpets combined in a blare.
            Aghast at it all, the pained owner paled.
The worst of it was, they left in a state past repair
The poor kitchen garden. Beds and frames, farewell.
            Farewell, chicory and leeks; farewell, all
            That lends soup savor.
The hare hid by a monstrous cabbage as redoubt—
Was pursued with a rush, found a hole and got out.
Hole! horrible gash the squire's horse had torn wide
            Till the hedge gaped from side to side.
Positively scandalous that gardener's toil
Prevent riders from backing through garden soil!
Our man murmured, "Kings' sport. Alas for insignificance!"

And was left muttering. Harm the dogs and horses had done
In an hour was mountainous in height by comparison
   With a hundred years of hares rolled in one,
   Congregated from that part of France.

Settle your quarrels among yourselves, princelings.
It is folly to ask the assistance of kings.
On no account invite them to take part in your wars
   Or cause them to enter domains that are yours.

v

THE DONKEY AND THE LAPDOG

   Don't ape what must be born in one;
You'll become a clown of awkwardness:
   A boor by birth is never less,
   Whatever his caparison.
Just a few upon whom Heaven smiled indulgently,
Seem blessed with the art of pleasing naturally—
   An art better not assisted;
So let us not be the donkey in my tale,
   Who hoped to seem more lovable
By proffering endearments which would be resisted.
   He said to himself, "Why not the same
   As that lapdog? Because he's a scrap of a thing,
   Have master and mistress been flattering
   And petting him the instant he came,
   Whereas I'm drubbed till the cudgels sing?
   His paw goes up, wheedling some benefit;
   He's kissed and promptly overrated.
If that's all one must do to be a favorite,
   It's not too complicated."
   So since initiated,
He lumbered up as his master shook with merriment,
   Raised a hoof which use had dented,
And dealt his master's chin a blow that was well meant,
To the music of a bray's accompaniment:
A dainty match for boorish intrepidity.

[81]

"Oh! oh! What a caress! and what a melody!"
Master shouted, "Martin, haste. This beast is pestilent!"
Cudgel-Martin rushed forth, made the tune different,
    And that ended the comedy.

VI

THE WAR BETWEEN THE RATS AND THE WEASELS

Those who comprise the weasel state,
No more than the nation of cats,
Are favorable to the rats,
And but for the latter's style of retreat
With narrow door through which to rush down,
The creature with elongated spine
Would bring about, I imagine,
A holocaust for the warred upon.
Now one year it happened
That the rats rejoiced in a gain
So great that their king, Ratapon,
Managed to have an army mustered.
Then the weasels, it would appear,
Flew the flag they used in war,
And it's said both fought until spent—
Word which reports authenticate—
With a loss of blood so great
That mile on mile was stained.
It seems that among those who remained
Of the twofold embattled host,
The grayer side suffered most—
It was defeated everywhere
Though heroic Artapax,
Psicarpax and Meridarpax,
Bore dust of warfare thick as fur
And supported wherever they'd gone,
Their troops which were being outdone.
Resistance had been vain
Since the Three Fates were untoward;
Captains fled at point of the sword—

And soldiers in an endless chain.
Every one of the princes was lost.
The rank and file got off best,
Stumbling rearward in rout
Down holes already made—
But the nobles were singled out
By a crested helmet heightening the head,
With horns or plume—marks of note
Such as men of authority wear—
Or as warning to weasels who fought,
That they had best disappear.
But the ornaments cost the wearers dear.
No chink, hoofmark, or dent
Was a refuge sufficiently wide;
Whereas the rabblement
Could crouch in a crevice to hide.
Most bodies with which the soil was strewn
Were those of eminent rats.

A plume that bespeaks renown
May presage severe regrets,
As a lane may incommode
A coach the width of the road,
Slowing it lest it be thrown;
While modesty anywhere,
Glides in as when silk is sewn.
Yes. Pride is a hinderer.

VII

THE APE AND THE DOLPHIN

Among the Greeks it was understood
That almost every voyager
Would provide as an interlude
Trick monkeys or dogs with his traveling gear.
Now a bark on which such toys were conveyed,
Went down near Athens, it is said,
And all would have perished at sea

[83]

But that porpoises mercifully
Are friends of mankind, as Pliny records,
And no one disputes this author's words.
Well, helpful dolphins swam about;
Even an ape who shared the mischance,
Possessed so human a countenance
That he was assisted to clamber out,
Instead of be drowned far from home.
A porpoise afforded him a chair,
As though a composer were in his care
And Arion been drawn from the foam.
Meanwhile in bearing the ape ashore,
The dolphin presently inquired,
"You are from Athens, the much admired?"
—"Ah yes; the same. I am well known there,"
The ape replied. "Permit me, sir,
To serve you; I am a favored man;
The entire world venerates my clan;
My cousin is Justice—a high officer."
The dolphin replied, "A courtesy.
Of course as a celebrity
Your fame has doubtless equally
Charmed Piraeus; a reputation gains."
—"Quite so. He's devoted to me
With an ardor that never wanes,"
Our impostor said—neatly caught,
By confusing inhabitant with home:

Many a fool plays aristocrat,
Not knowing Vaugirard from Rome;
Boasting he's seen this spot and that
Whereas his alps have all been flat.

The dolphin smiled and turned his head,
Appraised his gem, saw what he'd done,
And having saved from oblivion
An ordinary quadruped,
Swirled him right into the ocean
And swam back to save a person.

VIII

THE MAN AND THE IDOL

Now a certain heathen revered a god of wood—
One of those gods with ears who hear nothing said;
Yet the poor soul considered its power unlimited.
      It cost him three times more than it should
      Since votive offerings must abound,
And oxen for sacrifice that must be garland-crowned.
      Idols either false or true,
      Never had so rich a feast,
Though nothing desirable seemed to ensue;
No bequest, treasure trove, gains at play; Heaven did not
                              assist.
What is more, if tuppence worth of storm brewed
      In any spot, of any sort,
The man had his share of it; tribute had to be paid
Because gold for the idol must never run short.
Disgusted at last since afforded no gain,
The man smote the god with a crowbar, and as it fell
Saw gold pieces pour forth. He said, "You've caused me pain
But never gave me an obol for doing well.
Out from my dwelling—find another altar by which to dwell.
      You are like the savage, dull,
      Degraded, brutish, and made of greed.
Of no use till my club brought your life to an end;
The more I would aid you the more you seemed to need.
      Just retribution has made you my friend."

IX

THE JAY IN PEACOCK'S FEATHERS

A jay found plumes which a moulting peacock had strewed,
      Assumptively feathered himself out—
Rejoicing to parade up and down as peacocks strode about,

[85]

In what seemed an exalted mood.
Someone recognized him, and he saw the bird laugh,
    Was scorned, hissed, mocked, amid all kinds of chaff,
And their lordships the peacocks plucked off his feigned coat.
Even on taking refuge with jays when the game was too rough,
    The door was the reception he got.

There are plenty of ten-toed jays swaggering comically,
Purporting to be something which they cannot be.
    If terms like plagiarist alarm,
Why say more? I am not one to speak dictatorially
    Or do another author harm.

x

THE CAMEL AND THE FLOTSAM

    A man, encountering a camel,
    Fled, shocked by a sight so novel.
Another ventured near. A third then braved what they had
                    feared;
    The curiosity was snared.
We grow accustomed to what at first made us afraid,
Though before so alarming we had shivered with dread.
    Having seen it, we are prepared
    When we encounter it afterward.
Since I've broached this topic, a word might be added
    About some watchmen who were deluded
By a form at sea. They were so intimidated
    Each of them said he could swear
    That what he saw was a man of war;
Then concluded a fireship was being moored;
    Then a wherry; then something tied with cord,
    And then some flotsam that swung and swirled.

    Ah yes, how much I've seen in the world,
    For which these anecdotes account—
Far off, immense; but close at hand to what does it amount!

XI

THE FROG AND THE RAT

Wily Merlin, when speaking of chicanery,
        Said connivers are caught now and then—
Too bad that this word for them is not used currently;
I've felt its force, might I say, again and again.
But returning at length to my fantasy,
A sleek round rat sunk in materiality,
For whom Lent was not lean and Advent ever profane,
Lurked near a marsh in the hope of variety.
Then a frog hopped up and made some sounds that meant,
"Come share good cheer with me if you crave diversion."
        Master Rat welcomed the notion:
The frog might have nodded in modest assent,
But enlarged upon the delights of immersion,
Curiosity's harvest when threading the sedge,
All kinds of incidents at the morass's edge,
Marvelous sights to overawe one's grandchildren,
Romantic scenery, strange sorts of batrachian,
And a form of state undoubtedly unique
        For life in a creek.
Alas, the rat had not been initiated;
He'd never learned to swim and needed at his side
Aid which the promptly useful frog could provide.
She saw that his feet and hers were approximated;
        Grasses tied criss-cross made them secure;
Master Rat was dragged down. The frog, far too demure,
Towed the poor animal to the gravel below—
Against her sworn word and international law,
That she might crowd him presently into her maw,
Since he would be succulent as frog requirements go.
The conqueror was dreaming of tender rat steak.
As he calls on the gods, her smiles would shame a snake.
He fights; she pulls hard. While they thrash to and fro,
A hawk sailing near, who'd been watching the ground,
Sighted the half-drowned rat's unwilling round

[87]

And seized our pair—unwarned by sound or sign—
    Frog, rat, and aquatic twine;
    In fact two foods to combine
    By the double play.
    The bird had snatched the perfect prey,
    Having caught for delectation
    Meat and fish in combination.

    Snares woven impeccably
    Can be the weaver's executioner;
    And how often treachery
    Brings doom on its practitioner.

XII

TRIBUTE SENT BY THE ANIMALS TO ALEXANDER

In ancient times this tale was a favorite,
    Although I am not quite sure why it was.
That the reader may rightly interpret it,
    Here it is once again, clause for clause:

    They say that wherever news could circulate,
Jove's son, Alexander, saw fit to ordain
That any who valued peace, whatever their estate,
    Must neither hesitate nor explain;
    Worms, man, the quadrupeds persons maintain,
Elephants, even birds accustomed to flight—
    Must pay tribute, the royal perquisite.
    Rumor's multitudinous speech
    On behalf of the emperor
Terrified every species of beast to the core;
    Whereas till then one law had bound them each—
The law of appetite—they were obliged to subdue
    A species of fear entirely new;
So they met in the desert, forsaking nest or lair,
And after a colloquy the assembly resolved
    To pay tribute, also homage involved.
    For the latter aspect of the affair,

They chose a monkey as deputy to record proceedings formally
        Since records are necessary.
      As for the tribute they must obtain,
    Where could they get enough for all combincd?
        Then a prince with no object to gain
        Said he had gold that he had mined
    And thereupon the problem was solved
Except for those on whom conveyance devolved.
      The mule and ass said, if desired,
They could aid the horse and camel in bearing the gold
      And set forth with the tribute required—
    The monkey to offer credentials, as you've been told.
The cavalcade soon stopped short. A grandee had curbed its
                             speed—
My Lord Lion, whose prestige was what they least desired.
      "Precisely what I had required,"
He said. "Suppose we join forces as we proceed;
      I had to set out alone with my share;
But small as it is, I find I can't get on fast.
      Happily now, I need not be downcast
        If each conveys a fourth of what I bear.
Then no one's load will bow him to the ground,
And since left free, without tribute money in my way,
If bands of thieves appear, in which these parts abound,
      My forepaws are sure to have plenty of play."
Those who do not heed a lion's words are unique,
So all of them smiled and nobody was embroiled.
It was not Alexander for whom the great cat toiled,
So he devoured official food till his spirits were at a peak.
      Then they saw a rivulet
Watering verdant grass in which dainty flowers were set,
      Where knots of sheep were grazing peacefully
    And zephyrs played; in fact a nursery
Of the breeze. Suddenly the lion seemed to swoon
      But said no one else need be delayed;
      "Others of the deputation, proceed,"
He said. "I'm burned by a fever like the sun at noon,
And should seek a healing herb that possibly may grow here;
Whereas you are pressed and have to go on.
Return me my money in case an adversary appear."

They unpacked. Their liege lord sang a triumphant chant,
      Exclaiming amid excited purrs,
"By heaven, the productive dears have borne others—
What an increase! Observe; every precious infant
      As large as the mothers were.
The babes, of course, are mine." And he took all that his paws
                      could hold,
Which left but a few coins for the others to share.
      The monkey and bearers were appalled—
Had not a word to say, so went on toward the court
That they might tell Jove's son what made the tribute short.
      But it was they who suffered for not paying.

Lion attack lion? It is an old saying.
Pirates spare pirates? is what is meant there.
Neither would gain if each plundered the other.

XIII

THE STAG AND THE HORSE
WHO WOULD BE REVENGED

Men did not always have horses at command.
In the days when acorns served mankind as bread,
It was the forest that ass, horse, and mule inhabited.
There were no bridles answerable to the hand,
      Stirrups, corded panniers to load,
      Armor for horses knights bestrode,
      Formal coaches or carriages;
      Nor did anyone meet on the road
      Vehicles going to marriages.
    Now a stag whose speed was a phenomenon
      Had quarreled with a certain horse
    Who tried to overtake him, but the stag won;
Accordingly the horse made man his resource,
And the man, when mounted, decided where it should go,
      Till they had pressed so hard upon the foe
That the stag was overtaken, then dispatched ruthlessly.
    The horse thanked the man for his reciprocity.

"What do I not owe to you!" he said. "Since I am leaving you,
Farewell; I must return to my native wood."
—"But not yet, delay," the man said. "Work is best for you;
   I realize now for what you are good.
  Stay with me. After toiling, rest at no cost.
   You'll find fresh straw the height of your girth."
   Alas! What are comforts worth
   If independence has been lost?
The horse perceived that he had behaved foolishly—
Too late to repent; simultaneously
   A stable offered hospitality.
  The horse died there—ball linked to chain.
Though revenge holds out an illusion of recompense,
Count the cost of the thing you would attain
   Lest loss involved overbalance the gain.

XIV

THE FOX AND THE BUST

The great man's an actor who parades in a mask
And glamour is all that hero-worshipers ask.
The donkey judges by superficialities,
Whereas a fox sees all that there is to be seen,
And from all sides. Since his sensibilities
   Discern more than surface sheen,
He dares say what he once said of a hero's bust—
   A quip that certainly was just.
Though larger than life, it was a hollow affair.
The fox, in commending the sculptor's gift as rare,
   Remarked, "Fine head, but it lacks a mind."

How many grandees have fine heads of that kind!

[91]

XV

THE WOLF, THE GOAT, AND THE KID

XVI

WOLF, MOTHER, AND CHILD

In need of fresh grass that her withered udder swell,
      Mother Goat locked the door well
      Upon leaving the chalet
      And warned little Billy,
      "Baby goat, cock your ear
      As you hold your life dear.
      Anyone's words and the password must tally:
      'Plague on wolves and cubs they raise!' "
      Although she spoke the words low,
      Starved Master Wolf heard the phrase
      And thought, "Rich fare; I must go slow."
      He had found a secret to guard.
      The goat, as you have inferred,
      Went off, leaving Billy alone.
When he'd seen her leave, the wolf disguised his gruff tone—
      Arrant hypocrite—
And said the door must be unlocked; then, "Plague on wolves
                        and kin,"
      Thinking he'd instantly be let in.
But Billy quavered through a convenient slit,
"You must show a white foot or I'll keep you out."
Now there are very few wolves with white feet about,
It would seem; or at least so I have always heard.
Billy's speech was a shock which made Master Wolf absurd;
All the beast could do was hurry home to hide.
Just where would Billy be had he been satisfied
      With passwords our wolf might have found opportune
      To palm off on Billy as true?
      Two safeguards are better than one;
Too many precautions are better than too few.

The wolf of which I told you before
Brings to mind one of his clan outdone in a way still more complete.
He lost his life—as told here once more.

The spot was remote in which the farmhouse was set.
Master Wolf who lived by windfalls hung about
Since he had seen all sorts of livestock come out—
Calves, sheep, lambs, tiny and fat—
Multitudes of turkeys; so to speak, food in bulk.
The scoundrel, however, soon found the wait trying;
Then he heard a baby crying,
For when it was hungry it would sulk.
The mother told her bantling
He'd be thrown to the wolf. Now the beast was still lurking
And thanked the gods that he had been present to hear.
Then the mother, to quiet the little dear,
Said, "If he comes, we'll kill him; don't cry, little one."
—"How was that?" exclaimed the wolf whom her words seemed
to stun:
"Raise hopes, then dash them down? Keep me here at the gate
As a convenience? or trust my brain has been left out?
In the fall when there are nuts about
And that tot's in the woods, I'll be lying in wait!"
As the wolf was speaking the house door flew open;
A mastiff scared him back. Boar spears and pokers
Cut his hide to tatters
And then, "What were you lurking there for?" was
everyone's question.
He quoted what he had overheard.
—"Pity me heaven; devour one I've reared?"
The mother replied. "Raise a little son
That a glutton crunch its every bone?"
Poor wolf, he was clubbed till dead.
First, someone cut off his right foot and his head.
The chief man of the place had them nailed above his door as
an exhibit
With this proverb from Picardy printed under it:
"Good Master Wolf, do not sharpen your ears, not yet,
When mother calms baby with a threat."

[93]

XVII

SOCRATES' ANSWER

Our sage one year was something more—
A builder—though folk dared deprecate
What he built. Observers scorned the interior
As too cramped for one so great;
They disliked the outside; in fact all could agree
That the size of the rooms was a travesty.
How could he turn around! Too mean for one with his mind.
"May heaven see fit to provide me,"
He said, "with staunch friends to fill space I've designed!"

Good Socrates had justification
When he found his house overlarge for true friends. No pretension
More common than friendship—on which only fools would depend.
Not a word in the world more common;
Nothing more rare than a friend.

XVIII

THE OLD MAN AND HIS SONS

Any power is weak that is not born of unity:
As Aesop has explained. Listen attentively.
This is his tale, though with touches of my own,
Modernizing one who wrote inimitably,
As though my modest pen could augment such a man.
Phaedrus sometimes tried to appear spectacular,
Whereas that is something I never could have done.
But now for the fable or story I would share—
Of a father who wished his household to be a united one.

Aware that his life was about to ebb away,
An old man said, "My dears, dear sons that is to say,
See if you can break these darts and I'll explain

[94]

How it is that they resist you however hard you strain."
The eldest tried his strength, found he could do no more,
So said, "A task for one who'd crack iron at the core."
The second used full strength and supposed success sure,
But failed, as did the third despite competition's lure.
None could mar the sheaf although all three had tried;
Not a dart was splintered, the sheaf was so well tied.
"Frail lads," the father said, "since they have proved too stiff,
Surrender the arrows and watch me break the sheaf."
They smiled as at a jest; but the expositor
Took the bundle apart and broke the strongest there,
Saying, "Now that you've seen dissension cut like a sword,
Let love bind your hearts, sons; be all of one accord!"
Throughout his illness he did not again converse;
Realizing at last that his malady grew worse,
He said, "Dear sons, I join our forebears and depart.
Farewell; be of one mind—the wish I've most at heart.
In dying, I commend my prayer to you again."
They vowed fidelity and tears bespoke their pain.
He pressed each hand in turn and died. The sons as heirs
Found that the inheritance had imposed countless cares.
A creditor pressed a claim; a neighbor grew irate.
At first they got on well but tedium bred hate,
Good will tired of its role, then suffered disrepair.
Though blood had been a bond, each wished the largest share;
Self-interest stirred by greed filed suits that must be won,
Dissension, tricks, ill will, magnified dangers run.
The three were at swords' points, full of wiles and disdain;
The judge pronounced harsh sentences, again and again;
Creditors and false friends were pacing to and fro.
Errors crept in everywhere and payments were too low.
Of course disagreement gave way to despair.
If one would compromise, two thought he'd laid a snare.
Bankruptcy proved what had been shown them at the start,
That tied sheaves none could break can be splintered when
                                                    apart.

XIX

THE ORACLE AND THE IMPIOUS MAN

All who cheat God will fail, as fools find everywhere.
Labyrinths of the heart are bound to be laid bare
As soon as exposed to deity's piercing light.
Everything is as day in God's sight—
Even when sundown leaves the world crepuscular.

A man ripe for the stake—a pagan, I'd have you know—
Who believed in God, or at least would have it seem so,
      Provisionally, till all was laid bare,
      Went to consult Apollo, though the errand was
                        feigned,
      As soon as the god would be there,
And asked, "Is what I hold alive or has life waned?"
      Clutching a sparrow in his hand,
      Which he could smother to aid deceit
      Or, poor thing, could let go
      And thus belittle Apollo.
Apollo spoke, having discerned the trick of a cheat:
"Alive or dead, show us your sparrow.
      Don't try deceiving Apollo.
Do it again, and you will repent of your game.
      My eyes pierce any void, like the arrows I aim."

XX

THE MISER WHO LOST HIS HOARD

Only use gives possession. Let me ask one question then
Of misers, since the obsession which dominates such men
Is to add and add more till they have a surplus,
What have they, after all, more than the rest of us?
Dead Diogenes has as much in his grave
As penurious persons have who save and save.

Here, Aesop's miser's hoard, which had been of no use,
 Should certainly warn all of us.

  To profit by what he had
He would have needed earthly immortality.
He did not own but was owned by the gold he coveted
When he buried it out of doors secretly—
  His heart as well—having no other delight
   Than to brood on it day and night.
His obsession with money soon became so bad,
Whether he ate or drank, if he came or went away,
There was scarcely a moment when his thoughts did not stray
To the spot in which the hoard had been interred.
A ditchdigger saw him there intermittently,
So suspected a hoard and stole it without a word.
Then, as before, our miser went and found vacuity;
Shed tears of despair, groaned and sighed till all could hear,
  Tore his hair and trembled with fear.
A person passing paused to ask why such misery;
  The man said, "Someone took my hoard from me."
—"Your hoard? Where should it be?" —"By that stone
      heretofore."
  —"But why? We are not at war.
Why so far away? Could you not have been satisfied
To hide it in your wall cupboard there at your side,
  Instead of take it quite so far?
Your trips to it might then have been regular."
—"Regular? Heavens, man! Use some of it every day?
  Spend more than might ever again come my way?
I would not have touched it." —"Tell me, sir, if you please,"
Asked Good Sense, "why you should feel such piercing pain,
Since the money was a thing from which you must refrain?
  Bury a stone in the place,
  And be just as well off again."

XXI

THE EYE OF THE MASTER

When forced to take refuge with oxen, since nearly caught,
A stag was warned by the rescuers sought,
To find safer shelter or be killed.
"Dear friends," he implored, "do not give me away;
I shall show you a field where you'll find the best hay:
A promise, I assure you, which shall be fulfilled.
You'll not be sorry you rescued me."
The oxen at length promised secrecy.
With a corner for shield the stag could breathe as he should;
Then toward dusk grass was tossed where the oxen stood,
As in a barn anywhere.
Farm hands went about tasks here and there,
The foreman came and made a constant stir,
Not one saw antlers or newcomer.
Fresh from the woods and glad of sanctuary,
The rescued stag hoped to linger in a stall
While his friends toiled for Ceres as customary—
And stir forth later on as he saw darkness fall.
Chewing its cud, an ox said, "So far good, my friend;
But the man will come who has a hundred eyes;
Best be prepared for a rude surprise.
Don't boast, poor guest, before sure of the end."
The master came and looked at what the men had done.
"How is this?" he inquired of each one.
"I don't find fresh hay in the racks where it should be.
What filthy straw! To the rick; show activity.
An ox requires good care, needs it consistently;
Why those spiderwebs? Brush them down systematically.
Why should the collars and yokes be disorderly?"
As he stared hard, he saw an unfamiliar head—
A kind such as farmers don't see when at work;
Made sure, and found the deer. The hands each took a fork
And presently the stag was dead;
His tears could not save the poor creature from slaughter.

Pastor, squire, and neighbor shared with the master:
    Many enjoyed exceptional fare.

In this connection, Phaedrus—the height of elegance—
    Said the master has sight with which none can compare;
But believe me, there is sight that is sharper—the lover's glance.

XXII

THE LARK'S BROOD AND THE FARMER

Make the task your own is a maxim that is sound—
    Which Aesop, it seems, liked especially,
    As you shall see.

    Larks nest where grain is sure to be—
    When the blades first cover the ground,
    Just before summer has begun,
As love flames and young of all species abound:
    Even where marine thunders sound—
Tigers' in jungles and larks' in a blaze of sun;
    Moreover I shall tell you here
Of a lark for whom the spring had very nearly gone,
As though young love could never be alluring to her,
Who at last made up her mind to do as others would,
And assume home cares, like many more.
So she built, laid eggs, hatched them out as before,
Working fast; indeed did the very best she could,
But the wheat had matured as the brood was being fed
    With morsels for which the lark would soar
    To lay in the nest's interior,
Trying to fill starved mouths till they were surfeited.
Before circling aloft, she warned each little one
To be on guard concerning harm that might befall.
    "Note with care," she said, "what is done.
When the farmer speaks to his son, catch each word he lets fall
    Since what he says will determine what we must do—
    Remain or fly as others flew."
She had no sooner left her little family

Than farmer and son came as previously.
"That grain is right to cut," the farmer said presently.
"Beg friends with sickles to come ply them for me—
Tomorrow as first faint signs of dawn appear."
    With a whirr the lark flew near,
    Her chicks shrilling with one accord.
The first chirped, "At break of day, or so we heard,
His friends will be here in the morning, working hard."
The lark said, "If that is all he said, it's an idle threat.
We are not obliged to find another home yet.
But listen tomorrow; each word must be noted.
Enjoy these worms I've found; let us be animated."
The babes, mother bird, in fact all, slept free of care.
Not a friend appeared as the sky began to glow;
The lark was in the air when the farmer as before
    Came to make his rounds as proprietor
And said, "All this wheat still standing, row on row!
Our friends are in the wrong; we, still more to choose
As substitutes for ourselves folk who get nothing done.
    This time speed to relatives, son;
    Fetch them; we've no time to lose."
The young birds' terror was unprecedented.
"He said relatives, Mother. It's time, we are sure."
    —"No, birds, we have nothing to dread;
    Settle down once more, for we are secure."
The lark was right again. Not a sign of a man.
A third time beside the wheat he had come back to scan,
The farmer became vehement and said, "It is a shame
To expect from others what should be done by us
Who are better than friends or kinsfolk we might claim.
Note what I say, son. Is it not obvious
What we must do? Let us each, as a family,
Bring a sickle at dawn, and meet the emergency—
Our best course if we are to get the reaping done.
    Come, out with our sickles as soon as we can."
The mother replied to what she'd heard the brood repeat,
"Now, children, is the moment. It is time we were gone,"
    And the nestlings as quickly as if full grown
    Fluttered and flapped and then had flown.
    Not a larklet lurked in the wheat.

BOOK FIVE

I

MERCURY AND THE WOODMAN

To Monsieur le Chevalier de Bouillon

Your taste has made my own less crude
So I have taken pains that flaws should not obtrude.
You do not like a manner marred by self-consciousness
Or other sorts of tedious pretentiousness,
And I share your view. Forced charm is a despair;
Overdone masterworks are sadly amateur;
Not that I would banish each form of dainty wit;
You prize mentality and I too cherish it.
Any of Aesop's fables are ingenious;
   One can't match their felicity;
There's nothing like his charm and ingenuity,
So I shall not compete. My defects are numerous—
   Lack of smiting impact;
   Alien to me, in fact.
I'm not a Hercules, am of the minor school
And can but satirize vice, employing ridicule
As my one art—however inadequately;
   I've bared this weapon recently
That envy might seem absurd, as well as vanity;
Two vices which all but dominate our century—
   Seen in my frog, a little goose
Who in trying to be an ox was merely grandiose.
With antitheses to make me understood,
Virtue shaming vice's crew; wisdom, what folly's done;
   Lambs, wolves for causing blood to run—
Fly matched with ant, I have drama as it should,
Expand to all-embracing theater,
   With scenes of every character;
Men, gods, or animals, aiding me with a role—
Even Jove himself. Today it is Mercury,

[101]

Love's messenger, whom Jove found invaluable;
Although this time employed in another capacity.

A woodman lost his only means of gain—
His ax, I mean, and could not find it again.
Then all who had heard his lament were concerned—
The tool by which his daily bread was earned,
Without which he could not do any work.
Losing it seemed to have extinguished life's spark.
His face streamed with all the weeping he did.
"My ax! O my poor ax," he pled;
"O Jupiter, bring it back that I may hew,
And it will strike unswerving blows for you."
The woodcutter prayed and Olympus heard.
Mercury came, said, "It's not lost"; then inquired,
"Would you recognize the one lost as your own?
I found in the neighborhood what I think you mislaid."
When the man was shown an ax of gold as what he'd had,
He said, "No, I don't want it—not the one";
Then was shown one of silver instead of the first.
He refused; finally one of wood was shown.
He said, "There, this time it's my own;
If I may have it, my cares are dispersed."
Then the god said, "All—all three belong to you.
A man who won't lie should have a reward,"
And the woodman answered, "Then I'm glad to have all."
No sooner had the circumstance been rumored
Than scores of woodmen lost a tool and made an appeal—
A boon which Jupiter did not afford;
Once more he sent Mercury as messenger
With an ax of gold to lay impostors bare.
"We would be numskulls," each would have said,
"Not to assert instantly, 'Ah, it has been found!' "
But Mercury knows a specious word from a sound.
Response was a blow on the liar's head.

Take care of what is yours. Since lying harms everyone,
Best be sincere. But would you, if you strove
To secure by lies what is not your own,
Be a gainer in the end? You cannot deceive Jove.

II

THE POT OF CLAY AND THE POT OF IRON

A pot of iron's proposal
That a clay pot fare afield,
Met with a prompt refusal:
"Any joy that journeys yield
Is afforded by our warm hearth;
Brittle pots of breakable earth
Are inured to sacrifice,
Since jostles are far from wise:
I might be crushed by a blow;
But don't feel that you should not go.
Since iron is accustomed to strain,
No reason why you should remain."
Then the other turned arguer
And said, "As for shocks you'd incur,
Or objects you saw to fear,
If you felt that you'd come too near,
I'd expose myself instead
And you'd not be buffeted."
The clay pot was satisfied
So they fared forth side by side—
The iron, and the clay one protected,
Each on three legs as pots are constructed.
Clipper-clap-clip they tried their luck
And then at each jolt conflicted
If even pebbles were struck.
The clay pot suffered, in less than fifty paces, the worst that
could befall—
Left by the iron pot in fragments so minute you could not
count them all
And with only himself to blame.

Take as an equal a person who is not,
And your fate may be the same
As that of the earthen pot.

III

THE LITTLE FISH AND THE FISHERMAN

It would seem to have been God's plan
For fry to mature if spared human guile;
But what a foolish fisherman
To free what he thinks he may catch afterwhile.
He might catch it, of course, but cannot be sure that he can.

A carp so small he was nearly an illusion
Was caught by an angler where a forest stream ran clear.
The man viewed his capture with exhilaration
And said, "Aha, first of a mess for my delectation:
There it goes," since a wicker creel lay near.
The poor thing in a tongue too fine for our ear
Asked, "Of what use am I? Must I make a fire roar—
Half a mouthful when eaten!
Let me grow, I implore:
I'm certain to be retaken;
A gourmet will pay dear for a catch that is rare,
Whereas compare the exertion
Of catching a hundred such as I
For one meal. Meal? Mockery is the word to apply."
The angler said, "Mockery? Friend with the pulpit air,
Compose, if you will, a homily on despair.
You'll be laid in the frying pan. Preach till you tire,
You'll sear tonight on a roaring fire."

A fish in the creel, so they say, is worth two you've not caught;
The one, food in hand, and the second, for thought.

IV

THE EARS OF THE HARE

Horns wounded the lion so he lay on the ground,
      And as all heard his roars resound
      He vowed he'd not be gored again
      And banned from his domain
Every head with horns of any description.
Goats and bulls and rams were all compelled to go elsewhere;
      Stags and deer knew to disappear;
      All fled for fear of extinction.
Then a hare, observing the long shadows his ears made,
      Fearing that some inquisitor
Would confuse the shadows cast by horns and those by fur,
Which naturally cast the same kind of shade,
Said, "Farewell, dear cricket, I must flee
Or my ears will incriminate me.
Though I had an ostrich's head—almost as plain—
I would suffer the same fear." The cricket said instantly,
      "Horns, hare? Don't tell me that I am insane.
      God ordained what your ears should be."
      —"But the court would insist they are horns,"
Said Timid, "horns as tall as unicorns'.
However hard I argue, what would be the gain
      If I'm in a padded cell and they say something's
                  wrong with my brain?"

V

THE FOX SHORN OF HIS TAIL

      An old fox but one of the craftiest—
Devastating to hens, rabbits' ever-present pest—
      Had a look you couldn't mistake or, a league
                  away, doubt.
      In the end, however, he was trapped;

Then by desperate wrenching escaped—
But not quite, since at the price of a perquisite,
His tail. Alive, he nevertheless felt destitute,
Became adroit in having no brush to trail,
Went where his sort discuss whom next to persecute,
And said, "Why be annoyed by an unwieldy tail—
Fouled by drover's dust till we are in disrepute;
Of what service are tails? Each should make his tail short.
     If you agree, friends, outlaw convention."
—"Your counsel is fertile," was the ready retort,
"But turn, please, and then we shall have an opinion."
Derision followed, which made him a rogue—
Noise so great the curtailed creature could not be heard.
Pride's labor lost; talk of shortened tails seemed absurd
     And tails today are still in vogue.

VI

THE HAG AND HER TWO SERVANTS

An old hag had two maids spinning flax she'd prepare—
Each so skilled the Three Fates would not dare to compare
Their web with the maids' more concealed artistry.
Now the hag had no thought but the pair's industry
And providing the poor things with more and more flax.
Daybreak! with the sea ablaze where the sun had rested,
Spinning wheels contested, distaffs twirled and twisted,
     Droning, "Defter; you're belated;
     Don't stop spinning; don't relax."
Dawn's burnished car, as I've said, had not ascended
Till a rumpled cock had crowed; and thus reminded,
The far worse-feathered hag, more miserable still,
Fumbled on petticoats which grease made unwearable,
Lit a lamp and mustered a skinflint's energy
To rouse her weary pair who slumbered heavily.
     Soured by hard work done in vain,
One eyed her sullenly; the other's elbow stirred.
     Both out of sorts, since under strain,
Vowed in an undertone, "You're doomed, accursèd bird";

[106]

Then they seized the cock by whom rest was restricted
And cut his throat, as the vow they'd made exacted,
But murder never aids one as intended;
In fact our cutthroats' slumber was disrupted
By the half-lunatic sooner than before,
To keep them from lying in bed and cheating her—
   A result far from infrequent.
Sometimes by changing situations we abhor,
   We double the predicament
   As these tired girls killed care and brought on more—
Avoiding Charybdis, they had fled to the hag—
   Had swerved from the whirlpool to the crag.

VII

THE SATYR AND THE VISITOR

A satyr and his troop
In the den that was their inn,
Were about to share some soup
But had not had time to begin;

Seated upon the moss,
Parents and similar progeny
Had no carpet, and cave for house,
But hot soup they rejoiced to see.

When rain fell unexpectedly,
A drenched traveler fared near the brood
And, standing before them suddenly,
Was invited to share the food;

Nor needed to be asked again
By the satyrs to sit down,
Although every now and then
He would blow his fingers and frown;

Then before he had begun,
Blew his hot soup cautiously.

[107]

"Now tell us why that was done?"
The tall satyr asked diffidently.

"I needed my pottage cooled,
Then warmed my hands that were cold,"
The man said, and since unschooled
The satyr said, "Leave our fold.

"You daren't sleep here. God forbid.
You'd possibly do us harm;
Whose mouth did what yours did,
And can blow both cold and warm!"

VIII

THE HORSE AND THE WOLF

When warm spring winds make the grass green
And animals break from winter captivity,
A certain wolf, like other creatures grown lean,
Was looking about for what food there might be.
As said, a wolf after a winter that had been hard
Came on a horse turned out to grass. You've inferred
The hungry adventurer's thought.
He murmured, "Ha! marrow bones to crack.
Well, since it's not a lamb that must supply my lack,
I shall have to do some scheming that intention flower out;
Wily work." Meanwhile he advanced with measured tread.
Hippocrates' expositor
Said he knew which herbs could give an invalid aid,
And possessed every skill that could be employed
In each healing art, though modesty forbore
To enumerate. Master Horse need not be annoyed
That he had an infirmity
Since the wolf did not have to be paid.
Any surgeon was bound to agree
That grazing with no halter on his head
A horse ailed, as medical practice could convince.
"My foot underneath makes me wince

[108]

From an abscess that's formed," the horse said.
The wolf cried, "My dear horse, alarming; literally
      Nothing could be more dangerous.
I have served when horse grandees had one of those
      And they valued my surgery."
Our gallant surgeon had chosen the moment with one thought
                                          alone—
      To sink his teeth in the sufferer.
The other, who suspected what might occur,
      Kicked and left in a mass of gore
      A jaw with most of the teeth gone.
Much cast down, the wolf mused, "He was right to resist.
One should stick to the sort of thing for which one was made;
      I tried to be an herbalist,
      Whereas I should keep to the butcher's trade."

IX

THE HUSBANDMAN AND HIS SONS

      Work; for work pays—though the back bends:
      A resource that never fails.
A husbandman, warned that death would part him from his friends,
Called his heirs aside, as secrecy compels,
And said, "A fortune's been earned by those of our blood,
      Handed down from father to son
      And buried, but where is not known.
If each of you will search for it with hardihood,
You are sure to find it; you will come on it at last;
So plow when this next August harvest is past.
Turn, break, harrow, and smooth. Leave nothing as it was
      That work is able to displace."
He died, and his sons did as he'd asked should be done—
Dug and delved and harrowed everywhere, and thanks to each one
      Their profits left them open-eyed.
No gold, no hid treasure; but they had justified
      Their father's almost final word:
      If you'd find a fortune, work hard.

X

THE MOUNTAIN IN LABOR

As a mountain was forming a mound,
Birth groans reverberated about
And multitudes hastened toward the sound,
Certain that something huge would come out—
Larger than Paris possibly;
Lo, the striking monstrosity
Was a mouse! A fictitious tale
But one which I have held dear,
As being applicable
To bards who shake the hemisphere
And say, "Here is an expositor
Of Mars terrorized by the Titans' war."
One is promised marvels and finds one's hurricane
A fan.

XI

FORTUNE AND THE CHILD

A lad fell asleep on the ground
At the edge of a well and his sleep was sound—
Returning from some primary class.
Any bed seems soft to the young, even clay,
Though a man who had seen might have sprung away
A furlong and occasioned distress;
But touching him without a sound,
Fortune deferred the errand on which she was bound,
To whisper, "Little dear, I've saved your life, you see.
Better be prudent after this. Try to be.
They would have found fault with me if you had fallen in
And it would have been your fault,
For why should I feel chagrin
With so needless a result
Blamed on my capriciousness." And then her form faded.

[110]

More than right, if I am candid.
When we've done things for which we've repined,
We say that Fortune was unkind—
Blaming Fortune for what we did,
Reproaching her for the sins that cost us dear.
After being careless or turning a deaf ear,
We like to blame Fortune for what may occur;
Though ourselves at fault, we always blame her.

XII

THE PHYSICIANS

Now one of Doctor Fear-the-Worst's cases was sad,
Attended also by a Doctor Hope-the-Best,
Who swore he'd cure the man whose condition was bad;
Whereas the other thought he'd earned eternal rest.
Contradictory remedies failed to cure,
And Death interposed the sentence which all must endure.
Doctor Fear-the-Worst felt that he had been justified—
In fact, each thought he'd prescribed judiciously.
"Dead," said one, "as he was warned." The other replied,
"He'd be living now if he'd listened to me."

XIII

THE HEN THAT LAID THE GOLDEN EGGS

Take all that is there and forfeit increment,
Is a truth too clear for argument
In the old fairy tale in which golden eggs were laid,
One a day. The poor owner would stare
At the hen, till sure there was gold in her to share,
Then killed, spread out the bird, and of course was repaid
By no more than would be found in an ordinary hen.
He had cut the magic chain and she'd never lay again.
Think of this when covetous!
How many we have seen in our own century
Reduced to poverty by striving hard to be
Prematurely prosperous.

XIV

THE DONKEY AND THE RELICS

Since saints' bones had made his back ache,
An ass supposed himself revered:
The vain donkey, though bristle-eared,
Felt that incense and mass were for his, not for the bones' sake.
Perceiving the absurdity,
Someone said, "Now, Ned, curb your vanity;
Though sanctity awes all,
You're anything but wonderful
Or one to whom the world bows down.
It's the relics that are venerable."

Folk bow to the wig and gown,
Not the man, when a judge is a fool.

XV

THE STAG AND THE VINE

A stag had found somewhere a vine's arched tent
Such as one sees in some countries, dashed in to wait
And, spared threat of death, contrived to recuperate.
Seeing no stag, the hunt thought the dogs were off the scent,
Called them to heel and the stag escaped slaughter;
Then the ingrate browsed on the vine's leaves; yes, ate his friend!
The hounds heard, returned, the stag galloped farther,
Was forced back and slaughtered there in the end—
Saying, "My due; they've done what they ought to have done."
Ingrates, be instructed. The towering beast went down
And was torn by the pack. His tears were of no avail.
The tired thing was dismembered; their object, attained.

The stag's just punishment might serve as a symbol
Of asylum profaned.

XVI

THE SERPENT AND THE FILE

A snake, so they say, lived near a watchmaker
(Rather unfortunate for a man with just that work);
The serpent glided in for something to stay hunger.
      However, his flickering fork
Could find nothing but a file to endanger.
Kindly, with anything but an injured air,
    The file said, "Poor worm, aren't you courting despair?
      A great fool, little snake, although small.
      By the time my filings could yield
      The fourth of an obol in all,
      You would break your two teeth in.
      Only Time's tooth wears me thin."

Now this is meant for you, vapid second-rate minds,
Good-for-nothings who try to harm worth of all kinds.
      Your gnashed teeth imply nothing profound.
Do you think that you could leave a toothmark
      On any masterwork?
Bite steel or burnished brass or dent the diamond?

XVII

THE HARE AND THE PARTRIDGE

Better not disdain those whom prosperity fails,
For who can say how long he will be prosperous?
      Old Aesop put in his tales,
      An illustration or two for us,
      And in this fable such as it is,
      I am perhaps but quoting his.

A hare and a partridge had made their nest on a plain,
Went in and out in peace and life was equable

[113]

Till the hunting horn's refrain
Compelled the hare to flee where he need not quail,
To a thicket; then he had the dogs at an impasse,
      Even Brindle, the most voracious;
      But by exhaling the strange steam
Which hares generate when warm, he gave himself away.
Then Devil, snuffing hard to find out where he lay,
Barked that it was his hare, and unfair as it must seem,
Rushed after; though Double—famed for accuracy—
      Said the hare was off. A fatality.
The unfortunate beast was killed in his retreat
      And the partridge chirped in mockery,
      "You have been proud of being fleet.
Of what use was your speed?" She went on insultingly;
Her turn came; she was caught. One with wings need
                  not walk,
She'd supposed, in case something should cause her dismay,
      Not suspecting that she would be prey
      In the cruel claws of a hawk.

XVIII

THE EAGLE AND THE OWL

An eagle and an owl, by birth a hostile pair,
      Embraced and swore to forbear;
By kings' faith and owls' faith each declared his oath true;
Neither would wage on nestlings, war which either need rue.
"How recognize mine as mine?" Minerva's bird besought.
—"I might not," the other said. —"A mortal blow,"
      The owl mourned. "Then I shall never know
      Just when my nestlings might be caught.
Kings don't care if one is alive or dead;
What or why, and although entreated tearfully
      View all indiscriminately.
Farewell my baby owls if they are detected."
The king said, "Describe them or let them be inspected.
      I guarantee them immunity."
The owl said, "Baby owls are the sweetest things hatched,

[114]

Nicely formed, an angelic brood that could scarcely be matched.
Since those are the traits by which you would know them best,
Don't forget; bear in mind when food must be fetched.
      If thieves should invade my nest,
        'Twill not be you by whom my young were snatched."
Before long, Heaven blessed the owl with a brood to rear
And he'd flown forth to hunt when the evening was clear.
      Searching too for prey that might appear,
      The eagle chanced to circle near
      And up in a cliff that was sheer
      Or wall—I don't know which of the two—
      Spied a hideous little crew,
Tots with Megaera's voice and a fiend's morose air.
The eagle said, "These knaves are not owls' progeny;
I may dine," and an eagle can dine thoroughly—
He chokes down what he's caught and the spot is soon bare.
As the owl flew near he saw no pets to be fed;
An assortment of claws—that was all, alas.
He moaned and besought. The gods were supplicated
To punish the wretch who'd brought about such a pass.
Then someone said, though he was heartsore, "I blame *you;*
      It actually seems true
      That we think our species personable,
      Comely, well formed, irresistible.
The eagle, thinking owlets are as you portrayed,
      Was irretrievably misled."

XIX

THE LION PREPARES FOR WAR

Now the lion had thought of a country he might seize,
So counselors conferred and sent heralds forth by twos
      Informing subjects of the monarch's news.
All would assist in varying degrees:
      Elephant with enormous girth
      Carry armament to the war
      And in his own manner do as he dare;
      The bear would batter some foes to earth;

[115]

The fox was to think out a secret attack.
The monkey was to distract the enemy by japes they'd think
queer.
Then someone said, "Dull donkeys do not belong here,
Or hares who are subject to panic. Send the hares back."
The king said, "By no means; both can afford me aid.
Without them I never would consent to fight.
Good trumpeter ass's brays are certain to affright
And courier hare will bear news which must be conveyed."

With a leader's certitude,
Their king saw in what ways each's gifts would be good.
Potentialities were plain,
Since nothing is useless to one of seasoned brain.

XX

THE BEAR AND THE TWO SCHEMERS

Two schemers whose purse had grown thin
Sold to a nearby furrier
A live bear's serviceable skin;
As experts, they'd bring him down; at least they said they were,
And swore he'd be the best one ever subdued by guns,
A furrier's bonanza—immense wealth all at once—
Furred till impervious to frost however keen;
And fur for more than just one coat should be a boon.
Dindenaut prized his sheep less than these men their bear:
Theirs in their eyes, but not in bruin's sight.
They'd be back in two days and have had time to spare,
Then after the hunt, set a price that would be right.
The quarry was found, shuffled toward them at a trot;
The men stood as if halted by a cannonball.
The contract hung fire, and neither could recall
Why they'd come out or that the bear was to be shot.
One climbed a tree to the top (the one by whom the skin had
been sold).
The other, like marble—even more cold—
Played dead, face to the ground, lying prone,

[116]

Since he'd heard that a bear against which to guard,
    Is inclined to let alone
A body that has no life, does not move or breathe hard.
Master Bear, like a fool, was taken in by the ruse,
Saw the rigid form devoid of mobility
    And, fearing some kind of trickery,
Rolled it over, back again, brought his nose close
    To the nostrils to see if breath went in.
"It is a corpse," he said. "I'll make off, to escape the stench."
Whereupon the bear sauntered toward the woods again.
One of our two fur dealers came down from his branch,
Ran to his friend and said, "Narrow escape you've had,
But you weren't mauled, and suffered mere fright after all.
Well and good"; then, "What about the skin of the animal?
    When he whispered, what was it he said?
    His nose very nearly touched your ear
    As he rolled you here and there."
    —"What he said was, 'It might cost you dear
To sell a bear's skin before killing the bear.' "

XXI

THE ASS IN THE LION'S SKIN

Donning a lion's skin which shrouded his very feet,
    An ass terrified every friend—
    A plain donkey whose counterfeit
    Shook the whole world from end to end.
But the tip of an ear escaped the borrowed fur
    And the imposture made a stir:
    Cudgel-Martin sped toward the ass,
And those who had not perceived just what the creature was,
    Saw him cudgeled from the lion's den
    To aid a miller by bearing grain.

    Monstrous ado is made in France
By some to whom fables like this might be applied.
    Fanfare that's one-fourth justified,
    Merely magnifies inconsequence.

[117]

BOOK SIX

I

THE SHEPHERD AND THE LION

II

THE LION AND THE HUNTER

Fables are more than would appear;
The lowliest creature in them may be a schoolmaster.
Yet morals tire if not set forth ingeniously,
For a tale should preach and please simultaneously,
With the moral disguised by what takes us unaware;
A tale for the tale's sake is too slight an affair.
Combining fascination with vitality,
Certain pens so skilled that each is an authority
Took pains to avoid ornateness and diffuseness,
Excluding from their tales any word that seemed careless.
Phaedrus's were so succinct that critics objected,
And Aesop's were even more neatly constructed;
But improving upon them, one fabulist, a Greek,
      Of an elegance unique,
Tried contenting himself with four lines and no more;
Right or wrong, let the experts approve or deplore.
Let us see how this Babrius and Aesop tell the same tale,
One with a hunter; one, a shepherd to point the parable.
Each preserves the wording originally known
Although here, as resewn, some embroidering's done.
This is Aesop's story with what I've conjoined:

A shepherd, each time he'd count, found a sheep purloined,
So with indignation amounting to a passion
Laid snares near a cave, having had a suspicion,
Because wolves stole sheep, they'd committed the offense;

Then prayed, "O god of all that's glorious,
If I might catch the rogue who is causing me loss,
See the net heave, and gaze on the beast's countenance,
    My gift would be spectacular—
    Of twenty choice calves my herd chanced to bear,
    The fattest which I could select."
As he spoke, a lion sprang from the cave that was near.
The shepherd cowered and, incompetent with fear,
Said, "Alas, who knows, when he asks, what gift to expect!
I vowed if I succeeded—I need not know how—
In snaring the robber before I would depart,
O king of the gods, you should have a calf, but now,
I promise you an ox if spared what froze my heart."

That is the master author's treatment and what emerged,
    Now for his successor and how he diverged.

    A boastful young man who gave hours to the chase
Lost a pedigreed dog he was trying to trace
And supposing that it had fed a lion,
Saw a shepherd. "My man," he said, "show me the place
Where the robber lurks who has caused my dejection,
That I may obtain satisfaction."
The shepherd said, "Somewhere near yonder high ground.
I let him have a sheep as a concession
Each month, and since then my sleep has been sound
And I've felt secure wherever I've gone."
Just as he said this in an easy tone,
A lion rushed from some covert, tail aswirl.
The palsied boaster could only quaver,
"O Jupiter, grant shelter in which I may curl;
Show me a hiding place. Save me from slaughter!"

    The sign and seal of valor
Is how one behaves when cause for fright is near.
Some who took risks at first and sang bass, sing tenor
    The moment disparaged foes appear.

[119]

III

PHOEBUS AND BOREAS

The sun and the north wind observed a traveler
   Who was cloaked with particular care
Because fall had returned; for when autumn has come,
What we wear must be warm or we dare not leave home.
Both rain and rainbow as the sun shines fitfully,
   Warn one to dress warily
In these months when we don't know for what to prepare,
An uncertain time in the Roman calendar.
Though our traveler was fortified for a gale,
With interlined cloak which the rain could not penetrate,
The wind said, "This man thinks himself impregnable
And his cloak is well sewn, but my force can prevail
   As he'll find in the blast I create,
No button has held. Indeed before I am through,
   I may waft the whole mantle away.
The battle could afford us amusement, I'd say.
Do you fancy a contest?" The sun said, "I do.
   Mere words are unprofitable,
Let us see which can first unfasten the mantle
   Protecting the pedestrian.
Begin: I shall hide; you uncloak him if you can."
Then our blower swelled, swallowed what wind he could,
To form a balloon, and with the wager to win,
   Made demoniacal din.
Puffed, snorted, and sighed till the blast that he brewed
Left ships without a sail and homes without a roof
   Because a mantle proved stormproof.
It was a triumph for the man to have withstood
   The onslaught of wind that had rushed in,
As he somehow stood firm. The wind roared his chagrin—
A defeated boaster since his gusts had been borne.
Controlling clasp and skirt required dexterity,
   But the wind found nothing torn
   And must stop punctually.

The cloud had made it cool
Till the sun's genial influence caused the traveler to give way,
    And perspiring because wearing wool,
    He cast off a wrap too warm for the day
Though the sun had not yet shone with maximum force.

    Clemency may be our best resource.

IV

JUPITER AND HIS TENANT

One time Jupiter had a farm to be rented.
Hermes advertised it and applicants appeared,
    Comparing bids as they dared:
    A business not soon terminated;
    One said the farm was rugged, he understood,
And expensive to maintain; others spoke disparagingly
    But as they bargained busily,
A man with less wisdom than honest hardihood
Promised high rental, supposing Jupiter
    Would let him control the weather
    And stipulate whatever he chose;
Cool days, sunny, or the kind when a cold wind blows,
    Plenty of rainfall or limited,
    As soon as the farm was tenanted.
Jove agreed, then each signed the contract, and as weather
                                   king
Our man determined heat, cold, moisture, everything
Of the sort on his farm, though for no other man
Even nearby, any more than for an American;
A mercy for them, since they'd the best harvest they had had—
    Both of wine and grain harvested;
Whereas Jove's deputy's was really very bad.
    Asking the opposite instead
    Of what he had asked before,
    He received next year the reverse
    And results could not have been worse,
While his neighbor's farmland was yielding more and more.

The poor soul confessed that he had brought on a curse,
Pled inexperience,
And was kindly dealt with by his royal master.

And so we see that Providence,
Not we, should be our caretaker.

V

MOUSIE, THE CAT, AND THE COCKEREL

An unwary mouse, so young he scarcely knew where he was,
Chanced to nap near a mouser's claws.
This is what he told his mother of the affair:
"I had climbed the hills that bound Mouse Sanctuary,
Like some young rat with the world to see,
Although not exactly certain where,
When all of a sudden two beasts appeared—
One, the sweetest, kindliest ever reared—
While the other'd run and stop and shake his head;
You should have heard the horrid noise he made;
With a queer red topknot bare of fur,
And ragged arms with which he'd make a stir
As if going to fly and he couldn't wait,
Fluttering his tail tuft at a great rate."
Mousie was describing a cockerel scratch earth
As though of American birth,
So his mother'd be sure to know it was unique;
And then said, "His arms went up and he'd beat his fluff,
Bluster, and all he did was so rough,
He scared me. I'm brave, thanks be, but he made me squeak
And dart, he'd given me such a start;
I hated him with all my heart;
He had not left me any chance
To speak to his sweet friend who looked so generous
And was velvety like us—
Tortoiseshell with long tail, a gentle countenance,
An expressive glance—and oh, but his eyes shone!
Supposing a rat had grown and grown,

[122]

He would look like this grandee. His ears were silvery
        And furred like the ones on you and me
Yet I could not address him with someone making a noise
                                  like that,
        So I ran away from it."
The mouse said, "My dear, the sweet beast was a cat,
        A devious, hardened hypocrite,
        With a kind of malice that is innate.
        We are animals he would always hate.
        The beast who had a ferocious air
        Would never hurt us, would not touch a hair—
Might, when cooked and cold, provide a meal on which
                            we'd thrive;
Whereas a cat would be glad to live on mice alone.
        So don't, as you would stay alive,
        Take looks for a criterion."

VI

THE FOX, THE MONKEY, AND OTHER BEASTS

    Beasts who'd been ruled by him who lay dead—
    The lion's death brought together as one
    To choose a successor to the throne.
    They bore the crown from the place where it rested
    In a cleft which a dragon guarded
    And tried it on each, but found none it fitted
    Of any of those congregated,
    Since most heads were too little for it,
    Or too bulky, or horns would not fit.
    The monkey smiled as he handled the crown,
    Screwed his face into a thousand lines,
    Turned somersaults, devised monkeyshines,
    Even made it a hoop through which he took flight,
    While the whole realm observed him with delight.
    The fox alone looked on him with disdain,
    Hiding the fact that his heart had not been won,
    Yet paid respect as all the rest had done
    And said to the monkey, "Sire, there is a hoard

In a spot which none but I have explored,
And you of course have now inherited
What would have been the king's if he were not dead."
The avaricious upstart of a king,
Since he was afraid of being cheated,
Ran, himself, to the spot and into a snare he had not suspected.
The fox said in the name of the animals listening,
"Should any rule who do not know that the right to govern
                                        has been earned
By those whose passions have not mastered them?"
And the monkey was deposed. The beasts had learned
That only a few deserve a diadem.

VII

THE MULE WITH A PEDIGREE

A mule owned by the head of a large diocese
            Could be heard telling everyone
            About what his mother had done.
            This blood mare's proficiencies
Which took her here and there, made her a prodigy
            And he felt that in history
            Her deeds would shine forevermore.
To serve a mere doctor would be degrading;
But later, when old and sent to the mill for lading,
The mule recalled the ass, his other ancestor.

            Since misfortune had brought him pain
            Yet proved that it's folly to be vain,
            It was of use to the poor ass;
            Let us say plainly that it was.

VIII

THE OLD MAN AND THE ASS

An old man, on a donkey he owned, was journeying
    One time where choice grass chanced to spring,
So turned Grayskin loose and observed the freed serf
    Tearing over the sweet turf,
    Wallowing, rubbing, and scrubbing,
    Frisking, neighing, and nibbling.
    A pause meant he'd leave the spot bare.
    On seeing an enemy appear,
    The old man said, "Quick, we must fly."
    The saucy vagabond asked, "Why?
For fear I'd be bowed down by two and their weight?"
—"By no means," the man said while hastening toward the
                               gate.

The ass said, "But how does all this affect me?
    How should I care whose ass I am!
    French donkeys have an epigram:
    A master is one's enemy."

IX

THE STAG AND HIS REFLECTION

    Once a stag would haunt the brink
    To see reflected in the brook
    His tall tines at which he loved to look,
    While shrinking from shanks that seemed to shrink:
    Until shuddering with chagrin
That foreshortened fetlocks should spindle so thin.
"What disparity between head and feet!"
He said as he stared at the glimmer which falsified cheer;
"I've antlers with which a tall wood can't compete;
    My feet are unworthy of a deer."
    The soliloquy was short:

Confronted by a bloodhound's glare
And forced to dash off anywhere,
He made the forest his resort.
His tines caught the branches curving down;
In fact he was nearly thrown
By boughs interfering with his speed—
His only hope of being freed;
Then regretted his words, deploring the horns he had grown,
Renewed each season, on and on.

We love good looks rather than what is practical,
Though good looks may prove destructive.
The stag scorned his feet which were serviceable
And thought obstructive horns attractive.

X

THE HARE AND THE TORTOISE

If you don't start on time, you might as well not try:
As proved by the tortoise when a boaster finished last.
"Wager who'll be winner?" the tortoise said. "It's I.
You'll see which is the plodder and which is really fast."
The fleeter asked, "Are you sober?
Take herbs as a purge, good mother.
Say four grains of hellebore;
Sane or not, you have a competitor."
The two set forth and wickets were placed
To show them the goal toward which they raced:
As for me, I did not see the pair
Or the judging that was done.
Master Hare had no more than four leaps to take before he
would win the dare;
I mean the sort of bounds he makes when dogs nearly run
him down—
When he draws so fast he would take till Greek Kalends
to find,
As the pack noses ground he's left behind;
So he could afford to do some browsing,

Furthermore spare time for dozing;
Snuffing the wind while the tortoise came
Festina lente like a senator
Perseveringly toward phantom fame,
Following him who'd sped before.
Now the hare did not fancy a sinecure;
To defeat a tortoise is scarcely a lure,
So thought he'd allow her to think she could score,
And started late. He browsed and then would doze,
Amusing himself as a rabbit does,
And the race was deferred. But seeing presently
That the tortoise might win and there was no time to spare,
He was off like a dart. Belated energy!
The tortoise, alas, was ahead of Master Hare.
"Well!" she cried. "Was I right to say I could do what I've done?
Did your speed achieve success?
I've brought it off! And what of your tardiness
If you'd carried a tortoiseshell as you ran?"

XI

THE ASS AND HIS MASTERS

One time a truck gardener's donkey was grumbling
Because before the sun was up he had to stir;
Muttering to himself, "Cocks do some early crowing
But my eyes open earlier.
Why is a gardener's donkey rudely wakened?
Foolish to let them interrupt my sleep!"
Then kindhearted Fate listened,
Said that Sleepy-head's task was one he need not keep,
And that a tanner, not gardener, should drag him by the ear.
Damp skins weigh more than dry; foul scents hung everywhere
Till they almost stifled the pert quadruped
And he thought, "I'd a better master there than here.
Every time that he turned his head,
I'd nip greens as he slackened rein—
Say some tatter of chard that was an outright gain.
No bounties now, I fear; or if pay for what I've done,

[127]

It's a thwack." He obtained a place freer from strain
       And as humblest retainer
       Of a charcoal burner,
He still complained. But Fate can glower and glare.
       She said, "My! That beast again!
       A hundred kings are less care.
Would he have me devote myself to him alone?
       Does he think no one else is in despair?"

We are all alike and deserve Fate's reprimand.
We don't know what it is to be content;
       No test like our predicament—
Each pestering Heaven with an urgent demand.
If Jove gave us each what we wish that we had,
       Even then our complaints would drive him mad.

XII

THE SUN AND THE FROGS

When a tyrant wed, folk gave way to excess
       And, drowning care, would drink and drink.
Only Aesop thought it besotted to think
       Excess results in happiness.
The Sun had once pondered the desirability,
       He said, of marrying.
Instantly each frog community
       Was audibly worrying,
       And every frog wore a frown.
       "What if he has little suns to shine down?"
They asked Fate. "When one can cause us pain,
       Suppose six were drying up the rain.
Sea life would shrivel and every kind of sea spawn;
Farewell, reeds and marshes; soon there'd be no frogs
       And but for the Styx there'd be no bogs."
       Although a frog is a small animal,
What it said, I'd say, seems not illogical.

XIII

THE FARMER AND THE ADDER

Aesop tells how a countryman,
As imprudent as he was benevolent,
Had an estate he'd gone out to scan
One winter day, and observed as he went
A snake on the snow in a plight that was serious,
Mummied from head to tail till no longer venomous.
He dared not delay; it would die if left there;
So the man picked it up, took it home, gave it care,
And failed to foresee the result of an action
In which compassion had been complete;
He stirred circulation by friction
And laid the maimed form near heat,
Which no sooner had tempered the torpid blood
Than animus stirred and grew livelier.
The adder hissed, raised its head as best it could,
Coiled, and made a long lunge toward where the farmer
stood—
Its foster father who had been its rescuer.
The farmer said, "Ingrate! You'd be my murderer?
You shall die!" With indignation which nothing could foil,
He picked up his ax and the dastard was dead.
Two strokes made three snakes of the coil—
A body, a tail, and a head.
The pestilent thirds writhed together to rear
But of course could no longer adhere.

All should practice charity
Toward all? I've thrown some light on this.
Ingrates, I say with emphasis,
Will always die in misery.

XIV

THE SICK LION AND THE FOX

The sovereign lord of animals
Lay ill in the royal cavern's shade
And all were informed by seneschals
That formal visits must be paid.
The lion himself signed what he wrote,
Stating that none would go down his throat,
And sent each beast the document
Or passport stressing his intent—
Of not any more harming anyone
Than if his claws and teeth were drawn:
Since kings are importunate,
Each species sent a delegate;
Then since no foxes had honored the king,
As though to defend their reasoning
One said, "The pad-marks which circle the lair
Prove that any who visit the king in the dark,
Without exception, have left no forth-coming mark
Like those which enter. Singular.
A most suspicious circumstance.
All are guarded against mischance
And the king has signed his name with care—
A safeguard the foxes are glad he gave,
But all of the pad-marks enter the cave
And none of them leads to the open air."

XV

THE FOWLER, THE GOSHAWK, AND THE LARK

We scorn those who overbear
And condone our own oppressiveness;
While the principle holds everywhere:
We must, as we would be spared, spare those whom we could oppress.

A countryman fowling with beams a bird-glass throws
Allured by his bright mirroring of her a lark;
When a goshawk circling the plowman's even rows
      Dropped from the blue, finding his mark.
The fallen singer who had not yet been caught
In the malign mesh of the birdcatcher's twine
Was in the grasp of a bird with talons taut,
      Piercing her to the spine.
Meanwhile as the goshawk was tearing feathers away,
He had himself become the fowler's prey
And turned on his captor eyes full of alarm,
      Which said, "Have I ever made you quail?"
The birdcatcher said, "And this very small animal,
      When has she ever done you harm?"

XVI

THE HORSE AND THE ASS

If we lend no aid in this world of care
      When a neighbor is dying of despair,
      Then we find that his load is our own.

An ass took the road next a horse of marked surliness—
A beast with no weight on him but his harness;
Whereas the ass was so burdened that he was thrown.
He begged that the horse assist him in some way
Lest reaching the city be impossible;
Saying, "My prayer is hardly culpable;
As much as half my load would be to you but child's play."
The horse made a rejoinder so coarse it must be implied
While watching the ass plod and stumble till he died—
      A repercussion to deplore,
      Since afterward he had to bear
      Both the load that had been the ass's share
      And the hide of the former servitor.

XVII

THE DOG WHO DROPPED SUBSTANCE FOR SHADOW

Everyone is self-deceived:
Of all the fooled, agog to catch a phantom,
The number if you knew it would never be believed;
It is a permanent conundrum.
We ought to be reminded of Aesop's dog, who set out
With a bone, but, on seeing what he had in his mouth doubled
By water, dropped it for the shadow and just about
Drowned. The brook was instantly troubled;
And having worn himself out, he'd neither substance
nor shadow to thank
Himself for on regaining the bank.

XVIII

THE CARTER IN THE MIRE

Poor Phaëthon with hay heaped on his wain,
Found his cartwheels mired. There he was and would remain,
With no rescuer near. He was at a stand
In a corner of Brittany that is low land—
Quagmiry Quimper-Corentin—
The kind of place, I need scarcely explain,
To which Fate sends culprits she desires to goad!
Heaven defend us from such a road!
Say you'd heard our Quimper carter swear at the mud,
Scores of expletives would have come forth in a flood.
The man in his desperation
Was soon cursing the holes, raining oaths on each steed,
His cart, his occupation;
Then invoked the saint of the impossible deed,
Whose fabulous strength no one spurns,
And prayed, "Hercules, here is a toiler in need.
As pivot on which the earth turns,

[132]

Your pair of strong arms could save me."
Our man made the prayer and from clouds overhead,
A voice was heard saying distinctly,
"Hercules would have effort made,
Then assists mankind. Look hard, for patience can.
See what is hindering your strained span.
Scrape that mortar-like mud
From the felloes and the axle it has glued,
Spattering what should have mobility.
Pulverize with a pick rocks that could have utility.
Fill in that rut with hard grit. Done?" The man said, "The road
is restored."
—"I'll help you," said the voice. "Have your whip in position."
—"I have. Ha! My cart glides as for a magician:
Hercules be praised." The voice said, "No one used a harsh
word.
Your team pulled your cart from the slough in which it slid.
Exert yourself; Heaven betters what you did."

XIX

THE CHARLATAN

Go where you will, you'll find the charlatan:
His science is old as man.
Its practitioners lay siege to all.
Sometimes one will risk death in the theater, or one of the clan
Post bills on each hall,
Saying Cicero is outshone.
Here a fellow of the latter sort,
With a tongue to grace a king's court,
Said he could teach a booby how to speak in public,
A rustic, a boor, a jack whose head was thick;
"Yes, gentlemen, a donkey, an animal clown:
Let someone bring me an ass, an actual ass.
I shall see that he leads the class
In an academic gown."
The king heard him, summoned, and said to the hard boor,
"I've procured an ass from Arcady,

As rare a russet as you'd see;
I'd have him made an orator."
—"Consider the thing done, Sire," the charlatan said,
And the entrance fee was paid.
A don, as he told all concerned,
Was to see what the student had learned
In ten years, or the mentor be hung as a quack,
With a noose round his neck, as the phrase is, "till dead"
With his rhetoric on his back
And two ass-ears on his head.
It would be a scandalously fine affair which they would have
a chance
To attend, one courtier said. The sharper to be hung
Would carry it off with a smiling countenance;
Moreover would extenuate the circumstance
In the kind of discourse he made speciously long,
Full of terms that stir tears, and of course catch the ear
Of quack orators they would train—
Crooks, if I need to explain.
The quack said, "Death might interfere;
The king, the ass, or I might be stricken."

This was not mere effrontery.
In ten years how tell where we shall be?
So eat all you can, and drink the best that you own;
Each ten years Death bears off one in three, as we've known.

XX

DISCORD

The goddess Discord had been making the gods sigh
About an apple, till Heaven was in a fume
And she was cast down from on high.
Pseudo-kind mankind made room,
Spread his arms and seemed glad of one more,
With her brother Yes-No at the door
And Thine-is-Mine, her progenitor.
She did us the honor in the world down here

Of preferring our hemisphere
To the side of the earth where mortals are crude, since so reared
   Advantages have not interfered—
And are married without priest or lawyer;
   And thus without Discord, having no use for her.
Now Rumor would hurry to Discord in advance
   And bid her set forth in haste
   Whenever there might be a chance
  Of frustrating Peace or seeing her displaced;
Since the moment some shadow of ill will appeared,
Discord lit the spark for a fire difficult to suppress.
At last Rumor tired and said she must confess
   That Discord had so often disappeared,
   She should have a home,
Because when she was lost, search for her was troublesome.
She needed fixed arrangements—in a word,
Headquarters to which families of all categories
   Could go when members drew a sword.
There were no convents in those days for young ladies
   And to find a home for Discord was hard,
   Till eventually they declared,
   Any inn at which Hymen stayed, was to be one that
        Discord shared.

XXI

THE YOUNG WIDOW

Of course when a husband dies who has been dear,
One sighs brokenhearted sighs; then grows philosophical—
Sure to be healed by Time, whose flight cures all—
   Mourning's metamorphoser.
   The disparity is great
   Between a sufferer's state
Who's mourned a day or a year—supposing we meditate
   On how the two could be the same.
One will repulse; the other, attract; in a thousand ways scintillate.
The former abandons herself to sighs true or false—an eversame
Blighted air, to words—an unvarying monotone.

[135]

She says she is inconsolable;
So she says—a pretense to which such are prone,
As demonstrated by my tale;
As rather, truth shall demonstrate.

A siren to celebrate
Clung to her husband while life's flame came and went.
"When your soul must take flight, so will mine; they'll be blent,"
She said. "We'll both die—entwined too tight to separate."
It was merely the husband who died.
The belle's father was sound sense personified;
He waited for grief to abate;
Then lest his heir live disconsolate,
Said, "My child, you must not shed another tear:
How does blighting youth's charm help the dead you hold dear?
Think of those still alive; dry your tears; weep no more.
I don't say suppress your despair
Or instantly consent to care
As much about marriage as before.
But in time I'll present just the suitor in whom to rejoice—
Young, handsome, well built. You'll prefer him—a far better choice
Than your first." She murmured the words as one,
"Ah, I'm wed to the veil since he's gone."
The father let her feel that her mourning might last.
Thus a month came and passed.
One more; variety gave the young mourner an air;
Quaintly modish attire, white mull, an odd twist to the hair,
The smartening weeds that widows wear;
Touch on touch that's debonair;
Suitors were besieging her.
Once more the dovecote was thronged. A game, a smile, a dance,
Till our sufferer might be found—
Dawn or dusk—where young persons abound,
By the fountain of juvenescence.
Her father no longer praised lovers-to-be,
Since asked by his pearl whose loved ghost had dwarfed all,
"Where is the marvel you promised, who soon will be
marrying me—
Whom you said was incomparable?"

EPILOGUE

Our peregrination must end there.
One's skin creeps when poets persevere.
Don't press pith from core to perimeter;
Take the flower of the subject, the thing that is rare.
Besides, I'd best conserve my pen
And energies to write again
And sound another kind of praise.
Love, who inspires my fantasies,
Is restive and craves a change, he says—
The tyrant whom I have to please.
Let Psyche be my theme again; Damon, you ask that I express
Her mourning and her joyousness.
I shall try; I kindle when
She bids me tune and touch my lute,
So long as Love does not torment me again,
Setting similar tasks to execute!

PARTS THREE AND FOUR

TO

MADAME DE MONTESPAN

Fables were an invention of Heaven for us all
   Or if first devised by a man,
We should build him the best altar possible
    And then ought to do what we can
    To deify, as I have said,
Wisdom by which they were initiated.
The fable is a talisman, indeed magnetic thing
    So charming that it is ravishing,
    Of which we could never weary
Whether we are moved to the depths or made merry.
Olympia, graced by the glittering phrase,
Since my Muse has supped where the gods congregate,
Look upon her with kindness and render elate
The simplicities with which I enliven my days.
Although time can level all to uniformity,
You might, if you would, spare my book decrepitude.
Any work which would aspire to longevity
    Must be one which you think good.
I am asking if I have written worthily,
    Since there is no phase of beauty
Of a verbal kind which could take you by surprise,
You know so well in what the beauty of speech lies.
You listen or speak and one is charmed by you.
    My Muse, with a subject matched by few,
    Is tempted to amplitude;
Yet ambition of my own must be resigned
    To one of more majestic mind
    Upon whose praise I shan't intrude.
Olympia, grant this petition with which I conclude.

What a solace and defense your name would be.
Pray sponsor my book which has grown dear to me,
And might assure me immortality
   If you could say that you see here
   Worth which defies contumely
   And merits kindness everywhere.
To be prized for myself I could not have dreamed—
   Am but asking that fables be esteemed;
Such make-believe is loved by all, not just a few.
If there is in my verse something which you hold dear,
It should have a shrine which you inspired me to rear,
Though build one for you first is what I'd rather do.

BOOK SEVEN

I

THE ANIMALS SICK OF THE PLAGUE

A malady smote the earth one year,
Felling beasts and infecting all with fear,
To prove to them what grave offenders they were;
Although plague was the name by which it was known,
For it literally congested Acheron,
Warring on creatures everywhere,
It did not bear off all but all were endangered.
Any that lingered barely stirred—
Could merely breathe and that diseasedly.
Nothing aroused their energy.
Neither wolf nor fox disappeared
To stalk young prey as it sunned.
The demoralized doves scattered
And love starved; life was moribund.

When the lion had called his constituency
He said, "Dear friends, this is heaven's remedy
For the sins we have thought a boon.
So he who is guiltiest
Should sacrifice his good to that of the rest
And possibly most of us will then be immune.
In accord with the past, history suggests to one,
Penance as atoning for evil done.
So without subterfuge, braving the consequence,
Let each search his conscience.
As for me, I have preyed on flocks of sheep so often
That I have become a glutton.
Because they had wronged me? not once.
Moreover I would devour him when I mastered
The shepherd.

[143]

Therefore let me be sacrificed in recompense,
But first make a clean breast, not just *I* say how I offend:
We must have justice and detect the trespass,
      Then rend the culprit's carcass."
The fox said, "Sire, you are too good to rend;
Your sense of honor is excessively nice.
Eat sheep, Sire! Poor dolts, their loss is no sacrifice.
A sinful king? Oh no. You prove when you devour
      The beasts that you thought them superior.
      As for the shepherd, one would swear
      That he went where he ought to go,
Having become to any of us, high or low,
      A monster none can endure."
When the fox said this, applause deafened the cur
      And no one dared to consider
A tiger, bear, or other beast of prominence
      Guilty of any offense.
In fact, quarrelers of evident spleen
Were canonized for their innocent mien.
When his turn came the ass said, "To take a backward glance,
      I recall passing clerical domain,
The herbs and grass and hunger close to sustenance.
      Fiend take me, how could I refrain?
I nipped off as much grass as would lie on my tongue;
So sinned, if what we say must be disinterested."
They made too much noise to hear what the donkey said.
A wolf pronounced the verdict, to which he clung,
Convinced they had found the animal they must kill—
The battered rapscallion who had made the world ill.
He deserved to be hung as an example.
Eat another's grass! What could be more horrible.
      Death, only death was suitable
For the criminal—inflicted at once by spite.
And so, as you are weak or are invincible,
The court says white is black or that black crimes are white.

II

THE MARTYRED HUSBAND

Moral and outward charm are at odds as things go,
   Or I soon would be sharing my name;
For they aren't found together, and since it is so,
And the sweeter the soul the more faulty the frame,
   Choose one or the other.
Forgive my view that this sums up the matter.
I have seen matrimony and seen it to shun.
Nearly all sigh for bonds that will soon make them sour
And desire former days when they'd not had to cower,
When each has appraised the rash thing he has done.
One time a man whose wife had been making life dreary
   Sent her home to end worry,
   As a money-minded jealous
   Scold, abusive and predacious.
Nothing he did pleased her; nothing was opportune:
Oversleeping and then getting sleepy too soon.
It was too light, it was too dark; affront had become her pose.
The servants were fuming and marriage was her bane:
Men never notice things; squandering again;
   Precipitate; half comatose;
   She ranted until her consort, wearying
   And disaffected by her carping,
   Said, "Off to the farm if you must complain,
  In your birthplace where there is work to disdain
And Phyllis may need a turkey-matron
   Or a swineherd now and then."
Supposing he would find her changed presently,
He brought her back, inquiring, "Well, how were things there?
   You passed the time agreeably?
Is farm life a thing for which you could care?"
   —"Bearable," she said; "but the men!
They're lazier than those who work for you and me.
   Shepherds should not be leisurely;
When I said so, my mere tone of voice gave them pain.

[145]

To hire such idlers is a farce."
—"Fine, my dear," the man said one day and was curt;
    "Your disposition is so perverse
    That anyone near you is hurt;
If but met on some little late housekeeping tour,
    You're more tiresome than one can endure.
What is their fate whose whole lives you make harder,
    The domestics you've hired for your household and
                larder?

    And what shall that martyred man do
Who's compelled day and night to take orders from you?
Go back and be rustic: farewell. And as for me,
    If I ever bring you where I may be,
Punish my sins with one scourge when life is over—
Two wives like you shackled to me forever!"

III

THE RAT RETIRED FROM THE WORLD

    There are fine tales in the Levant,
And this is an account of a world-weary rat
    Who made a Holland cheese his haunt,
    Which not a sound could penetrate—
    Even some echo growing faint.
    In his round home which served each want
Our novel hermit kept gnawing now and again
    Till claws and teeth had hollowed out a den
That brought him near the rind while affording him food—
Both sheltered and nourished there, with a result so good
That he was curving out. God provides for the wants
    Of those who profess to be his saints.
    Certain rodents of fortitude
    Were known to a diplomat,
And one day they came begging coppers to spare;
    Having gone about everywhere,
Gathering funds for warfare against the cat,
    Since Ratopolis was blockaded.
The rat beggars had been sent abroad destitute,

State banks being in bad repute
When a country is invaded;
But they did not bear down or ask undue favor
For the siege would soon be over.
The recluse said, "Friends, could one share
Or give, in a place like this? I have no use
For coins. How could a recluse
Lend you aid except by a prayer,
Begging that heaven look down on you in pity
And aid you out of its tender mercy!"
Having played the orator
Our pseudo-saint fastened the door.
Was it, since I have curiosity,
Monkish life that had made the rat cold?
By no means. He lived fanatically.
The words monk and charity are synonyms. Or so I have
been told.

IV

THE HERON

V

THE HAUGHTY LASS

A heron on wary stilts, though where I've not found out—
Long beak thrust out on longer neck—stalked all about
Where a river cooled the air.
The water was as clear as the fair morning hour;
With Dame Carp circling near as under magic power
And a crony accompanying her.
The bird could not have found a more convenient bite
Since they'd veer in toward shore close enough to devour,
But his meals must be at an hour
When he might have appetite.
His tastes had been formed and his ways were regular.
Hungrier afterwhile, he wandered below
Toward some tench who swam to and fro

[147]

Not far from the bank where the sand had formed a bar.
No fish for an epicure primed for food less tedious.
      He had grown as fastidious
      As Horace's dainty rat.
"Reduced to tench!" he said. "A heron subsist upon that?
What sort of bird would think such refuse gain?"
Ate none, then found a gudgeon to disdain.
"A gudgeon! The sort of thing heron would detain!
God forbid! Spread my beak for spawn which fill me with
                            distaste!"
He spread his beak for less: all swam off one by one;
      Then no more upon which to frown.
The starving bird rejoiced to break his fast in haste
      On a snail, though a tiny one.
      Don't be irreconcilable;
The better the mind is, the more adaptable.
Demand too much and forfeit what you had.
      Superciliousness is always bad,
More than all when half grasping a thing whose lure was great—
Maxims we neglect—meant for men and not herons alone;
So be warned. Friends, I have something else to relate
Which certainly could instruct almost anyone.

      You'd find no damsel haughtier
      Than this lass who sought a mate and thought it her
                             right
That some handsome youth or other be in love with her,
Though not jealous (neat dual requisite);
      One of wealth—not acquired overnight;
      Estate, name, affluence;
Intellect; everything. Where secure the cynosure?
A solicitous Fate set itself to procure
      Suitors of worth and eminence.
The lass could merely see crass insufficiency.
"Wed me to wooden wits without intelligence!
Aspiring to my hand! Really! What absurdity:
      Taking men as a class, a dead loss!
Here but a dullard; there, positively gross.
The shape of that nose! So large it must get in his way.

This one a goose and that one a jay."
Are not the meticulous
Soon disgusted, whatever one does?
When the rare catches left, suitors a shade plebeian
Thought that the lass might be won
But their disdainer said, "Dear me! I've grown liberal,
Admitting these boors and bears; I'm not here to be bought
Like girls who can't wed anyone.
Thank God I am not distraught—
Worried sick lest I be an old maid."
The lass reaped the fruit of needless arrogance.
With charm impaired, she did not savor of romance.
A year went by. One more, and then she was dismayed;
Presently feared she faced a defeat; felt each day's smart,
Could not force a smile; since Love knew to depart,
She was soon a sight no one could bear,
Then undertook artifice with the most intense care—
To no effect, since Time had worked destruction.
We can change the fashion
Of a house; but not features ravaged by age—
Marred by pride and futile rage.
Torn by regret, all she could do was turn the page.
The mirror advised her, "Take any suitor in sight,"
And some mysterious force assured her that it had been right;
It can spur a fool too spoiled for any use,
To do what once would have been the surprise of her life—
Gladly seize in the end one whom no one would choose,
And be an uncouth fellow's wife.

VI

THE WISHES

India has a good fairy
Who never seems to weary
Of performing little tasks like polishing the carriage
Or cultivating cabbage;
But mortal interference
Can do endless harm. A goblin by the Ganges once,

[149]

Had been working for a citizen of some prominence,
Silent as a shadow, with speed and conscientiousness.
      He loved his master and his mistress
But especially flowers. Who knows?—the winds when pure,
Are friends of the elves and bring them a reward.
The fact is the fairy was always working hard
      And giving pleasure on each tour
      At inconvenience to himself—
Too affectionate to care to be uprooted.
      Though nimble-footed, he had stayed
      Despite temptations for an elf.
      Then his friends whom magic had bred
Stirred up the chief fairy by some sort of spell,
      Till whim or trouble to quell
      Sent our sprite from where he was situated
Far off to perform tasks near a Norwegian outpost
      In the house of someone
      Whose roof was furred with frost—
Though Laplander-Hindus seem an innovation!
The fairy said to his hosts, since loath to depart,
      "I must make a long journey.
      How I have erred I do not know,
Yet have been penalized and I must hurry—
Have but a month to stay. Let the time I remain
Advantage you. Make three wishes, but only three
      And they shall be fulfilled by me."
Now wishing is not a feat involving pain,
      Or a pleasure new to man.
Our pair first asked wealth in amounts fit for a prince,
      And abundance began to rain—
      Money mounting in consequence.
Cellars overflowed with wine; the loft was full of grain—
Almost burst. But alas, the maintenance!
Faulty books, dull hard thought; always more than one could do.
Conceive what large tasks were perplexing the two.
      They'd a fortune which thieves might devour,
      Sums they must lend to persons in power;
Were taxed by the crown; all their freedom was gone.
      Good fortune can be hard on one.
"Take away all this wealth. How I wish we had none,"

Each said to the other. "Oh, to be poor again!
Dire want is better than wealth that is distress.
Fly, Fortune, fly! Where is the goddess Happiness?
Dear Protectress, and sleep, rare bedfellow,
O Mediocrity, return at once." She did so.
Essential Sanity when brought home was put at ease
   And our two were again at peace;
But again as before, and two wishes had been used.
   Like all who have become confused
And waste time on dreams of castles in air,
Forgetting matters which should be their foremost care.
   The fairy and they were amused.
   Reminded by him that time flies,
They made a third wish known to him before he had left home
   And by asking that he make them wise,
Chose wealth that is not burdensome.

VII

THE LION HOLDS AUDIENCE

Their king the lion once called to a council of state
Beasts he ruled, to know whom he had to dominate.
   So deputies such as he had
   Carried a court circular
   To every creature good or bad,
   That it be read everywhere.
   His sealed edict designated
   A month in which he would be feted
   While holding court, and he would first appear
   At a banquet which all must attend—
   With turns by Fagotin [1] at the end.
   Since he ruled with benevolence,
The beasts could take pride in the wealth and brilliance of
         their prince
   And were to come to his Louvre to call.

---

[1] Fagotin—a monkey famed for drawing crowds to the marionette theater de Brioche.

His Louvre! Charnel house with a scent so perceptible
The bear's drawn-in nostrils denoted disdain,
A parliamentary sin as was plain.
And he frowned. The exasperated lion said,
"Down to Pluto; let him judge one so ill bred."
The monkey, content that the bear should lose his head,
Became servile and extolled the lion's ire,
His long claws and den, and said the bad air had a lure
   Like ambergris. No flower was so pure
That its scent could compare; but sycophancy
Failed through bad taste and was punished accordingly.
   How well such codes of moral flaws
   Anticipate Caligula's.
The fox stood near, so the king said, "Come, have no fear,
Bare your heart; I shall pardon mistakes made";
   But the fox feigned a cold, shook his head,
And since no animal could be the king's interpreter
   Who could not smell, he moved to the rear.
   You'll see the point, applied to man.
If you are at court and would be popular,
Praise must not burden the ear; though candor, too,
       requires care.
When you speak, best be as Norman as you can.

VIII

THE VULTURES AND THE PIGEONS

Once warlike birds made the heavens ring with hate,
Primed for trouble which ill will can create—
Not songsters of some vernal season,
Born in a bower which tender leafage makes,
Whose arts and brilliant choirs could all but dim the sun
As they announce that Venus herself awakes;
Nor Cupid's birds who bear aloft her car,
But vultures equipped as such birds are
With bentback beak and claws curved to tear.
It was said a dog's carcass had brought about the war.
The sky rained blood. There was no better term,

And if memory were not too infirm
To tell you all, I should faint from the tedium.
Captains succumbed and heroes breathed their last,
While high on his rock where fate had bound him fast,
Prometheus hoped that the end might have come.
What a sublime exhibition of ardor,
Though slaughter so great should stir saddened horror.
With courage, wit, shrewd forays, and force,
The ire on both sides transcended remorse,
For neither side left anything undone
That might have lessened the others' hosts,
Each being ambitious that it be the one
To fill the dim underworld with ghosts.
Yet the bird which compassion has made its own
Was disheartened to see dissonance sown.
Its rainbow neck bespoke a heart that wished its friends well,
So a flock of the good doves in unison
Tried to make the bird world equable
And somehow arrest what had gone on;
Therefore went forth to act as ambassador
And beg the vultures to end the dire war.
Truce was made and peace reigned presently;
But sad fact! It brought disaster to a brood
Which merited love and gratitude.
The scavengers forced the pigeons to flee—
Every one of them, and what was far worse,
Decimated towns, farms, killed each bird they could rend,
Since the injudicious doves had lacked common sense
In coming to terms with murderers.
Keep the malevolent divided. Don't bend.
The furtherance of peace that all may share
Depends upon it—on sowing among the malign, civil war;
Or your peace with them will not be peace at all.
A thought voiced in passing—all I'll say of the brawl.

[153]

IX

THE COACH AND THE FLY

Climbing a hill through sand, as though the load were lead,
Scorched by burning sun directly overhead,
  Six horses dragged a coach with a lurch.
Women, a monk, as well as old folk were walking,
Yet the sweating, blowing horses were balking
When a fly buzzed toward them determined to perch;
Convinced that noisiness could goad the horses on,
Stung one, stung all, sure that what she had done
  Could move the weight at a bound.
She rode on the coach pole; soon the driver's nose smarted,
  As the wheels were turning round
  And the vehicle started.
Then insisting that credit be laid at her door,
She would rush to and fro like a sergeant till spent,
Who must urge his men forward wherever they went,
While claiming the honor of winning the war.
  The fly complained that what she had done,
Was a task for them all and not for her alone.
Heavy work each should do had been left to her.
  The monk had let matins be his share;
They took a long time. A light heart overflowed,
But song can't move coaches along the road!
Pestering each ear, Dame Fly must incommode,
  Buzzing in foolhardihood!
At the top of the hill the tired horses delayed.
"Better stop for a time! Take a breath," the fly said.
"Since I've guided you up to the level again,
My good horses, admit that I've been under strain."

So consummate boors, too brash to be lessoned,
  Making disturbance everywhere,
  Worry themselves with a world of care—
As pests whose departure one longs to have hastened.

X

THE DAIRYMAID AND HER MILK-POT

Perrette's milk-pot fitted her head-mat just right—
      Neatly quilted to grip the pot tight.
Then she set off to market and surely walked well,
In her short muslin dress that encouraged long strides,
Since to make better time she wore shoes with low heel
      And had tucked up her skirt at the sides.
      Like summer attire her head had grown light,
      Thinking of what she'd have bought by night.
In exchange for the milk, since supposing it gone,
She'd buy ten times ten eggs and three hens could be set.
Taking care all hatched out, she'd not lose more than one
      And said, "Then there'll be pullets to sell.
I'll raise them at home; it is quite within reason,
      Since shrewd Master Fox will be doing well
If I can't shortly buy a young pig and grow bacon.
The one I had bought would be almost half grown;
He'd need next to no feed—almost nothing at all;
When he's sold I'll have funds—good hard cash to count on.
Then with room at the barn for some stock in the stall,
I could buy cow and calf if the pig had sold high;
If I'd not had a loss, I'd add sheep by and by."
Perrette skipped for joy as she dreamt of what she'd bought.
The crock crashed. Farewell, cow, calf, fat pig, eggs not
                          hatched out.
The mistress of wealth grieved to forfeit forever
      The profits that were mounting.
      How ask her husband to forgive her
      Lest he beat her as was fitting?
      And thus ended the farce we have watched:
Don't count your chickens before they are hatched.

      Whom does a daydream not entrance?
      Have castles in air no romance?
Picrochole, Pyrrhus, Perrette—a fool's or wisdom's mirth—

[155]

Every hearth can give them birth.
Each of us loves a daydream—the fondest thing on earth,
Illusion has a charm to which our minds succumb;
    Since it captures whatever has worth.
    All hearts are ours, we pluck each plum.
When alone, I tower so tall that the bravest shiver.
I crush and see Persian emperors suffer.
    I am a king, an idol.
My head is diademed with gems that rain:
Then the king's deep problems by some unjust reversal,
    Are Jean de La Fontaine's again.

XI

THE CURATE AND THE CORPSE

    The journey was a somber one
    Which took him to the graveyard gate;
    The curate's tasks were over soon,
    Enheartening him, whose greed was great.
His sad charge had a coach, since arrangements had been made
    For him to be carefully conveyed
In the garb called a shroud, at which hearts have despaired—
    For snow's glare, summer's shade—
    A dress which the wearer need never discard.
    One might have heard when the shepherd prayed,
    Such tones as showed how much he cared:
    Prayers familiar to the gown,
    Psalms and lessons on and on;
    And responses to the verse he would drone.
    "Poor mortal Clay, placed in my care,
All shall be done for you as it should be done,
    But it makes your priest Death's treasurer."
Curate Hard-of-Heart stared with uncanny power,
As though thieves had sighted a sum to devour;
    And greed become expositor:
    "Poor mortal Clay, don't forget my due—
    Gold and tapers and something more;
    Lesser things are important too."

The cost of a wine vat would now be met,
        Holding the best the region had grown;
        A niece lived for pretty frocks she'd get,
        As did the housemaid, Paquette.
        Each should have finery of her own.
        While charmed imagination played,
        Collision! A cart overturned the coach,
        And jolly Priest Hard-Heart, faith's reproach.
The leaden coffin had crushed the curate's head;
The weighty parishioner struck the shepherd hard,
        And a mercenary priest met his Lord.
        These tales are twins, it seems to me—
        Borne out universally:
Of Perrette's crashing milk-pot, with her sales not yet made;
        And of mercenariness repaid.

XII

THE MAN WHO RAN AFTER FORTUNE
AND THE MAN
WHO WAITED FOR HER AT HOME

        Who is not reaching for the moon?
Would that I had some vantage point and might watch foolish man
        Straining toward what will have vanished soon
        In the breathless race he would run
To capture at the North Pole or South Pole
A phantom that is without form or soul.
        When it would seem that the day is won,
Fickleness takes a turn with which he cannot cope.
Poor fool, I grieve for the faith of the wretch,
        Stirring tears not wrath by that at which he'd snatch.
He says, "Now this man had a cabbage patch
        And today he is pope.
Are such as we nothing at all? A thousandfold more wise.
        We have worth but does it count?
        Some power has blinded Fortune's eyes.
But then—to what would the papacy amount!"
Peace, sweet peace—it is peace on which the soul relies—

From the first an attribute of deities—
Rarely possessed by those whom we call fortunate.
     Don't search for but be sought by Fate.
What is feminine comes unpredictably.

Two friends who had worked and saved successfully
Were at length well off, but one was never at peace;
     Fate seemed unkind, so he said in despair
          To his friend, "Come, let us live elsewhere.
          What prophet is really thought great
Where he chanced to be born? There are towns that would value
                              our worth."
—"Search them out," his friend said. "As for me, let me wait.
     Neither climate nor place shall lure me forth.
But do as you like; make the search, since importunate:
You'll return before long. As for how my time's spent,
     I shall be dreaming of where you went."
     The quester—devoured by greed, you will infer—
          Found highways and byways down which he ran
          And compassed the distance he'd span
By next day—to the chief haunt of Fortune and changelings
                              like her,
If she stayed anywhere. He was at court, you may be sure,
Ruled by formalities which one must endure,
Attending the couché, the levee, at any hour
     When his hopes might be likely to flower.
There he was at his post, but she'd not been seen, or had gone.
"Why is this?" he asked. "I may find her farther on,
Since she is such an inconstant power.
I have seen her sometimes near yonder celebrity—
     Or some other. How can it be
That she is determined not to be addressed?
Although courts— I believe they say it is so—
Invariably adjudge modest folk best.
Fair sirs, farewell, courtiers; courtiers and fair sirs, I must go;
You'll be seeking forever what cannot be caught.
I have heard that Fortune has shrines at Surat:
I am off." No sooner said than he was aboard.
Men with wills of iron and armament as stout
Must have explored these seas and first dared beat about

In their tempestuous deeps where gales blow hard.
        Sometimes our voyager would brood,
        Longing for quondam quietude;
    Still more when the ship had been plundered
By pirates, was becalmed, aground, or storms thundered
And life seemed cut short. Worn to the bone again,
He sought fortune farther on, but in vain;
Whereas he might have found her where he had begun.
"Best go to Japan," said Hindus to whom he had run;
"Seek there if you care to see her shining face."
        Off again; by ship at a snail's pace,
        And then somewhat unexpectedly
        The reward for all he had withstood,
A lesson taught by folk whose life is rude:
"Best stay at home and grow wise intuitively."
The Japanese proved no kinder to him who'd left home
        Than such Hindus as he had visited:
        So the conclusion to which he had come
Was that Fortune had been where he should have stayed.
        Embarrassed by his plight,
He hastened back and, elate as loved objects met his sight,
Wept for joy and said, "How fortunate mankind
Whose castles in air are ones his feet can find:
        Who does not need to more than hear
Of the court, the sea, or Fortune—that conjuror
Who creates a procession before our eyes
Of offices and wealth which involve a ceaseless round
Of pursuits in which no satisfaction can be found.
I'll sit down here at home; and be sure I shall not rise."
        Bound he'd keep the resolve he had made
Against Fortune and the precarious leap—
        He found her sitting where the door-post cast shade,
By the friend who was sharing it, then fast asleep.

XIII

THE TWO COCKS

Two cocks got on until joined by a hen:
      And then ill will flared into hate.
Love, your power burned down Troy; so these cocks in a pen
      Made war which none could abate;
Xanthus flowed red with blood of gods the gods had slain!
Which fought best was in doubt, so spleen was roused again
Till the fight was one to which the whole cock world paid heed:
All with combs came to see their brother birds embroiled,
      And countless Helens of rare breed
Would be his from whom the defeated bird recoiled.
He suddenly vanished, embarrassed by defeat:
      Robbed of hens and power, he was forlorn,
While the powerful foe seemed to say, "Revenge is sweet;
All this plunder was yours." The victim's angry scorn
Would flame each time he saw his enemy parade,
Lift wings and beat his back when he'd sharpen his beak
      Till the very winds seemed weak.
      For the crushed to watch the one he'd degrade
Was needless combativeness. Victors must tower above the host,
     So ours flew to a roof and crowed till the region rang,
      But a vulture had heard the boast.
      Farewell to prideful love of which power sang.
The vulture's curling claws pierced the boastful bird,
      Whose rival's power was restored.
      The once humiliated fowl
      Made a courtier's commotion
      And was met with an ovation,
      Since hens and hens swarmed to his call.
Mere chance overturns what appeared secure
And vaingloriousness may work one woe.
Hold your fire; beware; you'd better be demure
      When you have struck a decisive blow.

XIV

MAN'S INGRATITUDE AND UNFAIRNESS TOWARD FORTUNE

A merchant had at last attained prosperity.
Despite typhoons, his ships were always fortunate;
Rocks, reefs, and whirlpools had not made sport of his freight.
Fortune seemed to grant the man immunity.
Though sea and ill fortune made others' trips inopportune,
It would seem that his cargoes were always immune;
Fate seemed to steer his goods ashore with special care.
Persons in his employ had been incorruptible:
His sugar, cinnamon, tobacco, had had sale
      At his price; and imports of chinaware.
Fashion's and folly's gold were his steward's despair,
      Showering as in a fairy tale;
Double ducats the smallest change he'd accept.
Coaches, fine. His hounds and his horses each a prize beast:
      His fasts were like a wedding feast.
When a friend admired the sort of table he kept
And said, "What about this fare? There is nothing daintier,"
The man replied, "Why not, I am a connoisseur.
What I do is well thought out. With too much to impound,
I balance chance with fact; then my judgment is sound."
But pondering gains made him covetous;
He hazarded once more what he had set aside
And this time nothing came of unjustified pride.
      He had been too impetuous.
A stiff breeze sank goods stowed with inexperience;
One good galleon lacked guns which he'd failed to afford,
      And sea robbers clambered aboard.
      A third that had docked without mischance
Excited no interest; idiosyncrasy
      And taste had changed to indifference.
      He was cheated whatever the circumstance.
Since passion for building made spending too free
At the same time that he was plucking every fruit,

He found himself destitute.
His friend, observing him in this distressing plight,
Asked, "What could have been the cause?" Was told, "Misfortune,
Alas." He said, "Bear it; you've one consolation;
Say you've failed; sound judgment gained can serve you aright."

Such words aren't gratefully received!
Each takes his own part when his goods can't be retrieved.
We think we have earned our prosperity
And if a thing we've done results disastrously,
Misfortune was our injurer.
It is typical of man.
We think we wrought our gains; misfortune wrecked our plan;
She is always to blame. Man is always unfair.

XV

THE FORTUNE-TELLERS

Mass opinion determines the tastes of a town,
Though in the first place influenced by accident—
Borne out by many an event
At each level of life from the loftiest down.
Fear and obsession and the willingness to oppress
Drown reason's voice as by a waterfall's force;
And will always do it of course.
In Paris once a woman passed for a sorceress—
Consulted about any worrier's bane.
Say one lost cherished lace or was lacking a swain;
Or a distasteful husband had outlived his use;
A mother-in-law or wife had been jealous without excuse;
Folk were running to her mansard
To beg that she make life less subject to hazard.
Able to see how a thing was,
She would use learned terms, and aplomb blinds the crass.
Her dice might fall aright; thus fact and guess concurred.
Every little while her verdicts dazed a dull clientele,
Until, though her ignorance was twenty-three-carat weight,
She seemed almost magical.

She lived in a garret and was illiterate
      But even so her livelihood
      Alone earned her an income too good
For her husband to seem subsidiary,
So she took a studio and a house less dreary,
      And a successor as sorry
Took the place which had lured the fashionable.
Magnates, belles, valets, folk with fine airs, everyone
Felt that the inmate could make the future known:
A sibyl's cave, so weak that the walls might fall!
Though the fraud had called the place the haunt of a witch,
Her successor declared she was no soothsayer:
"Sorceress! Sirs, you jest. Me an interpreter?
I cannot say my letters, don't know which is which."
Words were nothing. She read the stars since she lived there;
      Then grew rich on what she had spurned—
Making as much as a pair of attorneys earned.
Her furnishings and gear appeared mysterious—
Three-legged chairs and a broom which use had frayed—
Suggesting witchcraft and the things that a witch does.
      If she had meant all she said
      In a room well carpeted,
She would have been laughed at; but having inherited
    The garret, she seemed to work wizardry,
      While the seer died in misery.
      The sign insures the shop's success.
I've seen a barrister with his robe out of press,
      Earn vast sums and folk mistake worthlessness
For Barrister So-and-so, a man of consequence
To the crowd. Now should you say that it makes sense?

XVI

CAT, WEASEL, AND LITTLE RABBIT

    Dame Weasel with guile few attain,
    Captured a leveret's den—
    Entered one fine day without a sound.
Since the owner had gone she was sure of her ground

[163]

And had soon transferred what belonged to her,
While the rabbit stayed out as Aurora's worshiper
      Where thyme scents touched with dew abound.
After trotting his round, nibbling and sniffing each flower,
Johnny hopped to his den at his dozing hour—
Found Dame Weasel crouched by the window, alert,
And, "Merciful powers! Apparitions in my resort?"
The rabbit exclaimed, since robbed of his property;
      "O là! Madame Pointed Snout,
      Pack; depart; you've been turned out;
Or I'll summon all the rats in the vicinity."
The sharp-nosed lady said, "You cannot interfere.
      This den was mine first, and so is my own.
      What a place to set us by the ear—
So cramped that to enter you have to lean down.
      But if a kingdom," went on Madame Pointed Nose,
"Tell me if there is a law we'd call royal,
      Assigning forever each foot of this soil
To John, son or nephew of Peter or William—just those—
      Instead of to Paul or to me whom you'd foil."
Rabbit Jonathan argued that precedent stood—
That the law gave him charge of his patrimony—
"Bequeathed in due course as any could see—
Father to son, Simon to Peter, and so to me:
Ancient precedent stands; its provisions hold good."
      Then the weasel said, to end bad blood,
"Come, let Raminogrob end our perplexity"—
A cat recluse who'd proved to clients in sorry plight
      That he could be a hypocrite.
All sanctity, this well-fed, well-furred Velvet Claws
      Was a beast long conversant with the laws;
      So Johnny's respect for him was profound,
      And each with a culprit to impound
      Faced Judge Cat sitting furred and silken-gowned.
Velvet Claws said, "My dears, I do not hear a sound.
Quite near, quite near. In old age, you see, some words are lost."
Side by side they advanced, not suspecting the cost.
After he had had time to form a deep frown,
      Villainy sprang from clemency's cloak
And his claws without favor were pinning them down—

Both clients for his larder, at a single stroke;
As when two rulers relatively small
Select a king as referee and thereby forfeit all.

XVII

THE HEAD AND TAIL OF THE SERPENT

> A serpent has mobility
> Which can shatter intrepidity.
> The tail-tip's mental to-and-fro
> And tail-like taper head's quick blow—
> Like Fate's—have the power to appall.
> Each end had thought for years that it had no equal
> And that it alone knew
> > What to do.
> From the first, the head had guided the tail day by day
> > Till the tail accused God of folly
> > > And begged mercy,
> > Saying, "I've trailed mile on mile in this way,
> > Too subserviently.
> Was I meant to submit continually?
> > I appear to be but a servant,
> > Though providentially
> > A sister, so not subservient.
> > Twins from inception,
> > Each is each's counterpart
> > With the scorpion's power to hurt;
> > Each injects lethal poison.
> > Revoke the spell I cannot break;
> > Tell the head you had rather
> > The tail took us farther
> > And it regulate the snake.
> > I shall manifest a restraint
> > That can give no cause for complaint."
> Now granting fools' prayers can but presage ill,
> Involving harm not within the giver's intent;
> One must be deaf to destructive argument;
> But this time God heard; then, as new beadles will,

Our purblind tail could admire
As much as baked bread saw of fire;
Struck a statue in due course,
A boot, some bark; deaf to remorse,
Fell right into the Styx and drowned her sister.
Tragic rulers, hastening toward a like disaster!

XVIII

AN ANIMAL IN THE MOON [1]

We've two kinds of philosopher.
One says our senses never can be trusted.
The other is as sure
That they never are misguided;
And indeed both are justified. Philosophy
Feels rightly that the senses are deceiving one
If one relies on their evidence alone,
But when we offset what we see
By the distance of things away from one—
By the eye on which the image is thrown
And recall the impression's origin,
We are not deceived since facts are known.
Now whatever Nature does is wisely done
As I shall have demonstrated fairly soon.
I stare up at the sun. How does it look from here?
The monster's circumference is but three feet, it would appear.
But say I rose to its height in the air.
What would I have? Nature's stupendous eye to bear.

[1] This fable appears to have been composed about the beginning of 1677. The European powers were exhausted by wars and desirous of peace. England, the only neutral, became arbiter of negotiations at Nimeguen, and the belligerents each invoked her mediation. Charles II, however, was embarrassed by his secret negotiations with Louis XIV, which made him desire to prescribe conditions favorable to France. *Vide* Hume, who also says that the English king "had actually in secret sold his neutrality to France and received remittances of 1,000,000 livres a year—afterward increased to 2,000,000 livres; a considerable sum in the embarrassed state of his revenue." [From Elizur Wright's translation of *The Fables of La Fontaine* (Boston, 1841), with notes by J. W. M. Gibbs (London: George Bell and Son, 1903).]

Knowing its distance, I say its size can be inferred—
Something trigonometry can use angle and sides to define.
I make it a sphere; the ignorant, flat—which is absurd.
The earth spins around it, I say—a fixture in the heaven's design.
So—refuting my eyes—I am not taken in:
If we discount illusion, no harm has been done.
   In this way again and again,
I distinguish truth from outward circumstance,
   As corrective intelligence
Perceives that my glance had been a hasty one
Or that my ears were slow in conveying a tone.
When water bends a stick, refraction is the cause
   And Mistress Reason has earned applause.
   So, despite a misleading report,
My eyes convey fact which they need not distort.
Now I seem to have seen as I looked at the moon,
A woman's head—what some assume is one.
But is it one? No. Then what looked like a head?
Certain undulations by which we are misled,
Since the moon's crust lacks uniformity—
Flat at some points but showing diversity.
Light and shade will sometimes suggest by shapes thrown aslant,
   A man or ox or elephant—
Such as caused the British, of late, some dismay.
Something new in the telescope met the eye
   And roused a triumphant cry—
   Startling fact for science to assay.
Some sort of change up there had certainly begun,
Which perhaps had significance for everyone;
Did any suspect that it might have reference
To the war raging then? The king hastened forth too,
As one who followed science with diligence;
Looked at the moon and saw the monster which seemed
          something new—
A mouse on the lens as a source of the war—
Trapped by glass which had seemed to it a door.
People laughed. Genial folk. When will war bestow
On France time for employments of which all should know?
War has made us illustrious because of our power
Till we now intimidate every combatant,

Advancing where we would, since at that very hour
Mars' protégé, our King, was hearing the victor's chant;
His laurels inspiring verse which ages will devour.
      The Muses attend us at this hour—
Memory's nine as we enjoy pleasures which lend our lives cheer.
We long for peace but stifled moans are not heard here.
King Charles delights in peace but if he went to war
His sword would entice the English to share
Pursuits which they have been viewing tranquilly.
Incense to him would rise if he contrived to quell
This war for us! What deed more worthy of royalty?
Were Caesar's triumphs more desirable
Than Augustus' reign, in which Rome laid aside Rome's darts?
Enviable folk! Why may we not be blessed as well,
France sheathe her sword and turn, like you, to peaceful arts?

BOOK EIGHT

I

DEATH AND THE DYING

Aware that earth is hazardous,
The wise aren't taken unaware;
And since prepared when Death draws near,
Do not regard its coming as anomalous.
 Be courageous! Harvest, everyone,
Seconds, hours, and days—yours before they have flown.
  Where find me one who in the end
Evades Death's sovereignty toward which all footsteps tend?
Babes who saw the daylight first in, say, a king's household,
  Not even sure of where they were,
  Have died before so much as a day old,
  And with darkened eyes met the fate which they
         must bear.
  You need not dwell upon your power;
Integrity, good looks, or youth's inexperience—
  What merit does not death devour?
It's fearsome hand will claim all our magnificence.
  None can deny what you have heard me say,
  Although we universally
  Procrastinate, and in the basest way.

A certain centenarian pled injury;
Death at his door, he mourned, before life had begun?
He implored that it depart and leave him there
  To make a will, a thing he had not done.
If he were merely warned! "Why is haste your prime care?"
He asked the ghost. "Why not a more moderate pace?
My wife says wait till she departs as well;
Let me aid a grandnephew whom I ought to place.
Let me add a wing to the house in which I dwell.

Pitiless one, you are inexorable!"
—"Grandsire," said Death, "I'm here, and here advisedly:
As for impatience, your bad grace is what requires defense.
Fie! Aren't you a hundred? It would puzzle me
Had Paris two, or France ten, fitter to go hence.
Then how say that I summon you too hastily
   And bid you leave what you possess?
  Your will should have been made before today;
Your house have been enlarged, the youth have made his way.
Were you not warned considerately by distress?
   When pained by locomotion;
   By apathy—ambition gone—
By deafer ears, with taste almost illusory;
When your faculties failed dismally;
Are you sure that it is fair, when it is a fine day?
You are depressed that wealth does not advantage you.
   Is not each comrade who lent you aid,
   Dead, near death, or an invalid?
   Come, Grandfather; don't talk of health;
   Who would care in a commonwealth
   That a will's not been begun."
Death surely was right. When our powers are failing us,
Let us fare as from a feast; but like guests, first delay,
Thank our host for his best and then be on our way;
Wherefore complain that the path appears perilous?
Grandsire, you repine! Do young men despair?
   Look. See them running as if on air—
Although to Death that has grandeur in the eyes of all;
But cruel at times and inevitable.
I contradict the times. Indeed why should I cry
That those most like the dead are those most loath to die.

II

THE COBBLER AND THE FINANCIER

He'd sing from break of day till the sun would disappear,
  Like a seraph; any there
Stood still to hear the arpeggios sink

Deeper than seven sages think.
Nearby, a man quite sere though affluent thus far,
           Seldom sang and with careworn eyes ajar,
           Was a slave to fear of expense.
Before the sky could clear or one ought to start the day,
He would wake with a jerk, aroused by the cobbler's lay,
           And, "Oh, that Providence," he would say,
           "Could grant us the convenience
Of buying sleep as we buy provender—
           Food and drink that we require."
           Requesting the cobbler to come and confer,
Our complainer said, "Master Gregory, I would ask, if I
                                        may inquire,
How much do you earn in a year?"—"Do I earn, sir, in a year?"
           The dear man smiled at the financier
With a gentle air and said, "I don't know, am not quite sure;
I can't say what I earn; never count what's so poor,
     Just work for hire; but in the end it is plain
           As the seasons roll away,
           That I've earned our bread again."
—"Well then, how much might you earn, say, in a day?"
—"Sometimes more, sometimes less. A thing I deplore
(If it were not for this, what a round sum I'd make)
Is that every other day I lock the door
     And can't work, though the holidays we take
Seem alike, I swear; the priest, dear sir, should be blamed,
Since each new saint's day he has a discourse to drone."
The financier smiled as he said, "I'm ashamed.
Permit me to say that henceforth all your hours are your own:
Here are a hundred crowns—patrimony, I mean:
           To which to turn when times are lean."
The cobbler thought it the whole round earth's amassed dower—
           Say, the assets of each generation
           That were meant to advantage everyone.
Whereupon he went home and that very same hour
           Buried his gold and his joy at a stroke,
           Sang no more; in fact he could scarcely croak.
Then since he must guard the wealth which he had found,
           Slept by fits and starts, with uneasy
           Imagination busy.

[171]

His suspicions were stirred by each sound.
Both ears and eyes were alert all day, and at night,
If so much as a cat trod light,
He thought it would thieve his fund. In the end he had learned,
Poor man, and sped to him whose night's rest was really rest
To say, "Here are your hundred crowns, for I would have returned
The songs and sleep thieves don't molest."

III

THE LION, THE WOLF, AND THE FOX

A careworn lion, all bones and pained in each paw,
Craved a cure lest his disabilities progress.
(Better not gainsay a king or you are an outlaw.)
       In this case, to relieve his distress
The king had practitioners of any description
Come to attend him, from every direction,
Till all varieties of cure in the world had been brought
       To afford him the one that he sought.
But the fox paid no heed and sat at home, safely denned.
In paying court, the wolf said the fox had meant to offend,
Slandering the poor beast and creating a stir.
Plucked forth in embarrassment, the fox dared not demur,
So at last drew near and said what he had to say,
Aware that it was the wolf who was the slanderer.
He pled, "Sire, though I have been called malingerer
       As one the wolf wished to betray,
       My service to you has been delayed
       Since vows for you had to be paid,
Involving a hard journey day after day.
       Wherever my loyalty led,
I told surgeon and sage that you barely can prick up an ear
Lest your vestige of vigor should fail you some night.
       They said the blood cools from year to year,
       And since you lack heat through an oversight,
Wrap a live wolf's skin about the flesh you'd redeem—
       At the height of its natural heat—
       That should compensate, it would seem,

For energy years can deplete.
To make a long story short,
Try a wolfskin dressing gown."
The king welcomed the report;
The wolf was flayed, torn up, choked down.
The king devoured his former escort
And found the skin a constant comfort.

Courtiers, don't be slanderers; better turn a deaf ear.
Why must one compromise a fair career?
Evil hurries home faster than good we have done.
This is sure; slanders are laid at the slanderer's door.
Courts are places, furthermore,
Where nothing is forgiven one.

IV

THE POWER OF FABLE

To Monsieur de Barillon [1]

Might fairy tales have some allure
For so rare an ambassador as you are?
Dear Connoisseur, give ear as I murmur an air,
And if I aspire to literature,
I am not too presumptuous, pray concur, to bear.
You have many another snare
To ravel out besides the maze
A rabbit and a weasel wrought,
So read or do not, of their lethal ways;
Only let no new war be fought—
Affrighting threat these days.
I'd suffer any kind of war
That ill will brought upon me,
But one with Britain is unfair. [2]
Ah, that our kings might rule in amity.
How stand it were they to be foes?

[1] Ambassador to the Court of St. James's.
[2] Allusion to the negotiations that preceded the Peace of Nimeguen.

Should not our Louis at last enjoy well-earned repose?
What other Hercules would not wear down and yield
If this hydra [3] of his reared? Why must the beast disclose
A head that till now has been lying concealed?
     Should your friendship, versatile to bless
      By subtlety and seemliness,
Ameliorate ire and deflect the threatened blow,
A hundred sheep shall cause your altar fires to glow,
     Despite Parnassus' thrifty ways.
     In any case I'll sing your praise,
     With incense burned for you alone,
     To whom my thanks go on and on.
As for this little fable—just for you from me,
Why explain? I'm hoping that it may be pleasing to you.
     Even envy ought to see
     That though you say no praise is due,
     None praises you sufficiently.

To cure Athenian dupes of the senses,
An orator who dreaded dire consequences
Made ardent speeches reinforced by rhetoric,
To persuade the entire body politic
In favor of all as opposed to the few.
No one was interested. Using this and that cue,
     He tried stronger argument,
Convinced that a metaphor wins assent,
Thundered, honored the dead, mustered all that he knew,
Hearers heeded no better than if the wind blew;
     People with souls none could school
Were so superficial that all countenances
Were averted; his listeners were turning their glances
Toward a skirmish of idle boys playing the fool.
The rhetorician—well, changing his tenor,
Began, "Ceres one day, seeking crops to store—
     With a swallow and eel, they tell—
Came to a river. The eel crossed by swimming

[3] It was 1677. The situation in Book Seven, Fable XVIII, has become more serious. Charles has made a secret treaty with Holland and threatens to enter the war as a new head of the hydra, whose other heads are Holland, Spain, the Empire, and Sweden.

And the swallow by flying;
Both were over the water almost without trying."
"And what did Ceres do?" folk inquired as under a spell.
  —"She did what? Bent a stern brow
  On you in angered sorrow.
Why? That Athens' sons could take an interest
  In old wives' tales, with Greece hard-pressed;
That Athenians alone ignored their country's distress.
Ask if Philip advances or the threat has grown less."
  Athens came to its senses—
  Fairy lore so entrances—
  And gave ear to the orator:
  The power of fable does endure.
All are Athenians; I am the same,
Since the moment The Ass's Skin commences,
  Away with appearances;
  I am enraptured, really am.
The world is old? I agree; but to hold its attention
One resorts, as with a child, to fascination.

V

THE MAN AND THE FLEA

We worldlings harass the gods to listen whenever we plead—
In despair about what should not even vex mankind—
As though heavenly will were like our mundane mind
And it were everywhere, assessing each man's need.
Moreover it would seem that the puerile
Who wish something, however trivial,
Say, "Here's a state of affairs, O gods, for you to mend,"
As if the Greeks laid siege and the Trojans were forced to
         defend.

A flea drew from a fool's arm all that it could,
Then hopped between sheets; well? futile toil to seek all day.
The man said, "Hercules, there's our spring pest to slay,
Returned at the season at which hydras are renewed.

[175]

How is it, Jupiter, despite your altitude,
That you've not crushed the pest that did me harm today?"
Where there was a flea, a foolish man could say,
Ye gods with club and thunder, bear mortal servitude.

VI

HOW WOMEN KEPT A SECRET

Now when is any secret safe
With any sort of woman you can name?
Although I'd say, lest hearers chafe,
Some men are women with another frame.

Fearing that his wife's tongue might cause him discomfiture,
A husband dug a pitfall; woke her with, "Heavens! Torture!
Oh, what shall I do? Pained more and more!
Ye gods! I've laid an egg!" —"An egg?" —"See
here, to be sure,
It is still warm. Protect me. Could I ever endure
To hear myself called hen! Remember, honor bound!"
His wife's uncertain ground
Matrimonially made her swear
That she would guard his secret, and with the utmost care;
But her word was untrustworthy—
Like darkness but temporary!
Poor soul, she lacked self-discipline;
So hurried away—mischief made her sleep brief—
To inquire if a friend were in.
"Gossip dear," she said, "it would beggar belief;
Don't spread it abroad or my bones might be sore;
My husband has laid an egg heavy as four.
Heaven help me—I fear the consequence—
Don't mention to anyone what you have heard."
—"Now really," the neighbor said, "don't be absurd!
You are safe; realize my good sense."
One sought the home which had hatched the puzzle.
The other was instantly voluble,

[176]

Elaborating a lie threefold.
   He'd laid not one, three eggs, she told.
The number soon mounted; a new gossiper
Spoke of four—in a whisper to another's wife.
   Although why take especial care
   Since gossip was already rife?
Thanks to rumors which echoed from eave to eave,
   Each version meant an addition;
   By sundown it was beyond belief.
   The eggs laid taxed computation.

VII

THE DOG WHO CARRIED THE DINNER BASKET

When the eye has been charmed we are vulnerable;
   Much as fingers feel gold's power:
   Who in the world has ever
   Been true to his trust after all?

There was a dog who shared household fare, but not freely,
And fetched meals for master in a basket he'd wear.
While always moderate, certain choice provender
   He saw would tempt his probity,
Yet he was self-contained; I fear that we might find,
If tempted, that some of us would compromise.
Odd; self-control is something dogs must exercise;
   We cannot teach it to mankind!
Our choice dog, trotting forth with fare master was furnished,
Met where paths crossed a surly brute who was famished.
   Now that hopes had been foiled
Which at first had been fair—to defend the prey when he'd
          be embroiled,
Our mastiff set the food down as the others skirmished,
   For the snarling brought cur after cur;
   What a riffraff of them there were—
   Fearless and quick, an ownerless crew.
Dog Tray was aware of what the horde could do.

[177]

And that his life was at stake, as was manifest,
So said with sagacity that soon would be complicity,
"Stand back, doughty brothers, leave enough to feed me
      And you may take the rest."
Whereupon he led the way, filched a fragment or so;
The battlers and curs got in one another's way
    To be first at the food. A merciless fray,
      With nothing the horde would forgo.

It was like our own cities, do you not feel?
Where the state becomes the prey of untoward corruption.
      Guild provosts make inspection;
      Nothing is left. The sort that steal
Are models for all; a grim diversion
To see them engrossing the sums at disposal.
Yet saying a word lest the funds be run through,
      Could merely have made a fool of you.
      Your rectitude then seemed to bend;
      Before long you yourself were the first to offend.

VIII

THE JOKER AND THE FISHES

Humor—which, when forced, to me is just not wit—
Never allures unless strictly apposite.
      Surely those who care for bons mots,
      Were born with heads partly hollow.
      This may be an example
      Of that sort of fool, and my joker be
One with a jest for fools only—i.e., asininity.

      Dining where dainties were the rule,
    A joker one day was seated by his friend,
With some small fish at hand, saw large at the farther end,
So picked up some small ones and whispered as to an ear,
      Pretending that they murmured words he could hear.
The guests appeared surprised, then watched curiously
      To see what the outcome might be.

The joker, all seriousness,
Said that a dear friend's Indian journey
Worried him constantly;
No news meant a ship in distress;
He thought a storm should impress small fish, so listened.
But everyone said a small one would be helpless
To inform him what had happened;
Grown fish would have made more progress.
"Gentlemen," he asked, "might I question one of the big
fish I see?"
I doubt that the company
Enjoyed his raillery.
In any case he had his wish, for presently
They brought him a monster so agèd it would surely refer
To all the wanderers marine depths might know—
Besides drowned sailors down below;
And—seen through centuries of swimming to and fro—
Famous sea ghosts everywhere.

IX

THE RAT AND THE OYSTER

A rather dull rat who'd been farming a dell
Decided afterwhile that he was tired of home,
Of his household goods, his sheaves and swathes as well,
And departed one day, since determined to roam.
Free of tasks that were tedious,
He said, "The world is a tremendous place!
Apennines off there, and nearby the Caucasus."
Molehills looked like alps that stared him in the face.
Meanwhile as he fared he came to a sea beach
In a distant province where tides at farthest reach
Had strewn oysters. Because devoid of sea lore,
He thought he'd discovered ships the waves had washed ashore.
"Nowhere a life more drear," he said, "I would swear,
Than my poor father led in frightened innocence;
Here am I, by this time a daring traveler.
Sandy wastes and thirst are of no consequence."

The rat had got the words from a teacher and, with no sense
of what applies,
Used them hit or miss as he ran on—
Not a rat who gnaws any book that he can,
Who is cultured to the tooth-tips as a reading man
By reason of what he's done.
Oysters close like a vise
But one lay apart, for sun to inundate
As it drank soft air from the sea,
Swelling in and out with a sense of luxury—
The morsel a gourmet would call ultra-delicate.
From afar, prey so tender had caught the rat's eye
And he murmured, "Something into which to pry—
The tint of an oyster when it is just right to eat;
No wonder the tidbit makes one's heart skip a beat."
Master Rat's delight in it all was immense;
His nose neared the spread halves to test what appeared rich
And the strong muscled oyster shells snapped at his twitch.
He was trapped as a victim of ignorance.

The moral of this is a combined one:
First, as worth our attention,
When voyagers set forth without experience
Very little things stir their emotion.
And then there is this to be learned:
Catchers may find the tables turned.

x

THE BEAR AND THE GARDEN-LOVER

A bear with fur that appeared to have been licked backward
Wandered a forest once where he alone had a lair.
This new Bellerophon, hid by thorns which pointed outward.
Had become deranged. Minds suffer disrepair
When every thought for years has been turned inward.
We prize witty byplay and reserve is still better,
But too much of either and health has soon suffered.
No animal sought out the bear

[180]

In coverts at all times sequestered,
Until he had grown embittered
And, wearying of mere fatuity,
By now was submerged in gloom continually.
He had a neighbor rather near,
Whose own existence had seemed drear;
Who loved a parterre of which flowers were the core,
And the care of fruit even more.
But horticulturalists need, besides work that is pleasant,
Some shrewd choice spirit present.
When flowers speak, it is as poetry gives leave
Here in this book; and bound to grieve,
Since hedged by silent greenery to tend,
The gardener thought one sunny day he'd seek a friend.
Nursing some thought of the kind,
The bear sought a similar end
And the pair just missed collision
Where their paths came in conjunction.
Numb with fear, how ever get away or stay there?
Better be a Gascon and disguise despair
In such a plight, so the man did not hang back or cower.
Lures are beyond a mere bear's power
And this one said, "Visit my lair." The man said, "Yonder bower,
Most noble one, is mine; what could be friendlier
Than sit on tender grass, sharing such plain refreshment
As native products laced with milk? Since it's an embarrassment
To lack what lordly bears would have as daily fare,
Accept what is here." The bear appeared flattered.
Each found, as he went, a friend was what most mattered;
Before they'd neared the door, they were inseparable.
As confidant a beast seems dull.
Best live alone if wit can't flow,
And the gardener found the bear's reserve a blow,
But conducive to work, without sounds to distract.
Having game to be dressed, the bear, as it puttered,
Diligently chased or slaughtered
Pests that filled the air, and swarmed, to be exact,
Round his all too weary friend who lay down sleepy—
Pests—well, flies, to speak unscientifically.
One time as the gardener had forgot himself in dream

[181]

And a single fly had his nose at its mercy,
The poor indignant bear who had fought it vainly
Growled, "I'll crush that trespasser; I have evolved a scheme."
Killing flies was his chore, so as good as his word,
The bear hurled a cobble and made sure it was hurled hard,
Crushing a friend's head to rid him of a pest.
With bad logic, fair aim disgraces us the more;
He'd murdered someone dear, to guarantee him his rest.

Intimates should be feared who lack perspicacity;
Choose wisdom, even in an enemy.

XI

THE TWO FRIENDS

Two fast friends lived somewhere in Monomotapa,
And each regarded as both's anything of his own:
   True fantasists of a vanished day,
   Almost finer than some we have known!
It appears that the friends had been sleeping peacefully,
Utilizing the darkness appropriately,
When one of them woke terror-struck with concern
And sped to the other distractedly,
Where Sleep, that great master, had brought passivity.
The sleeping friend was stunned, seized sword and purse in turn,
Ran to the door and said, "What has occurred
That you come at this hour to your weary fellow men
Who were constrained to sleep that they be restored again?
Have you wagered your funds and found fortune untoward?
Then take mine. Has some fool been irascible?
I have a sword. Join me. You've been lonely too long—
A monk in your cell, doomed to nights that were dull;
I'll part with a slave who really is beautiful."
The friend replied, "Nothing at all has gone wrong.
   God bless one so lovable.
I dreamt you were sad, looked less well than you do.
Afraid it might be so, I have therefore run to you;
   My bad dream disturbed your repose."

Reader, which of these friends should you say loved the more?
Too hard to say, yet a true friend is, I suppose,
One of the very sweetest things one knows!
Discerning needs that are interior,
       He does his friend this favor—
       Interprets him by intuition.
       He'll dream, give a start or betray pallor,
       Merely on a supposition.

XII

THE PIG, THE GOAT, AND THE SHEEP

A sheep, a goat, and a pig then in his prime
Had been hoisted on a cart and were going to the fair
But not expecting the usual good time;
They'd be offered for sale, legend has it somewhere.
       The carter knew they'd not been sent
       Merely to enter Tabarin's tent.
       Don Pig was making lament
As if hundreds of knives had one pig to seek.
His mournful demur had soon outraged each ear.
The others, mere pets whose demeanor was meek,
Thought how strange for a beast to shake with fear
       And saw nothing of which to complain.
The man rebuked the pig, "How now! Are you insane?
You'll have this cartful deaf. Consider—quiet down.
That decent pair would not play the clown;
Are really persons of the world. Less uproar; don't you stir:
See that sheep? He thinks silence valuable.
       A shrewd soul." —"A shallow fool,"
Retorted the pig. "If he grasped what may occur,
He'd make a commotion one could hear a league away;
       And that endearing young goat
       Would have shocked you with roars from her
                    meek throat.
One thinks she'll be milked; the other, sheared today.
That they see nothing harmful in this is plain,

And they may have justification,
But I am food and food alone—
A portent meaning I'll be slain.
Farewell, pen, my erstwhile protection."

The worthy pig had become sophisticated,
Yet was he better off? If the worst must happen,
Why tremble in fear of what is certain?
It is sometimes wisest not to see so far ahead.

XIII

THYRSIS AND AMARANTH

For Mademoiselle de Sillery [1]

I had put Aesop away
But to please a goddess,
"Defer Boccaccio's lay"—
Honoring mortal loveliness
For Heaven's delectation.
Who could need persuasion
Or foil Beauty's purpose?
Could any be so callous
Toward a spirit from on high?
Certainly impossible.
What a nymph so beautiful
Would favor, so must I.
It was, if I'm to be precise,
Upon Miss Sillery's advice
That I tell more of Master Crow;
Draw Sir Wolf anew,
And let you hear them rhyme.
For Miss Sillery we construe
Her preference as law each time
Since her mind is matched by few.

[1] Gabrielle-Françoise Brulart de Sillery, niece of the Duc de la Rochefoucauld. She married Louis de Tibergeau, Marquis de La Motte-au-Maine, and died in 1732.

Who would not be ruled by her?
Well, our story's waiting there.
However inspired she may be,
She chides me for obscurity;
Therefore, since she does,
Let me in this fantasy,
Be perspicuous.
My shepherds confer, then as further attraction,
I shall rhyme a wolves' and a flock's disputation.

To sweet young Amaranth once, Thyrsis bared his heart
And said, "Ah, might you feel bliss that is unendurable,
Which charms as by enchanter's art,
You'd say that nothing known was comparable!
It is of this I fain would speak;
Do not distrust me or demur;
And how could I deceive you, assuredly unique,
In my sentiment for you. Could love be tenderer?"
Amaranth asked with response as quick,
"What is the name of this by which you have been undone?"
—"Love, comely word." —"What distinguishing mark
Could aid me recognize it? What sensation?"
—"Sweet distress compared with which kings' joys are stark—
Are wearisome; you dream where boughs meet overhead
And you may be secluded—
Mirrored in the brook as you gaze.
You do not see yourself. You see instead another face.
All else? as though it never was.
There is a shepherd of the place.
His presence, his mere voice, his name, so charms your ear
You've become a shy imaginer
Who blushes and sighs, though the reason is not clear.
When he's there you are perturbed; when not, you wish him near."
Amaranth in abandon
Cried, "Oh! You bid me feel an ill that I have known.
I'm aware of it now and by no means must wait."
Thyrsis thought himself fortunate
Till she added plainly, "It is the emotion
Which Clidamant stirs—the very one."
Poor Thyrsis was mortified, in fact he felt faint.

[185]

What a multitude we see
Who exert themselves for power which they would flaunt,
    And have, instead, advanced another's victory.

XIV

THE FUNERAL OF THE LIONESS

The lion's consort lay dead
And the motley of beasts she led
Sought the sovereign's sorrowful glance,
Mock consideration adding its pain
    To that which bore the beast down.
    It had been arranged in advance
    That a cortege wend its way
And burial follow on such and such a day,
    With marshals scrupulously
    On guard, that all be orderly.
    Judge if some subjects were absent.
    The king's howls became harrowing,
    Loosed till the den was quivering.
    What fane have beasts but a den?
    The rest would whine and whine again,
With courtly variations of roars in unison.
Are not kings' courts affairs where all that goes on,
Sad or gay, but proves that an automaton
Attempts to please a prince, and in self-defense
    Counterfeits subservience.
Apes and chameleons of no consequence
Set a pattern repeated in sycophants by the score,
Without care to defend the expositor.
    Coming back to where we were,
The stag shed not a tear. His disrespectful air
Clearly set forth what he thought of the queen's meals—
    His doe and the fawn at her heels.
No, he forbore to weep. An obscure gossiper
    Accused him even of laughter.
Kings' despair, as Solomon cautioned one,

[186]

Is severe; and lions' a phenomenon,
Though literature was a thing of which the stag was unaware.
The king said, "You would add a cheap note of scorn,
Foul deer? Not a groan, implying that you mourn?
Yet your carcass is one that my worthy claws disdain;
     They are a king's; hither, wolves;
     Avenge her, though lost yourselves.
     The queen's ghost would have him slain."
The stag had an answer. "Sire, forbear; no tear,
Since signs of outward grief would seem trivial.
Our immortal queen reposes on a bier
     Of flowers. Though supernatural,
     Her form is unmistakable.
'Sweet friend,' she says, 'command that eyes be dry.
Mingling with gods henceforth, I'm one whom naught can harm,
Elysium possesses many a charm;
Am I not with saints and are we not on high?
Should his tears somehow have blinded the king's eye,
I bless each tear.' " All those who had heard him speak thus
Murmured, "Spirits speaking! Her ghost here? Marvelous!"
The stag went unpunished, in fact received bounty.

     Devise a conceit to please kings.
Flatter them. Ply them with fabulous nothings:
However hot their indignation may be,
They'll swallow the bait and love you fervently.

XV

THE RAT AND THE ELEPHANT

I fear that appearances are worshiped throughout France:
     Whereas pre-eminence perchance
     Merely means a pushing person.
     An extremely French folly—
A weakness of which we have more than our share—
Whereas false pride, I'd say, has been the Spaniard's snare.
     To be epigrammatical,
     They're foolish folk; we're comical.

[187]

Well, I've put us in this tale
Which came to mind as usable.

A mite of a rat was mocking an elephant
As it moved slowly by, majestically aslant,
  Valued from antiquity,
  Towering in draped solemnity
  While bearing along in majesty
  A queen of the Levant—
  With her dog, her cat, and sycophant,
Her parakeet, monkey, anything she might want—
  On their way to relics they wished to see.
  But the rat was not one whom weight could daunt
And asked why observers should praise mere size.
"Who cares what space an object occupies?"
He said. "Size does not make a thing significant!
All crowding near an elephant? Why must I worship him?
Servile to brute force at which mere tots might faint?
Should persons such as I admire his heavy limb?
  I pander to an elephant!"
  About to prolong his soliloquy
  When the cat broke from captivity
  And instantly proved what her victim would grant:
That a rat is not an elephant.

XVI

THE HOROSCOPE

  Sometimes, take care as we may,
We die of that from which we tried to get away.
  A poor doting man, as prey
Of too fond parental love, had astrologers say
  If there were any fatal snare
  In store for his sole son and heir,
And was told of a thing the lad never must do—
Till of age; never venture near lions, they said,
  But later need not be afraid.
  To circumvent by this clue

[188]

What would have placed his son in jeopardy,
The father told the lad he must thenceforth obey
And not leave the palace for so much as a day;
Although in it he might be absolutely free,
Leap, run, walk with friends or keep ennui at bay
        By joining with them in boyish play.
        Before his majority, since the chase
        Allured him especially,
        It was proved to him unmistakably
That hunting is wrong and involves disgrace.
        Argue? advise? or try to tame?
        A disposition is ever the same.
The young man since restive—too headstrong to be
                      dismayed—
Was drawn to such sports as his compeers essayed,
        And pined for the thing more and more,
Since what is denied allures more than before.
Aware that he had been cursed by hindrances,
The prisoner in his sumptuous residence
        Would be going to and fro,
        Seeing paintings of his foe—
Or tapestries treating of hunts in a glade,
        Snarling beasts in embroglio;
        Or pursuers were portrayed;
So, on seeing a lion someone had drawn,
He protested, "Dastard! imprison me alive
In this depressing cage?" Unbridled thoughts contrive
To implement despair; and suddenly undone,
        The youth smote the beast with his fist.
Behind the drawing a nail protruded from the wall
        On which the clenched fist chanced to fall,
        Implanting it with venoms which persist,
And he died, despite all that physicians could do,
Of the safest precaution experience knew.

Aeschylus' own foresight was destined to fail,
        Since when alarmed by divination,
        Lest the house hurtle down,
        He left as soon as possible
And wished no other roof when he slept but the sky.

[189]

Possessed of a tortoise which she clutched as she flew,
An eagle looked down and saw the head in full view
Which had the appearance of a stone to her eye,
   Since on it hair no longer grew.
Hoping that she might crush what she'd caught, she dropped
         her prey,
And poor Aeschylus hastened his death in this way.

   Instances like these suggest
That star-craft—if it's that—precipitates a blow
   Which weak minds had dreaded when oppressed.
Astrology is false—undoubtedly is so.
   I feel that Nature would not care
To circumscribe itself; or fetter us still more
And trust to the stars secrets Fate has in store:
   Man, time, and place—upon which fixed laws bear—
   Determine what shall be done,
Though all the charlatans on earth spoke as one.
Could some star account for both herd and potentate;
A crook for the herd and scepter for the great:
   Jupiter indubitably
Arranged it? Jupiter? Stars don't know how they run.
How can they govern everyone,
Managing two types individually—
Exerting influence on me here where I stand?
Penetrating ether upon either hand?
Pass through Mars, old Sol, and every mile between?
Interfered with by what is too small to be seen:
Have events been foretold by seers of the horoscope—
   Wars with which Europe has had to cope?
Might not some predictions at least have come true?
Profound minds were neglecting what none of them knew.
The mighty distance, place, our human willfulness;
   And, too, emotion's hold on one:
   Can limited minds profess
To have understood all that has gone on
And call us the result? Life undoubtedly
Varies and never moves at the same pace.
   Make clear how trace by compasses
   Life through its entirety!

Now is there anything to say
Of these coincidences offered in my way?
Good Aeschylus' death and the lad chance seemed to kill
Prove nothing at all, since astrology, false from the start,
Foretells what one in hundreds may fulfill
    By some strange freak on nature's part.

XVII

THE ASS AND THE DOG

That each aid the other is the rule everywhere;
    But poor Gray was embittered
    And so failed in all that mattered.
    Though what won't the dear donkey bear!
As a dog ran along, they wandered where grass was young,
    Slowly, for donkeys are not high-strung:
    A pleasant pair which the same man kept;
The gentle beast grazed and the master slept:
    Exciting indeed for the renegade,
    Who found the best meal that he had had;
True, not a thistle, yet excellent fare.
How foolish to pamper the appetite!
    If the provender is not exquisite,
    Guests manage to eat whatever is there;
    And feeding where herbage sprang,
The ass did quite well. The dog, who'd felt hunger's pang,
Said at length, "Fond friend, will you not let down to me
The basket you wear, in which my dinner buns hang?"
No response; our Arcadian steed ignored the plea;
    Would not part with a modicum,
    Merely cared for pasture to roam,
    Callous toward one on whom hunger preyed,
And said, "Better wait, friend, until you are fed;
Hold out until Master's had rest as I've said,
And no doubt he will give you what you've always had—
    The customary piece of bread.
    He soon will have wakened; he is asleep."

[191]

Whereupon they saw leap
From the woods a starved wolf—another's hunger to be stayed.
The ass implored the dog to rush forth as rescuer.
The dog did not stir; the rejoinder he made:
"I advise you, my friend, to make off—to have fled
Before Master arises to give you your food. Dash ahead.
He will not drowse much longer. Quick; livelier.
Suppose the wolf attacks. Your sharp shoe as the cure
Will shatter his jaw; it is simple. Be sure
He will soon be knocked flat." There was no time to spare;
The wolf sprang at the donkey; the creature lay dead.

Let us each aid the other as I have said.

XVIII

THE PASHA AND THE MERCHANT

A Greek was forced to protect his trade
By enlisting a local pasha's aid,
Then was charged, poor Greek, as though a pasha paid,
Not as one who toiled for what he made.
Safeguards come dear. But since thus put upon,
The Greek talked of how he had been outdone,
And three Turks of little consequence
Proposed to serve the Greek in unison—
Substitutes who demanded less recompense
Than the pasha had charged the Greek alone.
He made the change; they protected his freight;
Then the pasha suspected perfidy
And was counseled at once to anticipate
The mischief of the unworthy three
By having them sent on some errand of state
From earth to Mahomet instantly,
Or perchance he would pay the penalty
And go there first, since these churls to withstand
Were of a sort who have poison made
Which sends one to safeguard a merchant's shade
In trading haunts of the spirit land.

[192]

Forewarned, the pasha used Alexander's ruse,
Went to the Greek with open countenance
And quickly too, not playing fast and loose;
Partook of food and showed such confidence
In what he said and everything he did,
That no one could feel that suspicion had been hid.
He said, "You have abandoned me, my friend,
And some bid me fear what this may portend,
But you are good, whatever you did;
No poisoner could have your open face
(A topic which could not be more out of place).
As for the three who promote your trade,
Give ear, for sour words are of small avail.
I'll not wear you out with a long tirade.
Allow me to tell you a little tale.

"Once a shepherd had a flock, and dog running to and fro.
Someone asked him what he intended to do
   With a mastiff whose daily fare
Was a whole loaf of bread, and said he certainly knew
He would have to give his mastiff to the village lord
   And get instead what he could afford,
   Replacing the dog with a small cur or two
That would cost him less and be yet more useful when
      trouble might brew
   Than one dog on guard, who must do it all;
They'd eat less than the one; but he did not think to say
   That wide jaws cause wolves to turn tail
   When about to dismember the prey.
The herd gave up the dog, and three little ones instead
Did not require much food; but when attacked they fled,
And the flock was dismayed; you'll feel the same dismay—
   Served by men who are not spirited.
If you are wise it is I, once more, upon whom you will depend."
  The Greek said, true.
      There's a thought in these things
  For small states that require a firm friend:
  It is that a monarch is in the end
  Better than scores of inferior kings.

[193]

XIX

KNOWLEDGE AVAILS

Of two respectable
Men, each had irked the other one.
He who knew more had fared ill;
The richer was a simpleton
But keen to outshine the other one,
So said that the world of intellect
Certainly owed him respect—
The apex of stupidity;
Only a fool would boast of mere prosperity
Devoid of aught to justify it.
Upon what grounds revere it?
"My dear man," he'd say now and then,
   "Aren't you men
Too sure you are phenomenal?
Do you entertain at all?
You're poring over books. Say where they serve a man?
Up three flights to shabby haunts hired by the poor;
June or December, wear threadbare velour
With merely your shadow for valet de chambre.
The commonwealth would disappear
Were never any business done.
Say what's more essential here
Than skillful men who make the wheels of commerce run?
We need the like; God knows 'tis so. Shrewd taste means
                clothes of note.
Clever hands, the merchant and shopkeeper offer the coat.
Good will tries it on. Does all your industry
Assist the bourse in any real sense?
Dead loss so far as I can see."
This foolishly obtuse offense
Fell flat very suitably.
The author was mute; speech can't match monstrous slurs;
War's better than satire as vengeance—more terse—
And demolished the scene of the arguers' rivalry.

Both left before the town would fall.
The dullard found no roof available—
Despised wherever he might be;
The other's words were prized everywhere—could never pall,
Making argument seem puerile.
Let the witless rail; wisdom asserts its sovereignty.

XX

JUPITER AND THE THUNDERBOLTS

Far from here, in heaven's redoubt,
Jupiter said, "I shall rear
A new race, for I must cast out
Folk who irk me everywhere;
Human error has waxed
Till patience is overtaxed.
Hermes, come here; fly down there;
Bring a Fury to me;
Procure from hell the worst.
Culprits ruled too leniently,
You must now die accursed."
But lest ire appear unfair,
Jupiter, although vexed, forbore.

O kings whom Jove made arbiter,
If you did not let thunder roar
For a night, or anger stir,
Your impetuosity
Would die gradually.

The god whose wings can never tire,
Whose silver voice can snare the ear,
Flew down where the Furies were;
But seeking a murderer
Other than Megaera or Tisiphon,
Chose Alecto the pitiless one.
Then pride led her to overbear
And she swore by Pluto's throne

[195]

She would smite without exception
Until all mankind was gone—
Dwelling where each is a shade.
Having heard her, Jove, dismayed
By harm she had prophesied,
Sent her back. No contrition?
His hardest fulmination
Smote mortals ruled by pride,
But paternal ire aims wide;
That powerful arm,
Brandished to do the world harm,
Had meant merely to perturb
Or to warn; perchance disturb
Deserts fairly far away.
Poor parents, how they play
At discipline. Since spared a curse,
Persons grew more and more perverse,
Testing Jove's clemency.
The lord of the air and the rain
Swore by the Styx he was he,
Man must be scourged again
By fiercer storms; the gods nearby
Smiled on him as a blusterer—
A parent whose threats fell through,
Who transferred what was his to do—
Forge darts that do not err.
There were two kinds to prepare,
Vulcan said; then made his fire glow
And brought forth these to throw:
A dart that never is lost,
Launched in showers furthermore
By the minor gods in a host;
Then some, inferior,
Which uproot a hill likely as not
Or now and then die in air,
And never hurt that at which they are shot—
Fashioned just for Jupiter.

XXI

THE FALCON AND THE CAPON

When caressing tunes intone some lethal spell,
   Pretend you're an automaton
Like that deaf dog who was, it seems, no simpleton—
   John de Nivell's by name. Note him well.

A citizen of Mans—capon some had dared say—
   Was haled to the magistrate with, "Come forth;
   He'll hear your case on master's hearth;
He awaits you with fire and spit; come forth without delay."
Whereupon the citizens, albeit mere decoys,
Called, "Birdie, birdie, birdie"; but he would not obey!
He was a Norman and let them call all day,
Answering, "Farewell; crude bait can not catch the prey.
   Your lures have failed and with good cause."
Meanwhile a falcon from his perch saw the byplay
   And how our bird ran away,
Since inborn cunning or perhaps experience
   Bespoke a lack of confidence—
Hard to catch although chased this, then that way,
Destined to be a bakemeat for a gourmet,
Garnished, seasoned, and fat. Such distinction is a thing to forgo
   And transfer with one's benison.
The falcon said, "Wretched phenomenon
Of limitation. Dullard, what do you know?
Such senseless clay lacks a mind; how lesson those who have
         none?

Now I, as a courser, bring master my catch;
   He's there at the window, see him watch.
Or can capons not hear?" —"I've no such affliction,"
Retorted the capon. "The meaning, it would appear,
Is that our neat chef would cleave me at a blow.
   Come back to be killed, I'd like to know?
   Let me go; your harsh mirth hurts my ear.
Am I intractable because I'd run away

[197]

When in honeyed tones they would bid me stay?
    If you understood the word roast
    And had ever seen a hawk eaten
    As I've seen folk eat capon,
Would you taunt me with so ignorant a boast?"

XXII

THE CAT AND THE RAT

Queerer four never were. Cat-claw-the-rind-clean,
Screech-owl-melancholy, Rat-gnaw-the-net,
    Weasel-flatten-out-till-lean—
    Quite an ominous quartet—
Dwelt in a rotting pine, by now only partly green.
Because there were four at the core of the pine,
A man had spread nets, and when the day was fine,
    The cat fared forth to hunt nearby.
Since nets about dawn have ever deceived the eye,
She was forced as their prey, to die it would appear,
Mewing to be set free, until the rat drew near—
She panting in despair and he with hopeful eye
On seeing in a snare his mortal enemy.
    The cat said, "Blest fortuity!
    Dear guardian, whose plans
    Often helped me in what I sought,
Come aid me tear this net on which I have trod by chance,
    Which snared my foot. Don't leave me caught—
You whom I have held dear and must evermore revere,
Are my favorite, dear to me as my eyes.
I am by no means sad, was offering sacrifice.
    First morning prayers brought me here,
Offered by cats of heartfelt devotion;
The net then bore me down: my life's at your discretion;
Gnaw me free." The rat inquired, "Might there be recompense
    To which you have not referred?"
    —"A pact of mutual defense
    Forever in force," the cat purred.
"My claws shall be yours; you'll always have the sense

That where I am your enemies dare not stay.
    I shall thin out harmful prey—
    Screech-owl males and weasels in wait,
Thirsting for your blood." The rat said, "What a thought,"
    Then hastened homeward obdurate,
    Where he found the weasel a-prowl;
And high on the bole the eyes of the owl.
Selecting the menace which meant him least hurt,
He returned to the cat and plied his art;
Chewed a strand, yet another, on and on
    Till he'd freed the ally he'd hate.
    When the trapper came at dawn
The confederates made off, precipitate,
But as time elapsed it was evident,
As before, that Rat-gnaw was watching every move.
Cat-devour said, "Embrace me, and seal fair intent;
    My heart is sore, since you prove
    You have thought your friend thinks you her prey.
    Could I forget that yesterday
    With God's help you set me free?"
—"And I," replied Rat-gnaw, "do I know treachery
    Or do I not? Could any say
How one may induce a cat to keep faith two days hence—
    Except by shifts for joint defense
    Favored in an evil day?"

XXIII

THE TORRENT AND THE RIVER

    With scattering spray and seeming wrath,
    A forest stream dashed down in foam.
All shunned its proximity or feared the aftermath.
    It had a name in every home,
    Such that none dared venture over
    Where the torrent was forced to spurt.
A solitary rider, on seeing bandits hover,
Interposed the current's force, made shore, and was not hurt.
The bursting spray and roar had been harmless, it would appear.

The one real barrier was fear.
Our man had escaped and his morale was good,
But the horde of robbers pursued as before
Where a river barred escape from the brood.
The picture of innocence—almost immobile—
It led the fugitive to think it fordable
For the banks were not steep and the bed was hard sand.
He rode in and his horse bore him off from the band—
The horde he had feared—but not from Death's watercourse.
Both drank the Styx, man and horse.
Both went down everlastingly.
Where our travelers fared, streams to ford are shadowy—
Nothing like fords they'd known best.
Among men one meets, the masterly
Are less talkative than the rest.

XXIV

BREEDING

Laridon and Caesar of heroic strain
Were two noble canine twins—bold, well built, and mannerly.
In the care of separate masters, long ago by some fortuity,
One roamed the forests; one, a kitchen for scraps that were
thrown.
Each lost the name by which he had first been known,
Since disparity in care
Encouraged geniality in one of the pair;
Whereas a scullion in charge of the other one
Soon had renamed him Laridon.
His brother scouring forth, before long created a stir,
Brought stags to bay and felled many a boar in its pride—
The very first dog to whom the name Caesar was applied.
His sons each had as mother some dog queen, no less,
That not one should discredit its origin.
Laridon, on the other hand, would pay address
To any back-door bedouin
And furnished France with many strains—
Sad turnspits of whom the evidence remains.

[200]

This merely servile breed who will hear a sound and cower
    Reflects none of Caesar's power.

Can all trace their birth or name their paternal ancestor?
The times and lack of care debase such more and more:
By neglecting gifts and their cultivation,
Sad that some Caesars will shortly be Laridon.

XXV

THE TWO DOGS AND THE DEAD ASS

    How fair were virtues to flower
    In the way that vices pair.
When we fall into one of the latter's power
We are the prey of all—yes, of any snare
That is not, combined with others there,
    Too incompatible.
Are virtues, however, companionable?
Have you ever seen one that really advanced
Or interfered, where another was entrenched?
He who is brave is brusque; those who are shrewd are cold;
As among animals, the dog's pride seems unjust.
    Though dogs are faithful to a trust,
    Good sense is lacking in a glutton:
One time two strays saw on the sea's horizon
An ass's carcass rise, and of course descend,
Each moment farther off than when it had first been seen.
"My friend," said one, "compared with mine, your eyes
                  appear more keen.
Start away over there where the colors blend;
Is yonder thing a horse, or ox perchance after all?"
    —"Why inquire what animal?"
The other starveling said. "As though we had it caged,
It must be brought ashore. Since swimming on and on
Would be too great a strain, with a wind opposing one,
Better drink each drop; our thirst will be assuaged
And we'll have a bonanza too, since after the beast is dry
    It is bound to augment our food supply—

[201]

Perhaps represent a week's gain."
So they lapped and lapped and lapped, till under the strain
They both burst from exhaustion.

As prey to folly, mankind is much the same.
Distraught because he cannot have what he would claim,
How many vows he makes as he wonders what to try.
Frantic with love of place, or frenzied till wealth be acquired—
He says, "I must find more land to buy.
Why not more gold to heap my coffers high!
Why not learn Hebrew, science, history—to which I have
aspired!"
A sea if he drank all that he desired!
Can mankind know satiety?
We mortals project plans that never satisfy.
Multiplied by four, life here would be too short,
And if it weren't, we'd not accomplish half we pledged.
Four Methusalehs even, successively aged,
Could not bring bales so huge to port.

XXVI

DEMOCRITUS AND THE PEOPLE OF ABDERA

Who can endure the crassness of the common herd!
Are folk not presumptuous, warped, and absurd:
Putting barriers between self and the thing they should see,
Self measuring by self the whole community!
Epicurus served apprenticeship (each does)—
Thought insane by featherweights! Where one was bred,
Who is appreciated?
They were insane; how useful, Democritus!
Warped Abdera sent ambassadors away,
To beg Hippocrates one day,
By script and person, for aid
In restoring their friend upon whom fancies preyed:
"Our Democritus," they said—weeping meanwhile—
"Has gone mad. It's his furor for books; that is it.
We'd like him better if he were not a bibliophile.

[202]

'There are worlds,' he'll say, 'which men inhabit—
      Philosophers possibly
      Are dwelling there—men like me.'
Dreams are only the half; sometimes other phantoms
Vex his disordered mind—even mere atoms.
He'll calculate the sky's span, nor move from where he's sat,
At sea about himself though not his habitat!
There was a time when he discoursed of this and that,
      But now broods upon some private theme.
Heal this demented man; wake him from his bad dream."
Though Hippocrates thought them persons to shun,
He went as requested. Note incidentally
      How mere fortuity
May serve one—since when he appeared, he came upon
The very man whose intellect they had said was gone—
      Wresting from man and beast a test
To see where Mind resided—in the brain or the breast;
By a rill in the shade, intent upon the brain,
      Dwelling upon each curved plane
Of the skull. Various volumes there occupied him.
He'd not seen that a friend had been on the way,
      Contemplation having made his sight dim.
Their greetings were far shorter than this takes to say.
Why should the wise be weaned from study of the soul?
Thus small talk was curtailed. Neither was voluble,
Yet what each had to say bore upon verity
      And desire that the truth prevail.
      How could retrospect avail,
      Of things said alternately?
      Have I not shown sufficiently
That human beings are unreliable?
      Who'll tell me it's believable
      That vox populi—where some so thought—
      Had been vox Dei; had it or not?

[203]

XXVII

THE WOLF AND THE HUNTER

The hoarding mania; eyes of a greenish hue,
As hard as a monster's, view the good that God can do.
I have remonstrated on each page, have I not?
How deaf you are to careful instruction
From seers or from myself: a hardened lot.
Never to say, "Recreation; work's done."
Poor thing, don't you see you have not long to live?
Let me repeat the thought, the best I have to give:
Joy: enjoy yourself. You say, yes, now and again.
Ah, really, friend; be careful; Death might thwart your plan.
Be joyous while you may. Take fright; my dreary tale
Of the wolf and the hunter has a moral for all.

Armed with a crossbow, a man shot venison,
Then brought down the doe's fawn which he had chanced upon.
Laid by the dead doe, it stained the grass in turn.
Now the doe and fawn he'd shot were beyond expectation;
He'd best have forborne, in moderation,
But saw a superb wild boar, and since he could not learn,
And liked pork mightily, he laid a third beast low—
Predestined for the Styx. 'Twas not a mortal blow;
The shears of Atropos were dull and she is diabolical,
So rained other barbs. Determined to prevail,
She persevered till the boar was defeated.
Satisfaction? Not for a conqueror till repeated;
What appeases him whom no hoarding can sate?
Time went on; then the archer from where the doomed boar
                                                    rolled
Saw a lone partridge running on new-turned mold.
          Though poor game to accumulate,
He picked up his bow to use it once more.
The boar summoned a final spark of vitality
In its extremity, gored the foe, squaring the score,
          And was thanked by the partridge accordingly.

Thus far it is greed I have exposed to view:
I'll treat hoarding next, that my promise be fulfilled.

When a wolf who chanced near saw that sight to rue,
He said, "O Fortune! You shall have a shrine I shall build."
Yet how stow four away? Could rare luck recur?
      Misers defend what they are.
"I've enough," said the wolf, "for a month, more than one.
One, two, three, there're four; yes, four weeks' clear gain.
      Is the evidence not plain?
In two days I shall start, but I might as well begin
And gnaw that stout cord—the finest to be bought—
Genuine sheep's gut as a mere whiff has revealed."
      So saying, he trod the bow taut,
And sure enough, was the one to be shot.
Our hoarder died that day; he had been disembowelled.

Let me return to the text. While you can, take your ease;
You've seen two victims of greed similarly slain:
      Covetousness robbed one of gain;
      Stinginess was the other's disease.

BOOK NINE

THE FAITHLESS DEPOSITORY

Since the Nine have loved my lyre,
Dumb animals whom we know
May have lent my songs a glow
Better than heroic fire.
In deities' dialect
Wolf answers dog at my dictate;
These creatures' rivalries reflect
Mortal conflicts dwarfed and great,
Fools' or those we venerate,
Though small minds, I own,
Outweigh by comparison
Any learned gathering.
They're a noisy following—
Ingrates and the tyrannous,
Past masters of despair,
Gross or fawning curs,
And far from incongruous there,
A horde of falsifiers.
All are liars—at any rate
Are said to be by Solomon.[1]
If it were only the profligate
Condemned by him alone,
We might exonerate man;
That everyone should share the ban,
Great and small universally,
I'd call a barefaced calumny
If Solomon weren't our falsifier.
Tales told in Aesop's way,
Or as though to Homer's lyre,

[1] Psalm 116:11.

Are not lies, you're sure to say:
Fraught with the daydream's charm,
Fairy-tale naïveté
Brings truth home and can disarm,
Feigning life as in a play.
These two masterpieces give
Mankind something that will live:
What we might say never ends.
Lies to match theirs are vain pretense
And the depository here,
Lying to an honest ear,
Was a fool and honor's foe,
To use the frankest speech I know.

The story now without more delay:

      A Persian trader leaving port,
Who had a neighbor to whom to resort,
Deposited a hundred weight of iron.
"My iron?" he inquired soon after his return.
—"Your iron? there is none: it has vanished, I fear;
      A warehouse rat gnawed it away.
I reproved my men, but what's to be done, sir, pray,
If there was a hole in the barn?" Though marveling to hear
So tall a tale, the merchant showed satisfaction
And then, when prepared, stole his false friend's son
And served a feast to which he bade his enemy.
The latter, in tears, refused the invitation:
      "You must excuse me. Pity me;
      Sweets are mere salt in a wound.
      My son was more than life to me,
My only child; I'm a man whose mind has not been sound
Since the lad disappeared: spare one whom griefs consume."
The merchant answered, "As yesterday waned in gloom
A screech-owl flew down and bore the child away,
Soaring, I think, toward a bastion in semi-decay."
The man said, "Now what owl that one ever knew
Could carry off children? It scarcely sounds true.
I really think the owl would be trapped by my son."
The first said, "Who could explain to you how it's done?

[207]

I'm merely saying he flew so near that I was convinced;
      And therefore if words are not to be minced
I'd reprove you for questioning my veracity.
      I don't say an owl's to blame for it all,
      But why an impossibility?
Say a rat gnawed a hundred weight of iron; if plausible,
Would a fifty-pound boy tax an owl's wing span?"
The thief caught the point of it, spun from air,
      Surrendered the iron, and the man
      Who'd regained it restored the heir.

Like two back from abroad, ambitious to score,
One was a kind of ceaseless bore
Exaggerating to heights with which the mind can't cope,
Making Europe, as under a microscope,
Rival the freaks in Africa's collection.
Bound that hyperbole reward his search,
He described a cabbage which defied conception.
The other said, "And I've seen pots the size of a church."
The first scoffed, the other answered, "Big enough
      To cook your garden stuff."

He was a wit; the iron merchant, clever. Ah well—
When speech forsakes sound sense, judiciousness forbears.
Don't aspire to right wrongs or be splitting hairs:
Best out-Herod your bore and surmount his ill will.

II

THE TWO DOVES

    Each's love for the other was unfeigned,
    Yet one tired of inactivity—
    Had somehow become feather-brained
    And must fly in search of novelty.
    Her partner inquired, "Tell me where.
    Abandoning one of a pair?
    Deserted—the summit of woe:
You have a heart of steel! What toil you'll undergo;

In tempests you might lose your head;
You cannot mean what you have said.
Later in the season I need not feel such dread.
Stay here till winds are fair: curb your haste, heed the crow,
Who insists that a bird will succumb to a blow.
I shall dream you're detained, never really rest.
The falcons, the snares. I'll say, 'Alas, it is raining now.
Surviving it, I hope; but how?
What food has she? What sort of nest?'
Should these heart-rending words not stir
A too intrepid traveler?"
Desire to explore, and impatience with her retreat
Were to bear her away with, "Forswear lament;
The fourth day from this I'll be back at your feet
And shall tell you how each hour was spent.
Ponder, dear dove, what I'll pour in your ear.
It will entertain you all day. But if I remain with you through
fear,
I'll scarcely say a word. You'll see everything,
And picture a paradise.
I'll say I was here; and there; as if on the wing,
You'll be seeing it with your own eyes."
Though both wept at farewell, one soared into the blue;
The sightseer was gone. A storm cloud presaged harm,
And, warned, the bird sought coverts of which there were
few—
The sole sheltering tree that could parry the storm,
Exposing its guest, whose feathers could not keep her warm.
When the rain had ceased, the martyred thing, soaked through,
Ruffled herself half dry though still surcharged and watery.
Then she saw a field where wheat lay in full view
With another dove near, and seizing opportunity
Felt the toils on her feet under food spread as bait—
A prey of bird catchers in wait.
The net was old, and as she fought it with bill
And feet and wings the meshes broke and out she crept
Although feathers came off. Worst of all to accept,
A vigilant vulture with claws curled to kill
Chanced to see our poor bird trailing part of the twill,
Like a convict in terror of further delay

[209]

As what hampered him seemed to give way.
The vulture closed in, when an eagle above
Digressed from his course and almost captured the dove.
While the two fought she escaped—at last free of the snare,
Thinking, as she sought a hut in which to be secure,
      No further crises could occur
      That might be too harmful to endure;
But an irresponsible lad (youth is hard, I'd say)
Took his sling, and a shot could have made the dove his prey.
      Poor foolishly valorous
    Sightseer, punished for her recklessness,
      Trailing twine that bespoke her distress.
      Nearly murdered, with wing hanging loose,
      She flew to the cote whence she'd come
      And for better or worse had reached home
      Free of threats and more abuse.
So they were rejoined; let your imagination play
On a contentment now that overbalanced pain.

Fond lovers, since love is all in all, if you go away,
      Come hastening home again:
Each a beautiful world to the other of the two,
      Forever strange, forever new.
Love the world in each of you, unaware of all the rest.
I who loved long ago, desiring nothing more,
      Would not exchange the Louvre's vast store
Of all that's rare—or heaven—for love confessed,
      Magic woods and magical byways
Scarce mortal where she walked, a fairy's where she'd gaze.
      Sheep had a sweet caretaker,
      For whose sake as her worshiper
I'd bound myself by Eros to serve her, her alone.
Shall ecstasy return that was, alas, my own?
Are lost delights that made life sweet forever gone,
Forsaking my soul in its dejected state?
Ah! might my heart take fire once more in the old way,
Alert even now to love's spark and, elate,
      Beat fast as in a former day.

III

THE MONKEY AND THE LEOPARD

Now since a leopard trod the boards
Matched by a monkey at the fair,
Both were in need of drawing cards!
The leopard said, "Connoisseurs, I'm elate, I've an air;
Am approved by royalty. The king who has been here,
Were I no more, would wish to wear
A muff of leopard fur, cream, yellow, black or gray,
With chained rosettes that interplay
On fairy-footmarked fur moirée!"
Singularities lure; each went in to see,
Gave a look, and came forth immediately—
The monkey meanwhile calling, "Come, if you please,
Come, my dear sirs, I'll whirl and twirl at my ease.
Praising his own cat coat to repletion,
The leopard there has mere distinction;
While I'm your slave Will, his far wittier foil,
Cousin and son-in-law of the clown
Whom the pope keeps near his throne.
Never before on your soil,
Conveyed here by three boats, I am yours for the day,
Charm all ears at a word, stage aerial play,
Swirls and twirls in reverse,
Crazy leaps timed for hoops, all for less than six blancs—
My dear patrons, a sou; if I've not earned your thanks,
I'll refund what you spent, and where you came indoors."

The leopard was outshone. Exterior diversity
Can never charm as the mind can, to infinity—
That sparkling fount by which enchanting gems are spilt.
We promptly yawn near any ostentatious dunce.
Ah, lords in leopards' pelts on which their fame is built,
Flaunt garb for gifts worth but a glance!

IV

THE ACORN AND THE PUMPKIN

Now God's way is the best; there's no reason to rove
The entire earth to prove that a person has seen
   What mere pumpkins are able to prove.

   A lumpkin who thought that his wits were keen
Pondered enormousness attached to a tiny thing
And asked, "Now of what was God thinking, who made us all?
How inappropriately he has placed that fine ball.
    Heaven for judge, if the marvel could swing
    From an oak, what a miracle
    Of supernatural care!
    Our trees should be known by the fruit they bear.
Too bad, Garo; He whom our curates expound each day
Might have inquired your views and not have gone astray.
We should all be better off; there are acorns on an oak;
One scarcely amounts to little-finger weight.
    Would pumpkins not be appropriate?
    God was deceived: the longer I look
At these fruits as disposed, the more surely I know
    That stems were exchanged on which they grow."
The blunder irked our hero until he was undone:
"Brilliant minds have no respite from activity,"
He said, stretching out for a nap where an oak veiled the sun,
When like a bomb an acorn hurtled from the tree.
He awoke and felt his nose as the injured place,
Discovering the missile in the beard he'd grown.
Dismay rejudged the acorn which had hurt his face.
"Oh! Oh! I bleed!" he wailed. "If the oak had thrown
A pumpkin from the branch and crushed my head,
    I might by this time have been dead;
But God has overruled me—no doubt in compassion;
    Perhaps He even foresaw my bruise";
    And Garo returned home in a muse,
    Praising God in heartfelt fashion.

V

THE SCHOOLBOY, THE PEDANT, AND THE MAN
WITH A GARDEN

Here was a youth symbolic of the school—
Up to his chin in what would mean the cane,
Fearsomely young and bearing out the rule
That pedants can impair anybody's brain,
Stealing fruit from a neighbor, old refrain;
Deflowering a tree. In the fall every time,
Pomona's gifts to the neighbor were sublime,
Superior to whatever others grew
As seasons led forth their retinue.
Where in spring find the flowers gardens bore,
Like Flora's own in bloom at his door?
He saw a boor from the school in the orchard one day,
Who'd got into a fruit tree and was making it sway—
Wreaking useless damage. Fruit and flowers. What defense?
Injuring buds that might later be sustenance,
The schoolboy maimed the tree, did such harm in the end
        That the fruit-grower, disheartened,
Complained to the schoolmaster of the scapegrace,
Who brought others until the orchard was overrun
        By boys doing what the first had done
Except that they were worse. The pedant—man in its most
                                worthless phase—
        Was adding to all the harm begun,
        Dunces who had been mistaught,
Saying his object was to discipline but one,
The marauder who was originally caught—
All profiting by the demonstration.
Then he droned Vergil and Cicero on and on,
        Each of course with reference.
Meanwhile boys swarmed through the orchard till the miscreants
Did the garden more harm than anybody could mend.

How I hate farfetched magniloquence—

Discursive intrusiveness world without end.
    If there are creatures who err
    More than boys at play, it is pedants as inane.
I declare, with either near, one or the other,
        God knows which inflicts the more pain.

VI

THE SCULPTOR AND HIS JUPITER

A sculptor was charmed by a flawless stone,
Bought it and, staring into space,
Asked of himself, "Shall I enthrone
A bench, a dish, or a deity's face?

"I'll form a god with a bolt held so,
Up in the air, as thunderer.
Man, pray and fear him from below.
Know that your master stands there."

At length he achieved what he longed to define,
Ever more dear to his soul,
A Jupiter there as though divine,
Save that he made no thunder roll.

Perhaps a myth, but people say,
Before the Jove had been displayed,
It filled its creator with dismay
Since he feared the very thing he'd made.

Yet sculptors are never in terror more
Than poets who conjure from air
Angry gods with revenge in store
As implacably as if there;

Children in this respect, we see,
Like babes who almost seem afraid
Lest mere dolls be refractory
When a careless word is said.

[214]

Existing as superstitiously
As the human race in its youth,
We inherit its fatuity
And still warp phases of truth.

Like the savage who suffered pain
From enemies who were not there,
Pygmalion carved Love and then
He found he was in love with her.

Men objectify, shall we say,
As real, some dream which they invent:
Cold as ice to truth each day,
While falsehood has their warm assent.

VII

THE MOUSE METAMORPHOSED INTO A MAID

A mouse squirmed from a screech-owl's beak. Why care where
it went
When it fell? I would not have cared
But a Brahmin automatically bent
And smoothed fur the beak had marred.
Let each country adhere to the code it's preferred,
Though some scorn a mouse's pain.
We are hard; while a Brahmin would as soon disdain
A relative's. He feels that he submits to a fate
That transforms one at death to a worm
Or beast, and lends even kings a transition state—
A mysterious concept to affirm,
Probed by Pythagoras, whose mind fed on such fare.
Born with this same belief, the Brahmin sought a sorcerer,
Eager to right what had been unfair and procure a key
To restore to the mouse her true identity.
Well, there she was, a girl and real,
Of say fifteen, who was so irresistible
Priam's son would have toiled harder still to reward her
Than for Helen who threw the whole world in disorder.

[215]

The Brahmin, marveling at the miracle,
      Said to the maiden who met his view,
"Say for whom you could care, merely furnish a clue;
      Any would thirst to marry you."
      She replied, "If credible,
      I would choose the strongest I knew."
The Brahmin kneeled as he burst forth, "Sun, it shall be you.
      Wed her and share my inheritance."
      —"No, for my face might be hid," it said;
"Clouds are stronger than I, I shall soon have fled:
      Choose a cloud for her defense."
—"Very well!" said the Brahmin while the cloud sailed on,
"Were you meant for her, cloud?" But it sighed, "Not the one.
I have no fixed abode and when whirled through the void
I might affront Boreas and be destroyed."
      So the distracted Brahmin cried
      To the wind he heard, "O wind, abide.
      Embrace my child in whom graces dwell."
Then Boreas blew hard, but met a mountainside.
      Deterred lest interests coincide,
The ground demurred and sparred, "Scarcely suitable;
      A rat might be incommoded
And weaken me by some tunnel he needed."
      Rat! at the word, Love cast his spell.
      Whom should she wed? At last she knew.
      A rat! a rat! Can names not do
      Love service? Ah, you follow well:
      Silence here between us two.

Everyone has the traits of the place from which he came. And still,
Admitting that this is the truth, a nearer view would seem good
Of what sophism never had quite understood:
We all love sun; yet more, what has a heart and will.
But affirm the premise? queer supposition
That when devoured by fleas, giants are outdone!
The rat would have had to transfer the maiden in his care
      And call a cat; the cat, a wolf-hound;
      The hound, a wolf. Carried around
      By a force that was circular,
Pilpay would bear the maid to the sun's infinitude

Where the sun would blaze in endless beatitude.
Well, return if we can, to metamorphosis;
The Brahmin's sorcerer, as bearing upon this,
Had not proved anything but man's foolhardihood,
In fact had shown that the Brahmin had been wrong
       In supposing, and far too long,
That man and worms and mice have in unison
Sister souls of identical origin—
       By birth equally exempt
       From change, whose diverse physiques, you'll own,
       Have gradually won
       Reverence or contempt.
Explain how a lass so fair, incomparably made,
       Could not earn for herself redress
And have married the sun. Fur tempted her caress.

       Now mouse and girl—both have been well weighed
And we've found them, as we have compared their souls,
       As far apart as opposite poles.
We are what we were at birth, and each trait has remained
In conformity with earth's and with heaven's logic:
       Be the devil's tool, resort to black magic,
None can diverge from the ends which Heaven foreordained.

VIII

THE FOOL WHO SOLD WISDOM

Shun fools or know what category you portray:
Tell me if there is something wiser I might say,
       Or more precisely to the point today,
Than advise you to flee a flyaway?
       Such as one sees at courts, to be sure,
Where princes would have boors jeered at by a boor—
Ridiculed as geese or yokels or fellow fools.

At a crossroads one time, using truth as a lure,
A fool pretended to sell it, and men are ready tools.

Scores hastened to buy, indeed almost everyone.
        As wry looks furrowed the fool's face,
        Folk swarmed up and got for money laid down
A buffet and two ells of thread in its place.
Buyers complained—ill adjudged to make an appeal,
And were all put to shame: it is best to disappear,
        Seeming to laugh with those who might jeer
        As though you'd not felt what you feel.
        Why reason out what no one knows?
All who do are ignoramuses and butts for fun.
        Best endure fools; and why expect reason
To account for their acts? We need merely suppose
That chance caused them to act in a certain way,
Yet the fool's thread and buffet led one of his prey
To go to a wise man who perhaps might explain,
        Who said nothing more plain
Than the seeming mystery which helped to ensure
That well-advised folk of good will near and far
Might know as a rule how to keep fools where they are—
The length away of the thread; and if not, then endure
        A similar caress.
You've not bought wisdom, and from the fool? say yes.

IX

THE OYSTER AND THE LITIGANTS

A pair of pilgrims who met by chance on a beach
Saw an oyster amid what rollers scatter.
Starved eyes dwelt on the find, indicated by each;
But before either tasted, both paused to bicker.
Then one bent down that he might possess it at least.
The other seized it, saying, "I must know, and here,
        Which of us shall savor the feast.
It should be his who saw it first; the other, merely there,
Must watch it disappear but not desire to share."
The other said, "Thanks be, my sight's extraordinary."
        —"Possibly but it can't surpass my accuracy,"
The other said. "I saw it first or murder me."

—"Well and good! I've touched its shell, so plead intimacy."
        Now as all this was going on
Nabob Nobrain the Grave came by; they made him judge,
And Nobrain downed the oyster without subterfuge
        As our pair of gentlemen looked on.
The then fed judge said in a patronizing tone,
"A word; the court assigns you each an oyster shell
Without charge; you may now depart, rewarded well."

Estimate the cost of a lawsuit and tell me
How much the family has left generally.
That Nobrain will take the money is a certainty.
The perquisite of the litigants is illusory.

X

THE WOLF AND THE THIN DOG

        Once a fisherman's fingerling,
        Despite grave words which charmed the ear,
        Was pained to learn that skillets sear.
Judgment is poor which lets your caught fish go, imagining
        You'll snare some year a catch to admire.
        That flint does not strike fire.
The angler was right. The carp perhaps even more.
Each defends his life and justifiably.
        Now at this point let me apply
        To a wolf and a dog what I've said just before.
        Spare Sir Wolf was untaught where the angler was
                     trained;
        Saw a starved mongrel they'd unchained
And was keen to devour him. The thin dog, since helpless prey,
Said, "A starveling disgraces your Majesty.
        Lest you merely mangle bones today,
        Defer me for there's to be
        A marriage feast to give away
An only child. I'll fill out and be at my best."
        The wolf was favorably impressed
        And let the spare dog delay.

Then he returned, having allowed its frame time to expand.
　　　　But the fellow answered coolly
　　　　Through a grille forged intricately,
"My friend, delay; I'm faring forth at your command,
　　　　With Warden, a dog whom none can resist.
　　　　Rest assured we shall join you for our tryst."
This person was a mastiff of extraordinary frame,
　　　　Whose way with wolves had won him fame.
"Good-by to both of you," the spare wolf said, since afraid,
Before disappearing. While his feet were nimble,
　　　　His brain was not fertile.
He still had much to learn about his wolfly trade.

XI

MODERATION

　　　　No one is moderate, I fear;
　　　　Among earthborn creatures, not one.
　　　　God devised a mean for man
　　　　And everyone he put here
Ought to conform, but will not in anything done.
Say he's done well or ill, he does not stop there.
The grain which golden Ceres binds for us
In spring sends up a speary overplus
Which absorbs substances which the crop cannot spare.
　　　　Thus the field in being overgrown
　　　　Lacks nutriment for the profitable grain sown.
Trees the same; such is luxury even there!
To curb the wayward grain God gave sheep permission
To reduce overgrowth in a good season:
　　　　So they foraged, but everywhere
　　　　There was grass, left pasture bare
　　　　Till Heaven willed that wolves thrive too,
Who ravaged folds and had soon left no residue;
If not devouring all, then anything there.
　　　　So Deity, to correct things again,
Had the carnivora slain: folk soon proved that there were
　　　　No worse servants of God than men.

Outdoing any beast, man is immoderate
        And goes to extremes that amount to a blight—
        So excessive that one must indict
Small along with the great. I don't exaggerate.
None is exempt. Is not moderation an old refrain
Ringing in our ears? from which we all refrain.

XII

THE CANDLE

It would seem that bees were born in cells near Heaven's throne.
The earliest swarms then congregated
        In fields Hymettus [1] afforded,
Feeding on flowers which conversing Zephyrs had made their own,
Till the chandler robbed Heaven's daughters of sweets the wax
                                    conceals,
        Leaving no ambrosia in the waxen rows—
        Or plainly put, since I'm verbose,
        He melted wax that had sealed the cells,
Formed tapers to flame resplendently
        And scores of dips for use each day.
A taper saw that brick is clay fired to durability,
Then mused upon longevity
Till Empedocles' [2] child seemed to think itself clay
        And in self-willed absurdity
Flung itself on the flames. Could logic's fool led astray
Have proved better its lack of philosophy.
Each differs from the rest: don't think that the folk you see
Who make up the world have been nursed as you were nursed!
In the pot, our wax Empedocles vanished instantly
        But was not more a fool than the first.

---

[1] Hymettus: a mountain in Greece extolled by the poets for the choice honey gathered on its slopes. (La Fontaine's note)

[2] Empedocles: the early philosopher who, when unable to fathom the mystery of Mount Etna, committed the folly of throwing himself into it to vanish as a god, defeating the success of the expedient and convicting himself of suicide by leaving his slippers at the foot of the volcano. (La Fontaine's note)

XIII

JUPITER AND THE WAYFARER

Oh, how often terror inspires prayer to the gods!
If only we would combine a deed done with the prayer!
But as fear subsides one's debt is a minor affair.
      Forgetting vows made, mankind nods
When involved in debts of mundane character.
"Jove will not collect debts on the day they are due," sinners say,
      "Calling and serving warrants on his prey."
      Wait! was it thunder rent the air?
Waive the divine implication if you can.

      As the waves rose, a voyager who was afraid
Vowed the Titans' vanquisher a hundred oxen slain.
He had not an ox. If he'd said elephants slain
      He could as well have kept the promise made.
Then he burned bones when they'd found a roadstead,
Soiling Jove's nostrils with the noisomeness engendered,
And said, "There, Sire; accept the homage I've tendered—
Ox perfume to be savored by almighty Jupiter.
These fumes discharge my debt; I am from now on a free man."
      Jupiter smiled, it would appear,
But afterward we hear of divine retribution;
      The god sent a dream which made clear
The whereabouts of a hoard, and the ultra-devout
      Flew as though fire had broken out,
Decoyed where robbers were, but his entire resource
      Was a crown. Fearing main force,
      He guaranteed ninety-nine more
From the sum he'd seen and counted heretofore,
Which someone buried—moldering where the dream said.
The thieves knew the place as one to treat with caution,
So one told the promiser, "Friend, I am afraid
You'd make fools of us. You're bound for Death's dungeon;
      Lay your hundred crowns on his throne."

XIV

THE CAT AND THE FOX

A cat and Master Fox, assuming a sanctified mien,
        Sought as saints the Grail or Rood.
        Veritable Tartuffes, outsmarting the most keen,
Neither white-wooled blackleg suffered dearth of food—
Sure to steal a fowl or cheese if in the mood
        As each did what he could to circumvent his friend.
Since in time it seemed that the journey had no end,
        Their wayfaring discourse grew tart;
        For an argument's a boon when bored:
        You'd fall asleep with no sharp word.
        So our pilgrims' throats began to smart.
All that mattered had been said, and in more personal vein
        The fox prolonged the endless chain
        To say, "You're fertile, sir, you feel,
Perhaps surpassing me, but I've trick upon trick."
The cat said, "I, dear sir, possess one master trick
        But observe that it is multiple."
Whereupon they confused by volubility
An argument worried into futility
        Till hounds hot on the scent foiled words.
Puss said, "You are prepared, friend; try your trickery;
        Worthy trickster, deal your cards,
Finessing the curs; I'll save my skin; do as well as you can";
And, a squirrel for speed, ran up a tree where she'd remain.
        Doubling a hundred times but without avail,
The fox went to earth, but with Brifaut on his scent
        Would dart and then recoil.
        Nothing he did could save the day.
The hounds swarmed in. Smoked out, he broke away
But shortly was brought to bay, and a pair whom he could not foil
        Were tearing his throat at a bound.
A thousand ways and means spoil prospects that are fair.
Attempting this, now that, one succumbs in despair;
        When trump take all is strategy that is sound.

XV

HUSBAND, WIFE, AND ROBBER

Despairing where no caress
Had inspired warmth worth the name,
This man who should be pleased, with his hopes fulfilled, mourned
loss.

Not a flicker of a flame,
No don't-you-dares, implied applause,
Smiles, or endearing ways. No overture
That fills a man with rapture.
Not a hint that his wife had found him necessary.
In short he was subsidiary,
Condemned by a hard destiny
To forfeit reciprocity,
Blessing the gods for as much as he got.
Why? If no tenderness is shown
By her of whom you've possession,
Have you a whit improved your lot?
In this case a marital nonentity,
Whose wife deplored what might enhearten memory,
Fumed one night till a robber who chanced to appear
Made short shrift of grief's eloquence.
The alarmed wife, weak with fear,
Rushed to her husband for defense
And arms whose warmth sufficed for two.
The husband said with grateful heart, "Robber, but for you
Could I have gone so far, so choose a recompense;
Select what you wish and at your convenience.
Take the house as well." Thieves don't demur, at any rate,
Grow shy or turn considerate.
Here was a hardened one. So I would infer
That of all emotions known
Fear stands first. Hatred, no comparison.
I'm sure Love quails at times; although it can make fear cower.

My authority is a man [1]
Who himself saw his palace charred to make his love afraid
　　And carry her through the fire he'd laid.
　　I'm all for risks that lover ran,
Delight in the tale, desire it told again;
　　What's more, it's true: with Spain in the role
　　Of the hero rather than the fool.

XVI

THE HOARD AND THE TWO MEN

A man with no credit and, what was still worse,
　　A resident devil thinning his purse,
　　In a word, a destitute one
　　Hag-ridden by care till undone,
Thought he might as well strangle himself in despair,
Since if he did not hang, starvation's verdict would be similar—
　　And few would care to die of dearth
If compelled to resign existence upon earth.
He chose for his doom a wall weak past cure,
Contemplating death in a spot somewhat obscure;
Had arrived prepared, and found a nail to use
From which as it jutted out he could suspend a noose.
　　The mortar was old, fell apart,
Exposed treasure which no one had disclosed before,
And our desperate soul then in haste to depart
Salvaged the hoard but left the rope on the floor,
And, gaining much or not, was changed by good cheer,
Nor merely elated but prompt to disappear;
Whereas the hoarder came and found that affluence hard won
　　　　Had flown,
So said, "Why suffer here who've lost such a sum?
Would that I might hang myself! Lacking a sure way,
　　I am forced to live, I daresay."
The halter lay at hand as if knowing he'd come.

[1] Count Villa-Medina, it is said, prepared a court entertainment, then had his palace set on fire that he might declare his love for Elizabeth of France, consort of Philip IV, as he carried her from the flames.

The aggrieved man hung it up, tied a knot, and then let go.
　　　Not needing to pay for rope
Should temporarily at least have offset woe.
So both halter and hoard aided one devoid of hope.

Where are there tearless misers to inter?
Tell me if they have buried treasure which they share?
　　　Booty for thieves or they prefer
　　　Kindred or bury it somewhere.
Might Fortune not muse somewhat quizzically?
Laughing likely, or smiling complacently,
And be all the more pleased that fool's toil was ill spent,
　　　Since caprice is her temperament—
　　　Relishing the perversity
　　　Of unforeseen suicide
　　　For one who found death compulsory,
　　　Who had been more than satisfied.

XVII

THE MONKEY AND THE CAT

Bertrand and Ratto, a monkey and a cat,
As birds of a feather owned by one householder,
Appeared paired for mischief and equals at that,
Since unabashed toward all, no matter who they were.
If small home disasters should savor of foul play,
Nobody need blame it on one with master keys
When threatened by a thief, and an imp not far away
Letting mice elude him while he grew fat on cheese.
The marplots veered toward the fire one day, then both sat down
　　　Before marrons the maid had set to brown.
Filching was a business in which the rogues might share—
Happily, furthermore, each be twice profiteer,
First for their own good, then damage to another.
Bertrand said to the cat, "It is the moment, brother,
　　　To effect a master stroke;
Steal me those chestnuts. If God had endowed my folk
　　　With paws to pull marrons from the fire,

[226]

You'd never know chestnuts had ever been there."
No sooner said than done. With curled-in paw the cat
    Maneuvered toward where he sat,
A sort of fluffy ash; again his claws
    Went through the grate, securing without pause
First one marron and then two, then even three at a stroke—
    Which Bertrand devoured as a joke.
A parlormaid's step; so, my gentlemen, begone.
    The cat, they say, hadn't one.

And many a prince has had to do without redress
    Because he found service flattering—
    Fighting in distant provinces
    To profit a king who desired something.

XVIII

THE KITE AND THE NIGHTINGALE

Where a kite molested any smaller bird
And was causing alarm throughout the neighborhood,
A swarm of lads had clamored for his blood;
Alas, a nightingale was caught in spite of all she'd heard.
Spring's herald begged of the great bird her liberty,
Arguing, "Dine on song, on melody alone?
    Consider by comparison
The tale of Tereus' murderous treachery."
—"How should Tereus, I ask you, nourish one?"
—"Not he, that lawless king whom passion wrought upon
Until his heartless fury makes us loathe the tale.
If you'd know sacred fire, then hear a nightingale
And learn what rapture is—as charmed as anyone."
    The cold kite's answer was all too bleak:
"A beautiful song, yes; but inopportune.
    The starved have no ears when they are weak."
—"I bring delight to kings," she pled. —"When a king has
                caught you,
    Why shouldn't you charm him as you say?
    Know from one who has overpowered you,
    That empty craws never loved a lay."

[227]

XIX

THE SHEPHERD AND HIS FLOCK

"So once more I have lost a lamb,
Another! The wolf has grown bold.
Cowardly fools to stand so calm!
When I counted last I'd a thousand in the fold.
Now they've got Robin, the dear, the pretty one—
Following me so dutiful
Down thoroughfares for bits of bun;
He'd be hard at my heel till stars and pasture blend.
Woe is me! If he heard me piping a tune
He'd come sauntering near from the field's farthest end.
Ah, poor pet, my dearest boon!"
As Willy made an end of mourning loss so sad,
His treasured one, Robin, the best he had had,
He admonished those left by the foe—
The rams, the many ewes, and all the lambs like snow—
Adjuring them to stand their ground.
That in itself wards off carnivora, he knew.
The flock declared that it was just what wethers do—
Crowd together and never be downed,
Since all would choke the insatiable one
By whom their Robin had been undone.
They laid their heads on the wolf's fate.
Whereupon Willy was elate.
As soon as the sun had left the lea
They imagined a monster moved—
A wolf perhaps; each sheep fled instantly
From what was not a wolf, but shadow as it proved.

Persuade poltroons to show a bold front:
They'll say they're made of courage;
But at a threat, farewell, courage that had been persiflage.
Stand like steel, exhort, and find you haven't a sheep to count.

TO IRIS: MADAME DE LA SABLIÈRE

Clear Rainbow, I would praise you if impulse had its way,
But that a hundred times rebuked, I mute my lay:
You are unlike all others I recall—
Mortals upon whose ears one's praise could never pall,
Alert to each word where honors are being conferred.
I don't condemn, indeed have not demurred.
Beauties, kings, and gods love praise; coldness irks them all.
Yes, toasts are stock in trade—a tool of the litterateur
Whose verse lauds Jupiter as thunderer.
If anything intoxicates gods of our mundane sphere,
Iris, it is flattery. You don't encourage it
Since you yourself, as we all know, love wit—
   Choice and daintily diverse,
Touching, if I may say, life at its very source.
   You love all kinds of sprightly fun,
Both great and small, but there—the world permits us none.
   Forget the world and its pretense.
   Wit that can follow a glance,
Science, airier things, have been flowers for us that combine
   In the conversations we've found so fine,
   Colors and fragrance too fused to define,
Where searchers for honey may find repose,
   And nectar concealed in every rose.
With some such point of view, I let my fancy play
In tales which are, if I may dare to say,
   Entertaining fantasy
   Now bold, now subtle possibly.
This sort of logic, labeled new, is old to you perhaps, or not;
   Certain arguers have thought
   Animals a mere machine,
Obliged to do this or that as servitor,
Soulless and mechanical, really nothing more;
   Like, say, a watch which we have seen
   Keeping time as a purposeless automaton.
   Look in at what it depends upon:
Wheels a-whir as substitute for what the soul might feel.

[229]

The first one turns an adjoining wheel
And it a third, till they sound the hour again.
They'd argue that beasts aren't spiritual,
That if you should tap one at some spot,
You'd perceive that reaction's been brought about.
Stimuli as we know, are transmissible.
The brain is sensitive to a stimulus brought
By some nerve, although how is it possible?
Matter; no more no less, they say;
Unreasoning unfeeling clay:
Creatures merely seem to betray
Certain states that are impersonal—
Tears, ecstasy, love, mirth, or the hours when one drinks gall;
Or perchance some other state.
Do not deceive yourself, mistaking this for that.
What is it then?—A watch.—And we?—Of another class.
This is how Descartes has dared to state the case—
Descartes, a man whom heathen would have made a god,
A sort of mean between spirit overhead
And man below, as the donkey's mind
Falls, I would say, between oysters and mankind.
Now let us judge of our logician's worth
By the only animal to whom God gave at birth
Power of thought—myself—who can think what his thought means.
Iris, heretofore they declared beasts were mere machines
That had no subjective way
Or any objective way
Of judging what Mind would convey.
Grown extreme, Descartes persistently maintains
That beasts do not use their brains
Though that they do seems clear, I'd say—
A view we share, we two. I know, moreover, and you,
That when staghounds bark and horns sound view halloo
The prey finds no compassion where he's crashing through,
And the much-abused creature will turn,
Since bewildered and pondering what to do.
Almost ill, old and worn, he will call from the fern
A younger animal to withstand the worst
And confuse the dogs where the trail is reversed.
What ingenuity! Then because besieged once more,

[230]

He retraces his steps and away as before,
    Weaves a maze tenfold more devious.
A king falls, who should die a conqueror,
        Torn by hounds to whom he was superior—
        Degradation for the glorious.

            Her still furry
            Brood, in jeopardy,
Spurs the partridge, in alarm, to let feathers trail,
Since the chicks aren't prepared for their warfare with death.
She wilts, feigns a limp, and half dragging wings and tail
Allures the hunter forward, and pack grown short of breath;
Defending her brood though it seemed impossible,
As the sportsman approaches to see what the hounds would kill,
        Then bids him adieu by sailing off easily
        While he stands there pondering, frustrated prettily.

        Far north where warmth is never known,
        Need I tell you that everyone
        Could know culture only in its dawn.
        Since seeds of thought were never sown—
Or at least by man; for they've creatures, we know,
        Who understand hydraulic flow
And master a stream from edge to edge,
Constructing a dam of mortar and sedge
That is sure to last, since strut reinforces stay
Where they've wattled saplings and added moistened clay.
One gnaws trunks in two; one sees that they are dressed;
All have tasks, seniors giving their juniors no rest
As foremen confer; then each with a truncheon takes command.
        The kind of state which Plato planned
        Undoubtedly ought in matters like these,
        To be guided by beaver colonies.
Where ice will form, they build high by comparison
        And cross upon dikes made of boughs they conjoin.
        Yet skillful procedure they illustrate,
        In constructing what we might admire,
        Is ignored by us who are bound to tire
        When no more than swimming a strait.

That the beaver is merely furred energy
Is a concept, rest assured, that I shall not acquire.
Once more encourage, do, my volubility
       Which concerns a king we may well admire,
The Sword of the North, to prove that I'm not being too fine-spun:
I refer to a king for whom Fame plucked her lyre,
Whose name walled in our world from the dreaded Ottoman—
A Polish king.[1] Now need I say, kings never deceive a man!

       This monarch of mine said that beasts with fur
In broods near his frontier, bred wars on and on—
Hereditary ones from parent to son.
       The broods would snarl from year to year
Like any fox, each stemming from that joint ancestor.
      Man never has waged a harder war,
      Despite his glorious dreams
      In this age of infallible schemes.
Advance guards, vedettes and spies' gantlets to run,
Ambushes, pickets, any ruse brains have spun
In the way of war and its accursèd consequence—
    Science born of the Styx, that mother of heroes—
      The creatures employed against their foes,
      With their den-bred intelligence.
To hymn that war, Acheron should renounce its sway
      Until Homer might fashion a lay
Of what happened there; how would Descartes furthermore—
Epicurus' rival—look on the hostility?
Merely reiterate what he has said before:
Insisting that wheels and gears actuate beasts we see,
      That memory is corporeal,
And urge us to infer what he had assumed was clear—
      Already incorporated here—
      That a creature can merely recall.
With recurring stimulus, it does what it has done,
      Working surely, he thought plain,
      Just as before in the selfsame way.
It would be sure to feel the same sensation
      And with no moral interplay,

[1] Sobieski of Poland.

Do the thing it had always done.
Whereas with human action,
We perform what we have foreseen.
The will sways or leads us. I speak, go out and in,
    Aware of some clear impulsion
    Which moves my mechanism, as power within
    Obeys intelligence. My own
Is something apart from matter, and certainly clearer to me
    Than matter is, however literal,
    Since master of all of which I'm capable.
Tools answer to my hand, my hand felt something lead.
Who guides the stars and the world? Who indeed!
Some angel perhaps as a deputy rules the air.
A spring that stirs in me, will touch some spring in there.
The impression is made. How, and why should I care
Until I read it in the heart of God some day?
If I am sincere about what the learned say,
    Neither did Descartes know why.
Really no more than we do, if I may say so.
Animals, Iris, I have by this time come to know
    Were born without the spark called spiritual.
As you will see when I tell you this tale,
Yet the animal is responsible, it is true
    As a plant scarcely is; quite true,
    Though sharing our atmosphere.
Now the story I've heard, which I'd like you to hear.

THE TWO RATS, THE FOX, AND THE EGG

Two rats while foraging at last unearthed an egg—
Sufficient to suck if one's content with half apiece:
And really as good as some immense tough ox's leg.
    They were an easy pair to please,
So rolled away their egg, willing it should be shared;
Then What's-his-name—yes, Master Fox appeared,
    Inopportune and ominous.
Bury or take the egg for fear it leak away;
Too slippery freight for slender forepaws to purvey;
    Eggs rolled awry cannot trail like hay.

[233]

Lacking an expedient suited to the case,
  With hazards of all kinds to face,
  Mere need suggested what be done.
Since not a league from home, one of them towed the other one,
Wasting no thought on what the miscreant fox might do—
Upside down, rear end first, egg in arms, got him back,
Hauled and mauled, with jolts and jerks, until both taut and slack
  Nearly wore his tail in two.
Now how, when I've proved their ingenuity,
  Speak of rat stupidity!

   For my part, I wish that God had wrought
Power in creatures to think as any small child has done
At the point when first aware that sentience has begun.
Children can think, although not knowing it is thought.
  Surely I would share with all—
  I would have assigned each animal
A mind like ours, though it might not quite compare;
And as no mere master spring that's nothing more.
I'd break up matter as it were molecules of air
Till very, very small as never refined before,
An atom's essence or fraction of atmosphere
That was as pure as fire and mobile furthermore.
We have seen a fire refine; is not wood when aflame,
Consumed? suggesting as much the same,
What might be called the soul? Say as a vein of ore
Bears gold and lead. The creatures I had made
I would have see, hear, and use judgment as I have said,
  Yet lack the conscious powers of man.
No monkey of mine would make plans as we plan.
  Well, as for me and what I am,
I'm born with thought but something besides, I am sure;
  Am clearly blessed in double measure.
To my fellow men I would accord the same—
  Babes, wise, fools, and madmen too—
Creatures so diverse that we're a motley crew.
Dissimilar souls were given the angels and us,
With common traits, yet may I say,
  Constituted in such a way
That ours is part of the world of spirit known to us;

[234]

It penetrates yet is not constrained in any way,
Unimpaired as when first exerting its sway,
       Actual but mysterious.
       This child of Heaven, shall we say,
Which appeared at first as a feeble ray,
       Was undecisive in the atmosphere,
But as the man matures, is able to make its way
       Despite the darkness everywhere—
       Gathering to restrict the play
       Of that coarser soul to which man is heir.

BOOK TEN

I

THE MAN AND THE SERPENT

The man had seen the coil move
And said, "Hah, fiend, I'm one of whom the world will approve
For saving mankind from a curse!"
Whereupon the creature who had been called perverse
(Serpent, not man, I would make clear;
One might easily be confused)—the serpent was captured
Before it knew it could be interfered with,
Picked up, slipped in a bag, and worse, since unused to fear—
It was condemned to death. As for justice, there's none.
Murder-bent then, to justify what he'd begun,
The man was soon satirizing:
"Symbol of ingratitude, compassion when shown
To a snake is poor sense. No more harm than you've done;
You must die," and heard from the nearly silent thing,
"Condemn a beast on sight without hearing a word—
Then not an ingrate hereabout
Could hope for reprieves implored.
Suppose you appraise your own deeds; bear me out.
You are my model. In my sins, see your own.
Cut my life short, say yes or no. Mere caprice
Dictates your verdicts—fair, unfair, or what you please.
Try me and my end is known,
But before my death, if you please,
Permit ten words and they are these:
'The best symbol of bad faith
Is the wayward mortal.' " A retort so cool
At first appalled the man but drawing a quick breath
He answered afterwhile, "The prattle of a fool.
My verdict is one which I have every right to sustain;
However, find a judge." —"Do," the reptile said with zeal.

A cow was standing near, came when called by the man,
Asked her view, and replied, "Why so dull
As to seek my advice for what needs but a word?
The serpent is right. On what ground should truth be spared?
I've nourished this same ingrate—for years and years reared
On my produce. Each day food I furnish appeared
That his hands might overflow—that his household might gain.
I've restored him when he has been shattered by pain.
      Though my toil and care of the man
Were all meant to please him and ease mortal strain,
When I totter with age he says browse as you can
Or starve. There are fields, if I dared to graze as one ought,
But I'm tied. If I were some slave a serpent had bought,
Tell me how he could be more ungrateful than man,
From birth to death. Farewell. No appeal; my mind is closed."
The stunned man who had been diagnosed
Said, "Serpent, are not such words calumny?
She's bemused, in her dotage, as any can see.
Trust the ox." —"Do; his opinion would be right,"
The snake said, head erect. With slow steps the ox came on,
      Ruminating and uninfluenced by spite.
      He said a beast's best years are gone,
Working himself weary for humanity alone,
Here, there, everywhere, while scourged and scourged again,
Man's faithful servitor, traversing hill and plain,
Hauling harvests, god-given free gifts; to him—oh no;
      He's trudging to and fro—
Dear compensation for man's cruelties and blame.
Lashed weak, nearly starved, yet when old he is of no use;
Man felt he conferred an honor when he came
To shed sacrificial blood which no ox could refuse!
At this verdict the man groaned, "More than I can bear.
      Quench this repetitive bore.
When asked to judge and tell us what is fair,
      The creature dares to accuse and gore.
I impugn the ox too! Let a tree speak the truth."
Worse for man than before. It had served him from youth,
Warded off heat and rain, and harm storms might have done,
Ornamented parks and parried smiting sun;
Furnished shade, then aided even more:

Its boughs bent under fruit, and in return for what it bore
It was felled by a lout. A severe reward,
It implied, "for a friend's fall-to-June ever-the-same
Cloud of bloom in the spring and ripe fruit when autumn came,
Noon shade, or hearth-wood which careful prunings afford.
Why cut a whole trunk down when mere limbs should be sheared?
I could have thrived for years; death was not nearly due."
Plain truth's unwelcome when what one always knew.
Since force tempted a mind which words could not retard,
The man said, "I've been too benign, am outraged by it all!"
Then brained the serpent he'd bagged against a stone wall
      With such force one could hear the bones break—
      As Grandiloquent always has done.
Justice offends him. Existing for him—snake,
Animal, mankind; everything and everyone
      Is his own.
      Yet one who'd reveal what all have known
Is a fool and must concur. What should be inferred?
      Withdraw, or take care that your words are not heard.

II

THE TORTOISE AND THE TWO DUCKS

A tortoise whose wits had deserted her
Was weary of her den and desired variety—
Impatient to leave home in favor of the rare—
Impatient, as cripples are, with domesticity.
      Now two mallards were dabbling there,
      To whom the tortoise broached her plan,
Who were certain she need not expire of despair.
      "Admire the universe? You can,
And have, when borne by our beaks which a bar will connect,
      America to inspect:
Realm on realm, strange folk, as we soar arm in arm,
Observing new shores and oddities sure to charm—
Ulysses did the same"—although you may think it queer
      That they introduced Ulysses here.
The tortoise approved what the pair thought should be done,

Said so, and a stick was borne to the scene
        To afford the pilgrim a palanquin.
"Grasp this bar," the ducks said, "as we shall, in unison.
Be careful; don't forget and weary or slacken, please."
The tortoise sailed, entranced by her cosmic view
        As folk stared, exclaiming, "Look! what are these,
        See that slow thing, as heavy as stone,
In her coat of mail 'twixt ducks! Now when were such things
                        known?
Marvelous! Quick, if you're ever to say you knew
        A day when queen tortoises flew!"
—"A queen," she said; "it is as you say, just the term;
I'm in no mood for jests." Too bad she could not conform
And travel silently; whereas she had been verbose,
Lost the stick when she parted her beak, so went down,
And her hard shell had shattered near those looking on.
Folly had dealt her one of life's mortal blows.
Conceit, false aims, fool's words that really harm,
        Envy which nothing can reform;
        All having the same parentage,
        Portend the selfsame heritage.

III

THE FISH AND THE CORMORANT

You could not have found a pond in the whole neighborhood
Which this cormorant had spared; his beak had probed each one:
Haunting pools and reservoirs, he'd lived on the fishing he'd done,
And his meals had not been lean; yet years can chill the blood,
        So the aging bird had grown small,
        Half starved as was natural,
Since a cormorant must work and support himself by his beak.
This one was too old to be peering where fish go,
        And lacked a net or line to throw,
        Till starvation left him weak.
How manage? Since need can find cures that are unique,
He resorted to a ruse. Where the shoreline catches rain
        There was a crayfish he had missed.

"Worthy crab," he said, "don't linger here. Begone.
　　　Tell your friends what threatens, what will be done;
　　　That soon they will not exist.
In a week the owner will drain the pond; they'll be but a memory."
　　　Then the crab expeditiously
　　　Spread the news. The excitement was great.
　　　Fish swarmed, then sent a delegate
　　　To say to the bird, "Sire Cormorant, explain.
We'd know who brought the bad news. Tell us who made it plain,
　　　Can you vouch for this word you bear,
Could you dispel the cloud? Say how combat despair?"
　　　—"Better move away," he said. —"But who would
　　　　　　　　　　　　　　　　transport fish?"
—"You need not give it a thought. I would serve you if you wish,
　　　And carry you all to my retreat;
Really such a pool as God and I alone have seen:
　　　One far removed from human feet—
Where Nature used her hands to shallow the rock in,
　　　Devising as foil for mortal spleen
　　　A fish republic so to speak."
　　　They relied on the bird's active beak
　　　And were rockbound, as I've said,
　　　Since every fish had been misled.
　　　The charitable offer bore fruit:
　　　Their bird lent the school on which he'd gloat
　　　A clear pool like his narrow throat;
Then caught them here and there in pairs, while spared pursuit.
　　　He instructed them at their expense—
That one ought never, never to have confidence
　　　In those who devour us. In consequence,
Would the doomed fish have fared worse if caught by man
　　　　　　　　　　　　　　　　perchance,
Who surely would eat what the bird ate, perhaps more?
Devoured is devoured by wolves' greed or men's.
　　　Why care if eaten last or first
　　　Or if the order were reversed?
　　　Time can make no difference.

IV

DIGGER AND PARTNER

A skinflint had so successfully
Scraped and saved, he was choked with affluence.
Avarice, companion and twin of ignorance,
Had made a miser finally—
Not sure to whom to transfer care,
Since he needed a trustee. Money weighed him down.
"If one spends, one's funds of course suffer disrepair,
And what lies loose tempts dispersion.
I myself would be thief of my hoard though my own."
—Purloiner? Come. Robbing yourself of what is yours to claim?
My misguided friend, you're in error. Miser is the name.
Here is something to dwell upon:
Wealth is not wealth if we never may spend what is there;
A curse in that case. Why hoard what you have conserved
Till you're old and to spend is no longer a snare?
We struggle for gains that must be preserved,
Then rob of value, gold we say is needed everywhere.
Worn by the search for some safe plan,
Our hoarder might have found an incorruptible man
But preferred to inter the gold, and with neighbor-digger
Set forth, plied the spade, and soon had interred what he'd stored;
But returned afterwhile to examine his hoard,
Could not find what he'd put by,
And thought, "I must question my friend with the spade"; so would I.
"Return, sir," he said, "we'll inter a sum as before—
Which I've saved since then and put it in the very same place."
Whereupon the thief returned the gold to the space
Where it had been and hoped to go again
To purloin all at once what the hole might contain.
But the owner was a thief's match,
For he took his fortune home to spend throughout the year
Since cured of forgoing it through fear;
And the purloiner who'd lost what he would snatch
Saw that he'd been an amateur.
Rob a wilier rogue than you are and you will not get far.

[241]

V

THE WOLF AND THE SHEPHERDS

If what I say can be credited,
There was a wolf whom conscience restrained,
Who deplored the life he had led,
And though wolves eat meat or are soon as good as dead,
Ours voiced a truth which my mind has retained.
He said, "I have been a creature who lives beneath a ban;
We wolves have been loathed by God and man.
Good shots, dogs, villagers, make a wolf's life short;
Jupiter on high is entreated till weary.
England's litters were large but no longer consort;
Bounties thinned us brutally;
Every country squire is obsessed
To spread tales that come his way,
Till, 'Murder those wolves' is the cry day by day
When some croup-bothered babe gives its parents no rest.
And all this for a mangy ass,
Poxed sheep, or snarling cur that guards their grass—
Fare I've detested heartily.
Well, suppose I renounce raw meat that has nourished me—
Graze, browse, or starve before I do as others do!
Is that intolerable?
Would it not be better than be hounded by all?"
As he spoke he saw shepherds devouring meat too.
They were eating lamb which they had just broiled.
"Oho! and my conscience recoiled
From bloodshed," he said, "although these curs and men
Eat the beast and are its guardian.
Should wolves alone keep the golden rule?
As there are gods in heaven, no! I'd surely be a fool.
Straggler Theobald won't need fire
To broil him in my retreat;
Or the silly ewe who stalks near at his bleat,
Or old Hornie, my young lamb's sire."

With justification. For a fact, is it just?
        We prey on what we choose—beasts held in trust—
Until gorged with meat; while we ask are dreams outgrown
Of an age when our own and wolves' interests were one?
        No hook for them, or turnspit over heat?
        Shepherds, shepherds! a wolf must devour—
        In the wrong only when he would forfeit his power:
        Would you have him a hermit and forswear meat?

VI

THE SPIDER AND THE SWALLOW

"O Jupiter, who bore my ancient foe,
Your own Pallas, though how we'll never know,
Except that she is your brain's progeny,
This one time, heed importunity!
Procne grazing clouds for flies, or sweeping low,
Serpentines o'er streams, weaving to and fro,
Filching the flies for which I wait:
My own, since caught in my snare, yet scarcely so.
It would be full were it not for my wingèd foe—
Such abuse merits action appropriate."
        Using speech with an insolent ring,
The spider bred choler, though once court embroiderer—
        Now a mere speck in her swaying snare
Woven for what she could trap on the wing.
Twin bird to Philomel, the swallow preyed at need
On food of the pest that spun, snatching gnats from the air
For her brood and heartless self; and her dives had speed,
Since the little mouths were agape for squirming fare
And were always chirping what when interpreted
Meant still more food, and more and more, poor helpless crew.
        The souring spinner, groaning like Job,
Merely got head and feet; but never worked, so was one to rob.
        Our swallow on a certain raid
Carried off flies in silk of the spiderweb,
With the spider dangling like a fob.

Jupiter sets two tables at which to feed us all:
Provides first for shrewdness, strength, and the bird with keen eyes,
    While those cursed with inferiority
    Must fare on the crumbs that fall.

VII

THE PARTRIDGE AND THE COCKS

Here a partridge was kept with cocks—in the same pen—
    Where noise and spleen imposed constant strain
    That made life an anomaly.
    Her sex and common decency
And the fact that cocks who can't pay court are a freak
Should have ensured the olive held out to one born meek:
Who might think her menage-mates would show her courtesy
Whereas the boors had forsworn gentility,
Regarded their guest as a target for attacks;
Then were torturing her with beaks hard as an ax.
    As a result she was almost sick,
Although she perceived that cocks are choleric,
Since each would fight the whole clan;
So said, "Traits such as theirs are deplorable,
But don't blame them; blame what mankind has done:
    Jupiter, foreseeing it all,
    Has spared birds uniformity.
I am not quarrelsome; cocks lack gentility.
Though I would have preferred to spend life trustfully
    With birds who mingle peaceably,
Our master confined me with fowl I would shun.
    He uses tunnel-nets for quail,
Clips us, then humbles us with cocks' wings like a flail,
But don't blame cocks; blame what mankind has done."

VIII

THE DOG WITH CROPPED EARS

"My own master deforming me,
How have I erred to be so harmed?
The man would make a fool of me!
Consort with other dogs? If I were not deformed.
O power who rules the beasts; or rather, fearsome man,
Doing harm that lasts for years."
The yet young boxer cowered and whined. It was done.
In spite of argument to harrow one,
Both his ears were cropped—notwithstanding his tears.
He mourned and looked despair, but as time went on
His case was very good; a dog disposed to force
And tearing others' ears soon would have been all scars.
Certainly his physiognomy
Might have been marred till there were scarcely any hairs,
Since a quarreler's ears are always scarred affairs.
The less ear the less to be torn by the enemy.
It was for the best. What would get the brunt of the blows
Must be armed when a dog defies his foes.
Warlike boxer with an air of disdain,
Spiked gorget and ears shorn, should make the moral plain:
Wolves can't catch what dogs do not expose.

IX

THE SHEPHERD AND THE KING

Now two demons dominate humanity,
Outwitting between them the goddess of reason,
And, I'm inclined to infer, have the whole world's fealty.
If you wonder who they are and by what names known,
One is Ambition and Love is the other one.
The former extends its sway almost anywhere,
Is even involved in love furthermore,

[245]

As I readily could prove; but I must show you here
How a king made a shepherd coadjutor—
In the good days long ago. Our own are not the same.
A king saw a monstrous flock—the pasture overrun
By nibbling sheep so well formed it meant wealth from each one—
Credit for which the good shepherd could claim.
Therefore the king, who thought him a phenomenon,
Said, "You should be a shepherd of men not sheep alone.
Forsake your flock for a breed of beast harder to tame—
      Chief justice henceforth, understand."
And our shepherd had, so to speak, scales in his hand.
Though all he'd seen was a hermit and wolves he'd fought,
He had good sense, and since he used the power of thought,
      He'd earned honors at last, bestowed upon few.
Whereupon the hermit he'd known made haste to inquire,
"A dream? Am I awake? You are nobly employed!
At court; live in state. Take care. Kings are folk to avoid;
Royal approval is fleeting and false; you acquire
What costs dear. When power is your spur
You thrive; then are even worse off than you were.
You do not suspect the snares in this on which you are bent.
I'm your friend." The judge laughed—once again counseled
                  uselessly.
      "Come now; face your jeopardy;
Court ways have already done your clear mind detriment;
I knew another as blind to his predicament:
      When a serpent hoary with frost
Somehow circled his hand like the snake-whip he'd lost,
Which it seemed had worked loose from the belt which he wore,
He murmured, 'Thanks be to God, sore heart could not ask more';
When a passerby called, 'God save us, how dangerous!'
—'Snake? There's none! Just my whip!' —'That will squirm, I insist.'
—'If I am mistaken, would I care to persist?'
—'You mean you treasure that pest, sir?' —'Surely none.
My whip was almost worthless; now I have a good one
      And envy dares to disparage me!'
      The blind man, ignoring advice to the last,
      Died in torment immediately,
Pierced by the thawing serpent which held him fast.
      As for you, I predict, sir,

That you will endure something even more dire."
—"So! What is there but death before which we must cower?"
—"Ills without end," said the discerning eremite.
His prediction came true—fourfold, what is more.
Court pests, devising plots hour after hour,
So impugned moral force and judgments that were right
That the king lost faith. Conspiring out of spite,
They stirred up foes. Estranged by his verdicts, some said,
"As for aid, he's reared a palace for which we paid!"
The king went to admire inferred magnificence,
Saw nothing to justify rumors which spite had spread,
And found modest propriety attested instead.
   Such was the owner's opulence.
They said, "He has a chest that's locked when we are nearby,
Bound with ten iron bands to keep his hoard of gems secure."
With the lid raised, all were chagrined by what met the eye—
   A fate slanderers must endure.
The folk who were standing there saw rags too weak to sew,
   Worn by the shepherd long ago—
Bagpipes, crook and cap, together with an old coat
   And scrip—if I do not misquote.
He said, "Treasured gear, in your day we weren't the prey
Of the serpent envy where lies wear one down;
Be mine again; marvels sicken; we'll away,
   Roused from nightmares of renown!
If you can, honored King, condone words spurred by pain.
I had forefelt defeat in trying to be great—
Charmed by ambition—seductive precipitate.
   In whom is there not just a grain!"

      x

THE FISH AND THE SHEPHERD
WHO PLAYED THE FLUTE

  With soul set on his pearl, Annette,
  Thyrsis sang like a wayside bird
  Songs to which the flute might be set.
  The very dead would have stirred

As he strolled where a streamlet purred
Beside flowers that dotted the lea
Fanned by breezes blowing fitfully.
Annette meanwhile sat fishing, dejected.
The wary fish were not attracted:
Our shepherdess couldn't catch one.
Her shepherd who charmed all he'd known,
On whom mere beasts poured forth to fawn,
Thought (wrong, alas), "I'll lure a selection,"
And chanted, "Fair citizens with fins, attend:
Forsake the naiads and honor here a fairer one.
You need not shrink from the creel you will presently fill,
Since you are not mortals Love can kill
But creatures she'll treat tenderly;
Don't seek her apprehensively:
You'll live in a fishpond soon, so clear it shows each gill;
If a few fish die from the hooks which her baits conceal,
To die at the hands of Annette is sheer felicity"—
Persuasiveness which he might as well have deferred
Since the deaf, it is certain, could never have heard.
Thyrsis had honeyed his plea, but each word
Was a murmur the breezes blurred;
So he lowered a net and immediately
Tumbled fish at the feet of the fair one angling there.

O shepherds as lords of men and not of husbandry,
Sovereigns who hope to adopt a concessive policy
In controlling swarms of the foreigner,
Do not suppose that fair words can win the day for you.
You need a more powerful snare.
Make use of your nets and the fish can't slip through.

XI

THE TWO PARROTS, THE KING, AND HIS SON

Two parrots—son and sire equally—
Knew regal care and shared their master's fare.
Two demigods, this king and his heir,

Had a passion for the parrots' company.
Linked by age, the sires were a faithful pair,
While as twins the young would associate,
And if at times in ways that were laughable,
When apart they were disconsolate,
Shared their meals and went to the same school.
He was a favored bird who had as intimate
And schoolfellow a prince with hopes at mortal peak!
Born with a love of birds undoubtedly unique,
The prince found a sparrow he might domesticate,
Who amused them all and in consequence
Gave the prince enjoyment that was intense.
One time when the two birds had fluttered and run,
       Youthful miscalculation
       Somehow occasioned ill will,
       And since sparrows affect disrespect,
       This one pecked but had fallen when pecked
       And was injured, so that his wing trailed
       And he could not be cured, folk concurred.
       The prince had them kill the stronger bird
And bury it. The parent's grief was severe.
When word reached him, his piercing protests rent the air,
       To no avail; complaints are of no use.
       The talking bird was then in Charon's barque
       Where words aren't heard. The parent's ire broke loose;
       And despairing resentment found its mark,
For the furious parent tore out the prince's eyes;
Then, flying to a pine to be inaccessible,
       Perched near the top and sanctuaried by the skies
Enjoyed revenge in atmosphere more equable
Where he was pursued by the king in his robes of state,
Who said, "Friend, return. What can tears ameliorate?
Crush hatred, grief, and spite? Obliterate what hurt?
       Though my grief can never abate,
       Honor compels me to assert
That we were responsible; my son was the first to err:
Son! No, it is Fate by which our hearts are made sore.
Years ago the Three, since it is their prerogative,
Said that one of our two sons would not have long to live;
       The other, have blindness to deplore.

[249]

Come; feel and be as we were; fly down to your cage again."
  The bird said, "King ever royal—
    After outrage that has left its stain,
    Must confidence not recoil?
You refer to Fate. Would you, on your faith, construct a toil
Of impious speech and snare me in its skein?
Say it is Providence or Fate that determined the design
    Of affairs upon this earthly plane,
I am destined to haunt the top of this pine
    In woods where I must remain,
Remote from the prince's destruction by Fate,
    Inflamed by animus which time cannot placate,
Which must be endured. I know kingly vengeance needs no
                                             defense—
A part of your prerogative; you live like a god, enthroned on high.
    You prefer to forget this offense.
I believe you; but distance is compulsory for me.
    I cannot thrive in your proximity.
Forbear to tempt; words are a waste of time; refrain;
    Do not insist as heretofore.
Remoteness, needful cure for hate's hot pain,
    Is shield for hearts hurt in love's war."

XII

LIONESS AND BEAR

    Here a lioness had lost a cub, a son
Whom a hunter had killed. The mother's sorrowing
      Shook the woods because of what he'd done;
Her lament that soared to heaven was harrowing.
      That darkness cloaked the light
      And quiet marked the scene
Had no influence on the unbridled queen,
Whose roars deafened every ear day and night.
      Mother Bear said at last, "One word more. We
                                        would hear,

      Good lioness; say, if you can,
      When you devoured a little one

That had no loved parent near;
All have fond parents; this being so, tell me,
Since no bereaved beast has been a plague such as you,
Though robbed of precious offspring too,
Why can you not suppress your misery?"
—"I forbear, under a dire curse!
Ah, my lost son! heartlessly dispatched by spite;
Then years of distress ever worse!"
—"Tell us, have you alone suffered mortal blight?"
—"It is Destiny, alas, that bears me a grudge." As usual
Protest in loud tones is the rule—nothing new.
Plagued humanity, my tale is meant for you.
Most of the plaints that I hear are trivial.
If those who feel that Heaven has been their foe
Will think of Hecuba, they will thank the gods, I know.

XIII

THE TWO ADVENTURERS AND THE TALISMAN

We don't find scented bowers on paths that lead to power.
The mighty Hercules is proof that this is so—
Never yet surpassed, I know,
In fairy tale or lore in which mere mortals tower;
Yet here we learn of one whom an old talisman
Inspired to attempt what no previous knight had done.
A pair set forth in company,
And the two knights saw a sign which told them where to go—
Posted above them, worded so:
Gentleman adventurer, if it is your fancy to see
A sight so rare it has not been seen by anyone,
You will leap the torrent pouring down
And bear off in your arms the elephant you see there,
Of marble which lies like a slumberer;
And transport it at a breath till you have reached the crown
Of the towering precipice which daunts heaven by its frown.
One knight turned back. He said, "What if footing can't be
found?
Rapids are deep where they make that sound.

Suppose we waded through and then resumed our way,
Absurd of us to select an elephant to convey.
    We'd look like fools to the wise!
An enchanter might propose such a hopeless enterprise
And we'd bear the marble possibly four feet;
But climb alps at a breath! We would surely court defeat.
No use, we're men, poor souls; unless we were meant to infer
A pygmy, dwarf, deformity we'd disdain,
    Or some mere elephant-head for a cane.
But tell me why a pair should struggle for such a lure,
Misled by words that are snares for us, I am sure—
Say a riddle with answer a child would have known.
Henceforth regard as yours our elephant of stone."
He turns away as our knight defies the elements,
    Closing his eyes to the torrent's flow.
    No undertow or violence
Can shake our hero's faith. Foretold, what he sees is so,
He finds the elephant slumbering on the farther bank
And staggers beneath the weight up the vertical mountain flank,
Across an esplanade, then observes a city.
The elephant's freed and trumpets explosively
    As the citizens suddenly shoulder arms.
Although the other knight would have shrunk from such alarms,
Our hero does not expose his back to the enemy now,
Prepared to sell life dear, with laurels on the brow—
Struck dumb as he hears the words reverberate from the court:
"Since death has taken ours, we have made you our emperor."
He humbly said he wished that he could play the part,
That his powers were too frail for the burdens kings bore—
As Pope Sixtus [1] had answered when offered the papal chair.
    (Would the burdens be more than one could bear

---

[1] " 'Tis a pretty tale: Sixtus Quintus, a peasant's son, became a cardinal. When old and infirm, he was asked to succeed Gregory XIII. With an air of humility he answered that he was unworthy of so great an honor. Upon being chosen, he feigned a cough to disguise sound lungs; then cast aside the staff on which he had seemed to support a feeble frame, stood erect, and sang the *Te Deum* in a voice that shook the chapel. Felicitated by Cardinal de'Medici, on his good health, Sixtus replied, 'When a cardinal, I was looking for the keys of Paradise and walked with a lowly look; but now that they are in my possession, my eyes are fixed on heaven. I am no longer in need of earthly things.' " [From *Fables of La Fontaine,* in the translation attributed to Robert Thompson (Paris, 1806), published by Nimmo & Bain (London, 1884).]

In assuming papal or royal throne?)
That he'd not been in earnest was presently shown.

Fortune, though blind, can reward blind fearlessness.
Wisdom's impulsiveness at times earns wreaths of bay
Though it does not pause in its impetuousness
To visualize a means or seek out wisdom's way.

XIV

THE RABBITS

For Monsieur le Duc de la Rochefoucauld

I tell myself frequently that man's counterpart
            In situations I take to heart
Is almost always some animal he knows.
A monarch's nature and his feelings are those
            Of the creatures he sways. Now I am sure
            That animals, however poor,
Have at least a semblance of mentality
In the mere corporeal self, energized by something there.
            I'll demonstrate this presently.

At an hour when stalkers stir, before the loiterer
Day has lighted their path upon the moor;
Before the sun's first rays are shining everywhere,
And it's neither night nor day, no one is ever sure,
Off where the tall trees are, I've climbed perchance
Like some new Jupiter and from an eminence
            I am thundering with my gun
            At the rabbits crouching unaware.
All disappear. I have startled them every one—
            On the green, in heather-sweet air—
            Bright-eyed, sharp-eared shadows that waited,
Then sported; nibbling thyme-perfumed fare, enchanted.
            When I made a terrifying sound
            They scampered, as if spirited,
            Underground where their tunnels led:

[253]

Soon the threat seemed harmless. Fear at first profound
Had presently subsided, and the rabbits as one
Were gamboling there again, even nearer my gun.

Now do we not present the same phenomenon?
  If wrecked by a squall we disperse
  And scarcely reach shore
  Before hazarding once more
  A wind never worse;
  Rabbits too, as scatterbrained
  As if we were Fortune's pawn.
Let me submit another scene I've drawn.

Sometimes strange dogs intrude on dogs in residence.
  Although they rue the offense
  You can infer how polite
  The old residents are, whose one delight
Is something teeth can gnaw. With yelps they set upon
  And imperil the unknown,
  Chase, and wage a relentless war.

An eye to the main chance, glamour's lure, and love of power,
Rule our monarchs of the day; and courtiers now and then
Constraining them to overbear. Let us everywhere
  Look at ourselves. Observe our heartless air.
Newcomers are despoiled, then stripped before they go.
Do not coquette and scrivener endure dire wear and tear?
  What weary hours young authors know!
How few can share when others have cakes to bestow;
  Then the larger the cutter's share.
Hundreds of stories would bear me out, I am sure,
  But when fables allure,
Rest assured they are short. Opinions coincide
As all masters of this special art have attested,
And although I might easily have persisted,
  This is enough to have suggested.

Whatever has depth in this discourse, you have supplied,
And modesty in you is greatness' counterpart.
Though compliments to you spring from the heart,

And certainly are justified in all men's eyes,
　　You shrink from praise in any guise;
In short, though contrary to your instinct, it is true,
That I inscribe again in reverence
A name which nations and past ages knew,
Which lends honor to France where you are sure to find
　　　　Names greater than elsewhere upon earth,
Permit me to tell the world that I have found in your mind
The theme which lends these verses of mine worth.

XV

THE MERCHANT, THE NOBLE, THE SHEPHERD,
AND THE PRINCE

　　Four explorers—ship aground—
Made shore half naked although more nearly drowned:
A merchant, noble, shepherd, and youth of royal descent,
　　Like Belisarius,[1] each a wanderer,
　　Shipwrecked and needing nourishment
　　That merely might arrest despair.
Yet to tell by what hardships they were united,
Or by what astral influences each had been defeated,
　　Would end in a tedious drone.
Say at last near a fountain they'd tired and sat down,
Then suggested in turn what should be done.
The prince thought court life harder than any known.
The shepherd, admitting that they had been afflicted,
　　Said wherefore now dejected;
Since at liberty at last, each should labor like a man
　　To support the others' common plan.
"Complaints aren't cures," he said; "say when has one struck home?
Exert yourselves and we shall surely get to Rome."
A mere herd discoursing—voicing an opinion!
Just how believe that Heaven gave wit and a shrewd head
　　To the king, no other person?

[1] Belisarius was one of the Emperor Justinian's captains who lost favor and
was obliged to beg (apocryphal).

[255]

Why need one who herds sheep think in their fashion
        And seem to us benighted?
This shepherd had seen and they had approved what should be
                    done.

Though near America when their bark sprung a leak,
The merchant said, "I'll teach arithmetic
At so much a month and receive remuneration."
        The prince was second to speak:
"I shall teach government." —"And I, heraldry,"
The nobleman said. Exceedingly practical!
As though Indians who live by activity
Could find heraldic jargon serviceable!
The shepherd said, "Friends, I assent. Well and good.
But what next? A month has thirty days. Sustenance!
        Faith, man! Are prospects food?
        Encouraging but the suspense;
Fair hopes that are deferred; meanwhile starvation, with your
                    plan.

Tell us what we shall eat tomorrow if you can;
        Hope based, rather, upon what assurance
Of a meal this evening? What is your guarantee?
        The moment is undoubtedly
        What matters most. And your plans
Are too unreal. My hand must staunch our need."
        Whereupon, with lightning speed,
He entered a copse and cut bundles of faggots folk bought.
Funds provided thereby, and next day from wood brought,
Saved them all from a fast by which they would have been un-
                    done,
And from having to labor in hell's oblivion.

        In view of what I've told you here,
Toil and don't put on airs as you hold your lives dear;
        The hand that works without demur,
Was ordained from the first to be our rescuer.

BOOK ELEVEN

THE LION

You may have read in some fairy book
Of rich Sultan Leopard's domain:
Scores of steers by escheat, scores of buck which he took,
    And scores of sheep swarming the plain.
Then woods not far off cubbed a lion destined to reign.
Courtesies back and forth by which each seemed to defer
    Were but courtly hide-and-seek.
The sultan bade his vizier the fox confer—
    A master hand and one alert to speak.
The leopard said, "You're pained at thought of the cub as king.
    Why fear a rustic orphan heir?
    I pity the poor beardless thing.
    He'll have his full share of worldly care
    If he maintains his power as king,
Without conquests on which to meditate."
    Twitched ears showed the vizier's state.
He murmured, "Sire, no orphan affects me in that way.
We must placate the cub and do it without delay
    Or efface him as a cause of fear
    Before his teeth and claws have grown,
For in time he would naturally overcome us here.
    We've no time to lose there's so much to be done.
I've cast his horoscope and war is prominent there.
    If treated as though he were your son
    He'll be a friend beyond compare.
    You must be his partisan
Or curb his power to harm." Wise words pronounced in vain.
The leopard drowsed, and where a ruler does, it is plain
That anyone whom he rules may do the same thing.
When the cub was crowned the realm was slumbering.

A flourish of trumpets; suddenly, and then again
      The entire kingdom was stirred.
The sultan sought the fox, who sighed at what he'd heard
And inquired, "Why now disturbed? Your choice has long been
                made.
With a thousand summoned to bear us aid,
So much the more to lose. Suppose each proved a glutton.
      We would find our byres and sheep gone.
He must be appeased. He is able to advance
Against allies armed by our wealth—with all contributing.
He has three potencies, each without purchasing—
Vigor, a brave heart, and ceaseless vigilance.
Throw him a sheep instantly; let him feed on mutton.
If insufficient, furnish a finer feast;
Give him your tallest ox; scrutinize herds you own;
      Toss him your fattest grazing beast
And thus preserve a few." Sultan Leopard thought not,
      Scowled and gained peace too dearly bought;
      Like each of his special friends, who paid dear:
      Failed and lost all, it would appear.
      Do what they would variously,
      He was master then and could deal a death blow.
Better make sure of a young lion's loyalty
      If you intend to let him grow.

II

THE GODS WOULD INSTRUCT JOVE'S SON

For Monseigneur le Duc du Maine

One of Jove's progeny was a son who understood
      That he was of divine origin,
      As his father had been.
Though youth loves but one, itself, this young god
      Had so affectionate an air
      His love needed no interpreter;
      He cared, young as he was, for contemplation,
And a tender heart sped the calendar

Until zeal had outrun expectation!
Flora's smile stirred his own; the charm of her very air
Took the heart by storm—even that of Jove's son.
With an intensity which inspired others' best,
All his sentiments were deftly, intuitively expressed,
Tears, reverie, each mood, for nothing is lost on such a one.
Since he was Jove's son, high inheritance
Conferred true mentality and signal qualities
        Not lent to all divinities:
He seemed as by hereditary sentience
To ply the lover's trade as one previously known,
        A master, whatever was done!
But Jupiter felt that he should be taught still more
And announced to the divinities, "Although heretofore
I alone have administered the world everywhere,
        It is a task the younger gods should share;
        Let me explain what I would have them do:
There is my cherished son of whom I have spoken to you.
Tributes to him as divine have been plentiful,
But to be worthy of his noble future role
He must know everything." The world's thunderer
Had no sooner ceased than he was applauded unanimously,
And a youth fired to learn never had finer opportunity.
        Mars who understood what weapons were
        Said, "I'll show him how to use the dart
        With which the gods have borne their part
For Olympus, that its refulgence should shine more clear."
        —"My lyre will refine his ear,"
        The golden Apollo chimed in.
—"I," said Hercules in his lionskin,
        "Shall arm him against immoralities,
That he may quell passions, those beasts with fangs to fear,
        Like hydras resurgent upon conscience' ear,
        Undermining us by ease.
He will learn from me a thing essential for him to know,
That virtue is the path to power, though trod by few."
        Then Love said there was no lore he could not share
        And teach all that the others would,
And surely could. For say what insight cannot do
        When love and it are brought to bear?

III

THE FARMER, THE DOG, AND THE FOX

Wolf and fox are dangerous neighbors for mankind:
Rest assured I'd be building far from where they are.
   Hour after hour, Master Fox watched lock and bar
For fowls a farmer raised. All his arts combined
Were of no avail to make so much as a feather fly.
Secure a fair meal yet not be murdered—
Headwork for him if that yard was to be plundered.
   "Tut!" he fumed. "Drat. Here am I
  Defied by the dastards without a qualm!
   I leave, come again, am mocked though I try
A hundred snares; while yonder rustic's life is calm
As he turns every feather to gold in his palm.
The glutton's engrossing capons, hens, the entire toothsome flock;
And I, a master thief, if I catch some tame old cock,
   Think, aha, what a genius I am!
Queer that crafty Jove has made me a beast of prey
And provides no poultry yard. I swear that when I've a chance
Olympus and the Styx shall hear some things I shall say."
   Vengeance fired his every glance.
He chose an inky night in which to strike a blow:
Sleeping as though opiates had made their breathing slow,
The farmer himself, both field hands and watchdog the same—
Fowls, pullets, capons, all asleep. Their featherbrained
   Owner had left the door unchained.
   What a thing in conscience' name.
Soon a whirl of carnage. The peaceful henhouse was profaned.
Relentless work. Slain citizens alone remained
   Where floor and roof were stained.
Saintly plumage was gore, nothing less, when dawn showed
   The maltreated forms from which blood flowed.
   The sun paled; even it refrained
From exposing the horror of that fearsome deed.
   Folk were similarly pained
On finding the slain in heaps, whom Apollo caused to bleed

To quench Atrides' horde—Greeks nearly in entirety
Destroyed—all, one night's toll of folk felled murderously
   As Ajax, pacing near his tent,
   Under the spell of wrath he'd vent,
Destroyed sheep and goats indiscriminately,
Hoping he might efface the master of all Greece,
   Ulysses, and those whose chicaneries
   Had won him the right to tyrannize.
Our fuming Ajax as fox of the holocaust
Bore some away, left others tossed from the roost.
The impotent owner's unfair reproaches rained
On his men and the dog. Such are rewards reaped by the good.
"Why have a dog! You should be drowned instead of chained.
Why not bark in time, 'Quick, a fox is in the brood'?
Why not frighten him off before loss was sustained?"
The answer: "And if you by whom the farm is maintained
Snore with the henhouse door ajar for fox's claws,
Why should a dog not dare to doze with nose on paws,
Who's never had charge of the flock strewn in the straw!"
   Worthy of an attorney at law,
   Such speech is that of an arguer
   And if voiced by the owner would seem fair;
   But as a mere dog's self-defense,
   It passed for crowning impertinence
   And Tray was belabored ruthlessly.
So when you have household responsibility,
(An honor to which I've not been known to aspire)
Don't hire a watchman, and rest. Harm done may be dire.
Close all doors yourself and keep yourself alert.
   Where failure might mean mortal hurt,
   The task should be yours, not for hire.

IV

THE MOGUL'S DREAM

Years ago a mogul dreamed there was a vizier
Inhabiting a heaven of bliss year after year,
As assured as exquisite, precious as it was rare:

[261]

Then saw in a dream an eremite somewhere,
      Forever surrounded by fire
Till even the damned thought the ills which he bore too dire.
Since sentence so hard could not be as would appear,
Had Minos perhaps confused two types of destiny?
Then the dreamer awoke in perplexity
And to master what had been stirring his fear
      Sought explanation from a seer,
Who replied, "There's no cause for astonishment:
Your dream has a point and inspires a presentiment.
      I would say that the gods desire us to brood
On a message from themselves; that in his mortal state
The vizier valued calm into which none might intrude;
The eremite, pomp reserved for a potentate."

I'd pause, if I may, to elaborate the thought,
Persuading you each that retirement should be sought:
Those who've found it have known contentment without
                        flaw—
At each turn, joys implicit in Heavenly law.
Solitude's elusive charm will bear me out,
Cherished by me from the first. Why not what I prefer?
Away from uproar, I'd know peace and fragrant air.
Ah, might I loiter with tempting queries to solve
Where the Muses touch my lyre, forget the cares which courts
                        involve;
And ponder the livelong day lofty thoughts which never tire,
With my hours at command for what the stars inspire;
Since their names and their powers as they spangle the night
Diversify fortunes whatever our plight!
If not meant for a glorious fate, I do not care
So long as I am the brook's interpreter,
And may have its bank of flowers for my poetry!
Fate will not weave a warp of golden thread for me;
I shall not sleep beneath a gold-embroidered canopy.
Yet who could say my sleep is not a luxury,
That it has not been deep and full of fantasy?
Despite my dearth, I shall make renewed obeisance
To it, and can say when changing the earth for Death's shores
Cares have not soured me: I depart without remorse.

V

KING LION, THE MONKEY, AND THE TWO ASSES

Wishing to govern in the best way,
The king knew that he must go to school,
So had the monkey come where he lay,
As an authority on how a beast should rule.
The monkey made this his first lesson to the king:
"I assure you, Sire, that a prince above everything,
  In all realms everywhere,
Takes care that a certain passion, self-esteem as it is known,
  Should yield to the welfare of the throne;
  Self-love would be fatal there—
  The main source from which vices flow,
  Notorious among animals we know.
To purge the mind of every vestige of conceit
  Is really a master feat
  And inconvenience for months, of course.
To overcome it requires the utmost resource.
  As monarch and worthy of trust,
  You ought to banish from your court
  All that is foolish or unjust."
  —"Better specify each sort,"
  The king replied at once.
  Whereupon the connoisseur
  Said, "My own kin play the dunce;
Each breed thinks its ways the ones to prefer;
  Calls other beasts incompetent;
  To tell the truth, impertinent.
I would conclude that the world's deafening din
Is not made by reputation but humbug in its place,
Intrigue, and an art of forwardness which is surely coarse,
Resorted to by the uneducated and those lacking mental resource.
  Shortly before this, as near as say a pace,
Two donkeys with censers were praising each other everywhere
And I heard one say in his companion's ear,
'My lord, do you not find man as unfair a fool as we know?

[263]

Wonderful mankind confers on the inane
   Our proud name, ass, prompt to disdain
Anyone ignorant, idiotic, or slow—
   And he dares deal our pride another blow
By describing as a bray our laughter and themes we set forth.
The simpleton mocks us and then walks away,
Scorning our sort. No, no, it is for you to say
   To him, "Suppress your words, they have no worth."
Such as he really bray. But let them rattle on:
   You're of my mind so we are one.
   Quite enough. And ah, how convey
With what angelic notes your song steals my heart away.
Trill as she will, Philomel is not your peer.
Lambert's is grosser art.' Said the other flatterer,
'And your voice, my lord, affects me in the same way.'
The donkeys engrossed in their back-scratching byplay,
   Then set out toward where a village lay—
That each might praise the other Gray, both well pleased
With what had come their way, which earned each a share
Of honor, since praise for one was the other's equally.
   Ever so many are known to me—
Not among donkeys but folk of consequence—
Whom Heaven intended for stations above the ordinary,
Who would change simple Your Excellencies, in their impertinence,
   To Your Majesties. Condone my temerity
If I have said more than is best, since it is clear
That Your Majesty will hold in confidence what I say.
His Majesty desired an illustration today,
Showing self-esteem making man ridiculous—a buffoon.
Injustice requires more time and we shall deal with it later on."
Whereupon silence reigned. Nor did I ever hear
That topic broached which would presently have made a stir.
Our Master of Arts, who was no amateur,
Regarded the lion as a monarch to fear.

VI

THE WOLF AND THE FOX

Yet why is Aesop sure that fox-brains are the best
And that the fox is first in all chicanery?
I am not positive that he has stood the test.
When a wolf is being menaced mortally
      Or falls upon an enemy,
      How prove his inferiority?
I make bold to say he'd surpass the other thief
And immortal Aesop alter his belief;
Although here is a case of that belief to include,
Concerning a fox of parts and the lure which he pursued—
A huge cheese so like the moon as to seem identical with it
      On the floor of a well which it lit.
      When a pail on a pulley-chain
      Was raised, another pail ran down:
Our schemer who'd grown nearly shadow thin
Tucked himself into the pail in which water had been,
      Which the other one had kept high,
      And was presently lost to the eye:
      Snared, though self-snared and more than pained,
      The fox faced his mortal end,
For he would starve if someone else who was famished
      Did not come to be nourished
      And duped by the selfsame despair,
Care to change places with the starveling down there.
He pined two days with no prospect of liberty.
Since Time never wearies, the moon waned visibly
      And although it was still clear
And burnished the well floor, would shortly disappear.
    Our starved fox scarcely knew his head from his feet.
    Then a parched wolf, whom hunger had lured from his retreat,
    Strayed near and heard, "Come down, friend, for food
I should like to share; look at what I have to eat—
A superlative cheese. The god Faunus churned the treat
      From Io's milk and it's as sweet.

[265]

Supposing Jove's health had not been good
And he ate some, his recovery would be complete.
Though it is no longer circular—
For I was starved—I have left you a sizable share.
Come down in this pail which just accommodates tucked-in feet."
Though the fox let no inkling of his thought appear,
The wolf was a fool to lend an ear;
But he went down, his weight hoisting the other bucket of the pair,
And the fox was soon breathing fresh air.

We need not plume ourselves. Our logic's poor when we are near
Something which we think we want,
As we accept all sorts of inane cant
If a-quiver with thirst or crazed by fear.

VII

THE PEASANT FROM THE DANUBE

We must not judge a man by outward circumstance—
An essential principle which is not new to you
But one already proven true
When I showed you young Master Mouse's innocence;
Though here I've been inspired again
By good Socrates, Aesop, and by a man
Born where the Danube flows—described more than well
As Marcus Aurelius tells the tale.
You know the two first, so permit an epitome
Which the third has suggested to me.
He was all hairs, like thistles at the root,
Till nearly as hirsute
As a bear, but a bear whose tongue worked in circles:
With brows thick enough to be shortened with sickles,
Thick lips, nose awry, glowering as it appeared,
In a goatskin shirt with the hair unsheared
And a belt of rushes to hold it in.
This poor creature from the Danube had traveled miles;
Not a village could be mentioned where Romans by their wiles
Had not bled the peasants thin,

Seizing what stirred their greed as they wormed their way in.
This delegate said to the authorities he found,
"Men of Rome and Senate, seated to hear a serf whom serfs
delegated,
I am first invoking the gods as I would be protected:
May my tongue do their will in each grievance I expound.
Heaven forbid that I should be guilty of falsity!
Without their aid anyone will automatically
Foment lies and injustices—
Always false to a trust when careless of their laws.
We can bear witness to Rome's greedy practices,
Though rather than her exploits, our own moral flaws
Inflicted our severities.
Shudder, Romans, shudder, for fear that you may endure
The same hardships you cause, and know tears and despair;
And finding tables turned, yourselves become poor;
While we as the powerful everywhere
Are Heaven's scourge and strip you bare,
As slaves of the secure.
Why are we your slaves? It is an anomaly.
If you think yourselves better than all of us, you err.
Why should you be master and the whole world defer?
Why interfere with us and our tranquillity?
We worked the soil cheerfully, content to sow and glean—
Skillful mechanics and skilled in affording food.
What have the Germans learned in your demesne?
If with their worth and hardihood
They had your cupidity,
Yielded to violence,
And were a country of your omnipotence,
They would make a better use of power in their state.
As for the cruelties your praetors perpetuate,
No one could conceive of our state—
Which even the imperial
Altars built by you must abominate.
Beware; there are no intervals
When divinity sleeps. As the fruit of your rule,
Objects of horror replace all that the gods hold dear—
Exposing their temples to ridicule,
Till Roman avarice is a madness inspiring fear;

No manner of bribe is large enough for men from Rome:
      Neither labor nor a lordly sum
Could satisfy their thirst, whatever we might do.
        Withdraw them: we shall not grow what we grew
        Or till the fields to afford them gain.
We shall flee to the mountains, leave our cities of the plain
      And partners dear to us; they must remain:
We shall consort with bears although they frighten us,
Rather than be progenitors of the inglorious,
Populating what the Roman world calls its realm.
      As for children already born,
We hope death may terminate lives bound to be forlorn,
Driven to crime by misery, with your praetors at the helm.
    Withdraw them, they merely give instruction
        In vice and spineless love of ease;
        And Germans will imitate their every action,
        Pillaging and thirsting for fees.
Arrived in Rome, I saw something that one should abhor.
      Folk must bring you purple to wear.
Those who don't offer gifts when treatment is unfair
Can't expect aid of the law. The courts make it their care
To prolong trials for years. These strong words, furthermore,
      May give you of the Senate a start;
      I cease. Yet if at death's door,
      So be it, for baring my heart."
He then sank to his knees and, astounded by what he said,
All admired the great heart, good sense, and eloquence
      Of this serf by whom they were venerated.
They made him a patrician; and outraged vehemence
Won him the station which he deserved. The country
      Chose new praetors and by a decree
Of the Senate asked that a copy should be brought them
Of the brave speech, in which all speakers were to be versed.
      Yet in time Rome grew tired of this theme
      Which had seemed magical at first.

VIII

THE OLD MAN AND THREE YOUTHS

An old man was setting trees out.
Three striplings jeered—all born near there—and told him, "Build
Rather than plant at your age, if you must be self-willed";
     Then said, "A dotard, no doubt.
     Asking by all that's heavenly,
Will you eat what's borne by trees which you are planting here?
An old man of your years should watch for Death to appear.
     Why work laboriously
Providing nourishment which you must needs forgo?
Best muse, and deplore the wild oats you've thrown about.
Curb ambition; your fancies can never take root—
     Are more appropriate to us, you know."
     —"And may never fit into youth's scheme,"
The old man said. "By the time our goal is won
We are mature and near death. The fateful shears, it would seem,
May cut short yours or my own career, either one.
Hope of long life for all here is minute.
Which of us is sure of other days to compute?
Of admiring the sky last? What assurance has one,
As a second flies, that he is to have another one?
My grand-nephews will live in the shade cast by this wood.
     Ah! Convince the wise if any could
That there's no point in taking trouble for posterity.
Thinking of fruit can give us twofold felicity—
Here, prospectively—then in the days Fate has in store.
     I may see the sunrise gild your graves more
     Times than one, for all we know."
The wise old man knew best. One youth was dealt a mortal blow;
Was drowned by a fall in an American creek.
Bound that he would distinguish himself in some way,
One bore arms for his land whose vengeance he must wreak,
But was sent without warning to Charon's corvée,
     And the third died when branches gave

[269]

And he fell with a graft which he was implanting—
All mourned by the old man who carved upon each grave
The story which I have been recounting.

IX

THE MICE AND THE OWL

While prudence scarcely would begin,
"You love wit," or "Here is something wonderful,"
Lest the listener feel chagrin
Before flimsiness, or find your tour de force dull,
This is a case to which you can't apply the rule:
A genuine prodigy, and though typical
Of the fable, it's surely more than a fairy tale.

They cut a pine tree down, where nobody could tell
How long the bole had housed an owl in melancholy state,
Mourning when Atropos would warn folk of their fate.
Then as years passed, the tree acquired, one by one,
Scores of crippled mice who could not run—
Nourished, although compelled to remain in one place,
Since the owl was feeding them heads of wheat he'd pull,
After biting off the feet to make them immovable.
It would seem that sometimes when a mouse was his prey,
He had had no meal because the legs were usable.
So to secure the mouse our shrewd bird took the legs away.
Each time he caught a mouse then, it was possible
For him to eat whenever he wished a meal—
At that time, or next day as he chose.
It would have been impossible to eat them all
Since too many would have been indigestible
And therefore afterwhile, reasoning as man does,
The owl piled grain, their staple,
Where they would be sure to nibble.
Might a Cartesian think it sound
To call the owl a machine or watch which someone wound?
What sort of mechanism could tell
The owl to curtail the mice while they filled out?

If the bird was not logical,
Logic's a thing I know nothing about.
His argument would likely be:
"The mice I caught eluded me
Unless I devoured them as soon as they were caught—
A thing I cannot do, and it therefore is plain
That I must hoard them. But if they must remain,
  Their maintenance requires some thought.
How manage? I'd best bite the feet off." Now for my part,
Inform me if man's logic could be more complete?
Could Aristotle's mind have performed a nicer feat?
  Please say, with your hand on your heart.

EPILOGUE

By water so clear 'twas not marred by a blur,
  My muse has borrowed Heaven's voice
  For beasts who grieved or would rejoice,
Setting their world forth, and as interpreter,
  Dramatized them as they are;
So that everywhere they are heard and understood,
  Each in his vernacular.
  Since all have speech however crude:
Although their dialect is one my verse might mar.
If the animals find me unreliable
And their character is not depicted well,
  You will admit that I've begun
What more daring minds might carry on.
Master of the Nine's own lore, may your proficiencies
End my task and teach the truths I've failed to seize,
Resorting to this form used by me in my way,
Though you are overoccupied for energy to stray.
Meanwhile, with my muse detained by what is innocent,
Louis, our King, was subduing the continent
And effecting the noblest projects of our day,
  Which even gods might emulate.
Masters of the Nine, your achievements, may I say,
  Are sure to vanquish Time and Fate.

[271]

PART FIVE

TO HIS GRACE

THE DUKE OF BURGUNDY

My Lord,

There is no protection under which I could place my fables more illustrious than your own. Although you are at an age when other princes are barely alive to the glamour of their surroundings, the taste and judgment shown by you in all things, together with my desire to obey you and ardor to please you, have led me to offer you a work for which my model has been the admiration of past ages and of the wisest minds. You have bidden me proceed with the task, and if you can permit me to publish the fact, I am indebted to you for many of these subjects, which you have invested with a charm that has made the whole world your admirer. We no longer have need to consult Apollo, the nine Muses, or any of the deities who dwell on Parnassus. Nature has endowed you with every gift which it could bestow: skill in adjudging intellectual things; also knowledge of the laws which govern them. Aesop's fables afford ample scope for such gifts, since they include all kinds of persons and incidents. These fictions are indeed a species of history in which no one is flattered; nor is the content as unimportant as it may seem, since animals, as employed here, are preceptors to mankind. I need not expand the statement, for you, better than I, could say if the purpose is served. With a live comprehension of poets and orators, you will the better be able to evaluate statesmen and generals later, and will judge men and reward effort with equal shrewdness. I cannot at my age hope to see the day, but must make up for the shortcomings of an imagination which years have enfeebled: when you ask for a fable, I shall try not to disappoint you. If only you might find in what I say tributes worthy of a monarch who is responsible for the destinies of peoples and nations; whose conquests, victories, and auguries of peace are the hope of the world; who stipulates terms with clemency as great as any foe could desire. I see him a conqueror who is willing to limit his own power, of whom one could say yet more fitly than of Alexander that he is about to hold a Parliament of the Universe, and persuade innumerable princes to meet and terminate a war which could not be other than disastrous. These are matters too high for me; I leave them to better pens, and am with the deepest respect,

My Lord,

Your very humble, very obedient,
and faithful servant,
DE LA FONTAINE

BOOK TWELVE

I

THE COMPANIONS OF ULYSSES

To His Excellency the Duke of Burgundy

As a prince, my Lord, prized by Heaven above all,
May your shrine find the incense I burn acceptable.
My tributes are the work of a too tardy muse;
Toil and advancing years must serve as my excuse.
My faculties decline while in proportion your own
Grow stronger, as is evident to everyone.
They don't proceed, they dart—indeed seem aerial.
The parent that lent you traits that are incomparable
Burns to excel for Mars, as brightly as your gifts have shone.
If left to him to implement his desire,
   He would have seized Victory as his own,
   With giant strides inspired by interior fire,
Restrained by a god from effecting his design—
Namely our king—in possession and master of the Rhine—
Before a month had passed—speed essential to its conqueror;
Foolish as we would be if we tried to be his imitator.
I cease since Mirth and Love, as I can but infer,
So dislike a long discourse, I'd not be a trespasser—
Though the highest stations are not held by those two,
But by Reason and Judgment, as arbiters attending upon you.
Imagine the latter's view of onetime wanton Greeks—
  Changed instantly to besotted freaks
   When they had surrendered their shape
To a magic power which could make them inhumane.

Ulysses and his friends after many an escape,
The sport of winds for ten years, had wandered about in vain;
  Then when anchorage seemed good

[277]

Dropped sail in a certain port
Where Circe held her siren court,
Luring victims to drink what she brewed—
A delicious potion to numb the will till gone.
Soon reason itself had flown
And each found his exterior growing rude;
Before long they were beasts as different
As lion and bear and elephant—
Some prodigiously deformed
About which others swarmed:
Diminutive as the mole, curious species.
Just one Greek was normal, Ulysses,
Since he'd scorned the draught which he knew to be
treacherous.
Now having been both sagacious
And valiant, with comportment so finished that he shone,
He prepared for the enchantress
A drug not too different from her own.
A goddess bares all that is in her heart:
Here, the passion by which she herself was hurt.
Ulysses, not being one to cast opportunity away,
Bade that her magic power restore
To each falsified Greek his true exterior;
But the sorceress rejoined, "Let the wild beasts say
If mishap lent them shapes they would care to give up."
Speeding to them, Ulysses said, "We have escaped the cup;
I have come to inquire if you would not prefer,
Cherished friends, to be men as you formerly were.
Please say, since speech is possible."
With a kind of intimidating purr
The lion said, "Laughable;
Why renounce gifts to which all whom I know must defer?
My claws and teeth can match the most ferocious jaws.
I am king; why submit to Ithaca's shriveled laws
And a soldier's tedious round of indignities?
I shall stay as I am and be at ease."
Off with speed to the bear, our hero said, "I am heartsore.
Brute, my brother, once a fair sight to me,
What a contrast; honestly!"
The bear answered with a roar,

"Now how should I be? All bears have harsh fur.
Who shall say that one beast excels all the rest?
    Should perfection of your sort afford us a test?
Judge me, then, as a bear who is loved by a bear.
I uncouth, sir? Begone. You be human; I, rude.
I am free, glad to be—without cares to intrude;
        Am blunt but whoever disagrees,
        I shall stay as I am and be at ease."
Undismayed still, the royal Greek dared persevere
And say to the wolf at the risk of rebuff,
        "Friend, you estrange me by being so rough
        That a lovely young shepherdess burdens the ear,
    Complaining here, now there, that gluttony leads you on
    To master and feed upon
Sheep that, before, you would have guarded faithfully;
        Your life bore out your honesty.
        Leave the woods; change, since you can,
        And instead of a wolf be an upright man."
—"Is there such?" asked the wolf; "I see none for my part;
You have just now pronounced me a brute with no heart.
But who are you? Except for me would not you too
Have eaten those sheep whose loss grieves the neighborhood?
        Could you swear, if I were you,
        That I would have less thirst for blood?
To set you at one another's throats, a word is pretext.
What man does not leap like a wolf at the next?
All in all—whatever I may have become—
        Iniquities matched with iniquities—
        Best be a wolf with the woods as my home.
        I shall stay as I am and be at ease."
Ulysses gave each a similar chance,
        Which each scorned with vehemence.
        Great and small unanimously
Would range the woods and live self-indulgently
        Till the moral sense was drowned.
They had lost all power of comparison
And thinking that license emancipates one,
        Were slaves whom they themselves had bound.

My Lord, I had wished to offer you today

Something pleasant as well as profitable;
      It would please me more than I can say
      If doing so had been possible.
Then the friends of Ulysses appeared at my door,
Types of whom our world has many more,
      Whom I bring you in my fashion
      For scorn or correction.

II

THE CAT AND THE TWO SPARROWS

To His Excellency the Duke of Burgundy

A cat and sparrow just able to flutter
Were household pets and had been brought up together.
The basket had stood by the cage every day,
So when the cat was annoyed by his feathered neighbor
He'd return pecks with pats from paws blunted in play
And took care each time to spare his comrade injury.
      All his rebuffs were meant playfully,
      And whenever the ferrule was his tool,
      Deflecting its force had been the rule;
      Whereas the sparrow was direct
      And pecked with some force when he pecked.
      Forgiving injuries done,
      Master Cat had learned to condescend,
Convinced that ill will should not get the best of one
      In brushes with a perfect friend.
Since they had been associates from babyhood,
And lived side by side, neither had seemed afraid;
Even in fencing, felt that temper had not been displayed;
      Then a sparrow from the neighborhood
Flew in, tweaked pert Pierrot and could not refrain
From tweaking Raton, who had dignity to maintain.
Soon the birds disagreed and ire was palpable.
      Raton growled protectively,
"Delightful guest! This stranger who has come to call
      Has dared to insult one dear to me!

The scamp who has fluttered in may kill my compatriot.
Never while cats are cats." He took part in the fight,
Ate the strange bird and said, "The world is right!
A bird is certainly a bite on which to gloat!"
It was not long till both were down his throat.

What moral can I deduce from what has just been said?
Fables aren't fables if not brought to a head.
I seem to detect outlines which escape me; no use;
Discerned by Your Grace at once where I have been misled.
Conundrums are for you, not for my groping Muse;
So she and her sisters are invoking your aid.

III

THE MISER AND THE MONKEY

A man was hoarding. You know how when people hoard
   Madness throws reason overboard.
He dreamt of nothing but ducats and pistoles, this fool—
For when they lie idle, I'd call them unprofitable.
   That safety for his hoard be assured,
Our miser dwelt where the sea was the one thing in sight,
That from every direction thieves might be deterred.
There, with zeal which would seem to me childish appetite—
To him, ecstasy—he massed his spoils until they towered:
   Thus his days and nights were devoured
As he'd cast, calculate, and reapply the rule,
Calculate, and cast like a cipherer in school.
A good-sized monkey more intelligent than the man, I suspect,
Would hurl from the window doubloons as they'd collect,
   And every day cause a deficit.
   A lock to the room where the miser would sit
Made it safe to leave coins on the board where they were tiered,
But one fine day, thanks to the notion on which he had hit,
Sir Bertrand sacrificed to the sea wealth his master revered.
   As for me, when I compare
The monkey's pleasure with the miserly man's share,
I think both deserved a fool's prize equally.

[281]

Some might think Bertrand had priority,
Though to say exactly why would be rather hard;
So then with not a thought but to waste what he should guard,
He picked up a doubloon and was hurling money down—
      Jacobus, ducat, or crown,
      Then rose noble—in jubilant throws.
With force and skill the monkey soon dissipated
Those minted disks by which man is inebriated,
      For which thirst grows and grows.
If he'd not heard the key of the miserly man
      Scratching at the padlock's aperture,
Bertrand would have gone on hurling as he began
      Till no coins remained to be hurled, one is sure;
Whirling them fathoms to the ocean bed—
A gulf where shipwrecked treasure upon treasure's hid.
God help the scores and scores of financiers motivated
      To do as that misled miser did.

IV

THE TWO GOATS

      When they have found grass nourishing,
      Goats are disposed to wandering
Where pasture bars are down: impelled by capricious mood
      Toward what might promise solitude,
      Remote from meadows owned by man.
On hilly, indeed inaccessible terrain—
Say, upon a rock almost sheer to the base—
Two nanny-goats resolved that they would rear and race;
And since nothing deters a goat athirst for fun,
      Each outdid what the other had done.
      Then having known privilege,
They spurned the grass as at some secret word,
Converging on one spot though you might say absurd,
And came to a stream with a plank for bridge.
Paired weasels could never have passed head on,
      If hair-thin;
And the deafening force of the stream coming down

Was enough to have warned each Amazon.
Nonetheless, and aware that they might be thrown,
One set foot on the board as the other had done—
Like Philip of Spain and our Louis who dimmed the sun,
     As each would pause and then advance
     When bound for the Isle of Conference.
     The two were treading cautiously—
     Noses opposed with determined air—
     Rivals in danger which they must share,
Working along to the center gradually
Since neither would retreat. Of illustrious birth,
Each, it seems, was the flower of a strain of sovereign worth.
One boasted Galatea's goat as ancestor—
Gift to the nymph when Polyphemus wooed her first;
     The other, the goat by whom Jove was nursed—
     Amalthea as progenitor.
Both fell. Each lost her life since neither would give ground.
     The chasm devoured the two—
     A dire result but nothing new;
     Similar accidents abound.

TO HIS GRACE
THE DUKE OF BURGUNDY

Who requested of Monsieur de La Fontaine a Fable to be called

THE CAT AND THE MOUSE

Desiring to show a young prince her esteem
     And bow here literarily,
Fame asks that Cat and Mouse be my theme.
     Cat and Mouse—let me see.

Ought I to portray someone beautiful
And charming, but so sportive and unmerciful
That she tortures the person in captivity
     As cats the mice they will not free?

Or should I take as my theme the whims of Fate?

[283]

Nothing more to the point than demonstrate
How smiling Fortune treats folk contradictorily,
      As cats treat mice they will not free.

Or should some king, a great one, be my simile,
At whose word even Fortune's wheel stands still,
Undeterred by all sorts of hostility,
Who makes sport of the mightiest if he will,
      As cats toss mice they will not free.

But the windings of my thought have imperceptibly
Brought me out where each step I take will be a loss
If I let myself drone on suicidally
And make my Muse a mouse for the young prince to toss,
      Like one the cat pretends to free.

V

THE OLD CAT AND THE YOUNG MOUSE

A young mouse of little experience
Imagined that he could argue in his defense
And that hard old Rominagrab would set him free.
      "Why not grant me liberty—
      Too minute to be an expense
      Amid such prodigality?
      Say by what possibility
      I could hurt you, your lady, or friends?
      A grain of wheat's enough for me,
      A mere nut makes a mouse immense.
Since I am thin at present, wait till I expand.
Your offspring will need food, as any mouse would understand."
When in straits, that is what a poor mouse found to say
      And was told, "Your logic is astray.
Who am I to listen to your unseasoned fears?
Your logic is wasted upon one of my years.
A cat, an old cat pardon? Never anywhere.
      Realize, mouse, that you will go
      Where dead mice congregate below.

[284]

Logic is not a thing about which the Three Fates care.
My young heirs must find other mice on which to grow."
And that was all.
As for my fable, well,
This is the moral that seems applicable here:
Fond youth flatters itself that all must heed its prayer;
Old age is inexorable.

VI

THE SICK STAG

In a region where stags abounded there was an invalid.
His friends came to ask how he did,
Surrounding his sickbed to stare and inquire
And express fervent grief, till weary of everyone
He begged, "Depart, for Death is my desire;
Sirs, let Death end Life when done—
Bid her do it now, and moderate your tears."
But not so; his too morbid peers
Stayed to grieve and mourn, and none left the sick deer
Before God ordained that they forbear;
Then the beasts must drink a stirrup-cup.
Anywhere they stood, they were cropping the grass,
Stopping and browsing on leaves they chanced to pass
And all signs of aliment were swallowed up.
Naught was left which the stag might require.
Ill, taxed by famine more and more dire,
He grew faint from fasting till fordone,
And died since all his food was gone.

Aid comes dear when one is ill.
Doctor and clergy charge what they will!
O time, time-servers, and we their helpless prey—
Even in death compelled to pay.

[285]

VII

THE BAT, THE BUSH, AND THE DUCK

A bat, a bush, and a duck unanimously
      Hoping that they might outwit poverty
      By using funds they could combine,
Invested in a ship to further their design.
Accountants, managers, and men to go between
      Were as scrupulous as they were keen,
Setting debits down, and cash to the last jot,
      Till the bank was full; but a cargo they'd bought
      Was sunk where currents bore the freight
      Into a rock-bound narrow strait
      That made short work of the pilot's skill.
Ballast and those on board were seeking shops again
      Next Tartarus and souls in pain.
Our three voiced plaint on plaint, futile to right the ill;
      Though everyone, to be exact,
Even the smallest merchant is acquainted with the fact
That loss is a thing about which to be covert.
Here, alas, their good name had been mortally hurt.
The loss was capital as the world was aware;
The partners had failed, so with neither funds nor friends,
      Debtors' bonnets of green counseled people beware,
      Since one who can't earn cannot dispense.
Interest and principal to dwell upon each day,
      Lawyers and their fees to pay,
      Collectors bound they will not depart,
      Back at daybreak rattling the door,
Trained them in ways of eluding a creditor;
      And also in verbal art.
As its briars detained persons who tried to push through,
The bush would say, "Dear sirs, advise us what to do;
      Reveal in what gulf our shipping lies
      That we may salvage our merchandise."
The duck dived to recover what was belated.
The mouse that wears wings refused to be baited;

Hanging furled all day, he declined to stir.
Though sought with warrants everywhere,
He clung to his chink well closeted.
Some debtors I've known were not bats with court cares,
Bushes or ducks who have, as we say, speculated;
But respected grandees who used the servants' stairs
For egress when solicited.

VIII

THE QUARREL OF THE DOGS AND THE CATS

Since everywhere on earth Discord has been a curse,
You'll find thousands of adversaries in pairs
Whom the goddess has enslaved and made her worshipers.
Taking the elements—if I may comment—
We are startled to find that every element—
Each pair—is inherently adverse.
Besides the four potentates,
How many besides, of all degrees,
Foment war that is interminable!

A house full of cats and dogs—there have been such
curiosities—
Under injunction which lay like a pall,
Were at last constrained to keep the peace
Since their masters regulated their tastes and activities,
Threatening with the whip any who were irascible.
Amiable as cousins might have been,
They seemed fraternally inclined and compatible,
Edifying the neighborhood by their mien.
The truce then ceased. We'll assume that it was food.
Say a bone was tossed with too much partiality.
In a towering rage, the injured complained of the indignity
And bade Justice punish an act so rude.
Chroniclers attribute the hostilities
To unfair favors shown a nursing hound.
In any case, difficulties
Arose in hall or kitchen, which made the house resound.

[287]

Everyone took sides and viewed the opposition with disdain.
Judgment was rendered, and the cats in full choir
      Deafened those near with their uproar.
The attorney said procedure for them was plain—
Refer to the decrees. Futile search everywhere.
They'd been hid in a corner by agents who gave them no care—
      Eaten by mice—or so folk infer.
Then more lawsuits were instituted against mice
And some died: veteran cats bore down with their advice,
Waging war, mind and claw, on all mice and rats,
      Who were robbed and then killed by the cats
And the master of the house made no complaint.

Coming back to our theme, not a species is current
Without a foe as check, which Nature's laws require.
The cause is something with which I have nothing to do.
I'd merely say that results are good when God is through.
      But this I know; it would seem the rule—
Three-fourths of the time there need be no quarrels between men.
Mankind, even if you are three score and ten,
      You really should be back at school.

IX

THE WOLF AND THE FOX

View life in its entirety;
Who likes the work he has to do?
A soldier makes us wish to be one too,
And views civilian life enviously.

The fox would play wolf, stories run.
What a thing! Do wolves desire
To wear the wool the sheep would shun
And know the comfort of a byre?

It is really a phenomenon
That a prince of eight should compose

[288]

A better fable than old age can
As it merely labors on,
Writing verse less judicious than the prince's prose.

Touches which lend his fable zest—
Missed by the poet, or less neat
Where he was striving to do his best—
Make the prince's praise the more complete.

Since mine is a kind of homely art—
Songs to the bagpipes' reedy drone—
My hero will cause me soon, we'd have known,
To resort to the trumpet's counterpart!

No seer but sufficiently alert,
I discern in skies which his star makes luminous
A succession of deeds so illustrious
Clustered Homers will need to mass their powers—
Few though they be in times like ours.

    Forsaking the portent as it towers,
Let me think how to say what the fable portrays.

"Worthy Wolf," said a fox, "my poor fare's a disgrace—
Some tough old cock or scrawny hen who never lays;
    I am tiring of my fast.
You have better fare and your risks are not dire.
I creep toward a house; you take what you desire.
Tell me, friend, how I too may secure a repast;
    You will have stirred gratitude at last
In the first fox to taste a fat sheep's toothsomeness.
You'll not be complaining of my forgetfulness."
—"By all means," said the wolf. "I have some fur for you to wear,
Of a brother who died. Slip on his hairy dress."
When done, the wolf said, "Now in your new character,
You'll be safe from brutish dogs who protect the fold."
    The fox who'd done as he was told,
Learned, in so far as he could, the lesson set.
A crude wolf at first, he became a more natural one,
    And in the end a paragon.

[289]

No sooner initiate in the wolf's alphabet
Than a flock of sheep teemed forth. This fox a wolf had reared
Induced dementia the instant that he appeared.
　　　　As when Achilles' shield
Hid Patroclus, the Trojans forsook the field,
Mothers, daughters, sires, rushed to shrive themselves:
Dog, shepherd, and sheep sought the town, in fact flew,
And as forfeit left the wolf a ewe.
The robber fell on it but as soon forsook the prey
When he heard a cock crow in some neighboring brood.
Our fox-wolf pursued the bird lest it get away,
　　　　Casting off long fur and claws,
Heedless of the sheep and of advantage won;
　　　　Fast as a fox's feet could run.

　　　　A counterfeit is a doomed cause.
Disguising one's self can never advantage one.
　　　　One soon returns to what one was,
　　　　Almost before the change was known.

　　　Your Grace, whose wit stirred me to write what I tell,
You have given me all I have tried to express—
　　　　Theme, vehicle for what I'd stress,
　　　　And moral hid in it as well.

x

CRAYFISH AND DAUGHTER

The almost backward walk of crayfishes,
Rear end first, recalls a philosopher;
And oarsmen face the stern; sound strategists no less
Will concentrate their power while making noise elsewhere,
At another point from the one where they are,
To magnetize an adversary here or there.
My metaphor, though slight, portrays a heroic man;
Or should I say one who has done what few have done—
Who alone dispersed a hundred-headed pact
And conceals what he'll do or not, from everyone,

Preserving his secret till an accomplished fact.
Don't probe for plans he makes and does not care to give
away;
When Fate ordains results we might as well obey:
As combined rains descend in a roaring waterfall,
A hundred gods are powerless when matched with Jupiter.
Together, destiny and our King concur
To rule the universe. Now for our tale, lest I pall:

A crayfish's mother said to her one day,
"My, my, you are grotesque! Why must you lurch awry?"
—"Much like yourself!" rejoined her progeny.
"Since shaped like my mother, how should I walk differently?
When you advance backward, should I walk forward?"
            And logically the standard
            Has a far-reaching effect
            Upon all able to reflect.
For good or ill, it can make wits lag or glow
Though for the most part lag. But a moment ago
I spoke of how crayfish walk. It is how most wars are won;
            Yet a method we had better shun
            Unless precisely apropos.

XI

THE EAGLE AND THE MAGPIE

Unlike in birth, speech, thought, audacity,
And more ways, an eagle or, to speak accurately,
            Majesty,
        And a magpie walked toward the sea
And no other birds but themselves shared the long promenade.
Fear smote the jay, but hunger having been stayed
The eagle reassured her and said, "Converse with me,
Bird. If the mightiest god in his sovereignty
            Over all finds life hard to bear,
I think, having served him, I might seek diversion somewhere,
So chatter away unceremoniously."
There was no bit of news Limber-Tongue could not dispense,

Here or there, far or near. Her words were numerous
As those of the man in Horace, too voluminous to appraise.
Nobody could have made a more nonsensical fuss;
She offered to report anything that might pass,
          Hopping and flying from place to place,
As the best of spies, God knows. Her offer was an offense.
          The angered eagle said to her,
          "Do not leave home, precious bore,
Chatterbox jay, adieu. Know that I do not care
          For babblers at court, indeed deplore
          That sort of time-waster."
          Margot was glad to be dismissed.

Life among the great may be hard on the guest.
We perceive that it sometimes means mortal distress.
Informers, spies, folk by whose charm we are impressed,
Are at heart unequivocally what we detest:
But if, like Margot, you are a visitor, I would suggest
          Adopting a magpie's two-toned dress.

XII

THE KITE, THE KING, AND THE HUNTER

To His Serene Highness the Prince of Conti

Since the gods are good, they would naturally expect
          Kings to be, and kindness in kings
          Is the kingly trait we most respect—
          Sweets of revenge being paltrier things.
Your Majesty agrees! And surely it is true
That you suppress your wrath as soon as it bursts forth,
Whereas Achilles' anger, famed throughout the earth,
          Has made him inferior to you
As hero, a title only for men who come
In a golden age and bring the world what strengthens it—
Few enough in our time in which nothing is the same
And kings are praised because of crimes they don't commit.
          How different, you by whom we are blest,

[292]

Showering good which earns for you a shrine in every breast.
Sounding from sacred fanes, Apollo's song ascends,
Exalting you as one whom even gods revere.
Though where they assemble, you mingle as with friends,
Our own age must serve you upon our mundane sphere
Where Hymen longs to dwell an age with you,
        Since joys such as no other knew
        Presage a happiness ahead,
        That is like heaven, unlimited!
In view of charm the Princess and yourself possess,
        Heaven itself is moved to bless
        Extraordinarily as I have said,
By setting you apart to be a refulgent sun
So brilliant that it outshines all other luster shed,
        Though you are but a youthful one.
In Her Highness we have grace and wit combined,
        Such that the world reveres her mind
        And a self as sweet as spirited,
        Lovable as venerated:
Yet I must not dwell further on your happiness;
        I shall stop since my lines are dedicated
        To a bird of prey from the wilderness.

A kite had built a nest somewhere year after year,
        Then was caught by a falconer
Who was tempted to offer the fruit of his enterprise
To the king as perhaps a thing which rarity made a prize.
The bird, the falconer's gift humbly made—
        If legend is not suspect—
        Took as perch it had chanced to detect,
        The king's nose, on which it preyed.
—What? perched on the king's nose! —Exactly that, I find.
—Ignoring crown and orb, or was the creature blind?
—The result was the same, had he had them or none.
It was as though the king's nose were a common one.
To try to describe the court's dismay and its expressions of pain,
Would be misguided effort with nothing to gain.
The king was self-contained; kings don't shock everyone
        By admitting it when in pain.
The obsessed bird stood his ground, motionless on and on,

As though paralyzed where he had flown.
Trying to break the spell, the master called, made a feint,
Held fist and lure toward what seemed turned to stone,
                    Which dawn might find had not yet gone;
The fiend's claws, it appeared, were permanently bent.
                    Though clamored at incessantly,
He would clutch the king's nose all night apparently;
Dissuasion indeed had effect in reverse.
As the hawk at last took flight, the king was heard to say,
"I pardon both. A king daren't have a grudge to nurse.
One wild; and one, a hunter from some mountain pass.
As for me, their king has a Sire's intuitiveness.
                    Let neither be under a curse."
The courtiers approved—thrown into an ecstasy
By words which seemed to shame lack of liberality.
For a time it became to kings a parable.
                    The forester had got off well,
But there was a sense in which the pair was culpable;
Neither'd mastered procedure concerning royal birth.
                    One, young and without a trained standard of worth;
Each a child of the woods; but was that criminal?

We've a Ganges setting for Pilpay's tale of the bird—
                    A land where not a soul has heard
Of an animal's blood shed in any way.
Kings themselves have no quarry which they may slay;
Reasoning perhaps, "This hawk which we possess
                    Bore arms for Troy in her distress;
Perhaps is some great man or prince we do not know,
                    With casque or plume or furbelow,
And might again be the thing that he has been before;
                    Accrediting Pythagoras' lore
Whereby a creature will change form now and then—
                    Be a falcon, perhaps a dove again,
                    Be born a man; or aerial,
                    Perchance, with heaven for domicile."

We have two versions, and that is one
Account of the hunter's mishap; the other follows here:
Although a feat which had almost never been known,

A falconer saw a kite which he contrived to snare—
      A gift for royalty alone
      Since a triumph of skill that was rare.
In a hundred years no such thing had been done—
The *ne plus ultra* of falconry.
The hunter strode through the crowd, elbowing his way in
As though a supreme felicity
      To bestow the prize he had managed to win,
      On the king and be a favorite:
      The gift—the bird with bell, complete—
      The savage-eyed, big-shouldered bird of prey,
      Sank his scimitar talons halfway
In the hunter's nose, lending the poor man's nose hawk's wings
                            to wear.
      Loud cries: loud laughs rent the air,
Monarch's and courtiers'. Who wouldn't have laughed? If in
                    their place,
I would not have kept a straight face. Though perhaps not dare
      To say the pope laughs, I'd not swear, I confess,
That he does; but don't cheat kings of happiness.
      A life all frowns would be despair.
Laughter is the gods' delight. Although shrouded in solemnity,
Jove and his court might be mankind, they laugh so heartily.
Old chronicles declare that laughter smote the ear
When limping Vulcan bearing nectar would appear.
Whether the Olympians showed wisdom or had none,
I think my digression makes a moral plain
      And morals are indispensable.
If you hope that the one here is unusual,
Who could claim that it is? Obvious as the sun—
Fools outnumber the favors that kind kings have done.

XIII

THE HEDGEHOG, THE FOX, AND THE FLIES

Despite his years and native wiliness,
      A fox whom hounds contrived to press
Till blood darkened his fur, sank down where insects swarm
On a quagmiry path and there the poor thing bled,
      Devoured by flies as I have said.
He asked why it was that a beast must bear such harm
And be the sport of a fate which left him all but dead
      In filth upon which flies are fed.
"A fox! Devour at will the wiliest animal
      Of any the woods have bred!
Since when were foxes refuse upon which pests have preyed?
Lash at them with my tail? It cannot move at all.
Merciless insects, begone; Heaven itself curse your clan!
      Feed upon anything scavengers can!"
      Now here, someone new to my verse—
      All over spines, with the forest for nurse—
Burned to rescue his friend from the relentless brood
      Who stayed though surfeited with blood,
And said, "I shall impale each pest upon a spine,
Good Cousin Fox, and you shall be yourself again."
Reynard replied, "No, friend, please do not stir a quill:
Best let the dastards feed till they have had their fill.
If you impale these pests, now full as they can swell,
Thin fiends will take their place and be more unbearable."

Profiteers swarm the world; no one could count them all—
If you are at court or if you are making your will.
Aristotle applied this fable to mankind;
      Examples could be enumerated—
      Reflecting pointedly, our own French mind.
      Such persons plague us least when they are sated.

XIV

LOVE AND FOLLY

Love is a curious fire
Set by torch, quiver, darts, and air of innocence.
Love is a science to acquire
By degrees and by vigilance.
To expound it even in part would not be easy;
I am pondering here with a diffident air
The blind god hurt by folly
Though he is a god, cursed by the loss he must bear
Of his eyesight; well, possibly a service was done;
Let lovers say. A lonely man has no criterion.

Folly and Love were playing together one day
When the latter had not yet suffered loss of sight.
A dispute arose and Love said lay what they had to say
Before the gods in council; let them judge which was right.
Folly lost her temper in consequence,
Dealt Love a blow with all her might
And he was blinded out of spite.
Venus sought to avenge the little prince;
As woman and mother she deafened even deity:
Protesting outrage incessantly.
To Jupiter, Nemesis, each kind of divinity—
Judges of the underworld, nether gods and sublime—
She stressed each phase of the case,
Said Love leaned on a cane if moving but a pace
And how his grudge could never be repaid:
No sentence could be commensurate with the crime.
Civil damages as well must be defrayed.
All studied the accusations made,
As affecting society and him who pled injury.
Then the gods' supreme court judge ordained, to end the stir,
That Folly as her penalty
Lead Love and let him lean on her.

[297]

XV

THE GAZELLE, THE TORTOISE, THE CROW,
AND THE RAT

To Madame de la Sablière

First, my work would enshrine what you are:
And then endear it to folk everywhere
With poetic art as my support,
In founding which the gods themselves took part,
I'd honor a person revered in every heart,
For whom I would make a temple of my art
And carve above the door for all to see,
SHRINE OF IRIS, rainbow-hued divinity;
Not the nymph whom Juno had as maid
Beside her throne. The goddess, one may guess,
And Jove himself would think it happiness
To be your Mercuries if you lacked aid.
I would have as apotheosis for my Muse,
Olympus' arc which would be luminous
Round Iris' throne in the bright atmosphere.
I'd have her life portrayed on walls for us
Where we might ponder scenes which we hold dear.
One does not of course expect her to abound
In official exploits calculated to astound.
I would have a likeness of her displayed
In the shrine of shrines—and her smile that blazed
When she was pleased, unselfconsciousness when praised,
Her glance toward those by whom homage was paid,
Who in reverence for her would kneel—
Heroes and deities surrounding her,
Both gods and men intermingled there,
Burning incense for one who is irresistible.
I would have her eyes on fire with her soul's flame
And its rare traits, though of course not every one.

[298]

Since she cares acutely for her fellow men,
In her heart, warmth has compassion as twin.
Friendship with her is a bond that can't wear thin.
Indeed her mind of heavenly origin,
Called virile, with a charm of which to dream,
Is one for which there is no counterpart.
O Iris, you who master every heart,
Love for you makes other love but esteem—
As deep for you as for one's self, 'twould seem.
(Speaking impersonally, since I have sworn
To curb these strong emotions which you scorn,
Postponing my sketch; but sometime authorize
My Muse to complete this imperfect exercise.)
My short preamble, meant to stand apart,
Is as it were a smile before I start,
In reality but an anecdote
Told with my kind of informality
Which you may like for its simplicity—
Not quite the sort of thing we hear kings quote,
Though you'd repudiate even kings' wit
If unaffectionate. To you he's counterfeit
Who would not die for his friend willingly—
Rare man whose friend's life's dearer than his own.
Now four beasts living affectionately,
Are about to expound a truth we should be shown.

A gazelle, a rat, a crow, and a tortoise
Lived together in peace and had nothing to dread.
By choosing to dwell where they were inconspicuous,
      It was a charming life they led.
Then man, the dastard, must investigate.
      Though miles of desert guard your lair,
      Or ocean depths or upper air,
You'll never escape the hazard of that enemy in wait.
The gazelle sprang about with no thought of the risk she ran,
      Till a dog, joy of man the barbarian,
      Circling ahead where she had been,
Caught the scent of her hoofs upon the grass.
She fled and at dinner was not at her place,
So the rat said to the others, "Help me to explain

[299]

Why only we have come to be fed.
Could the deer forget us so soon, and the life that we have led?"
　　　　　The tortoise replied at once,
　　　　　"I wish I had been there—that my dwarfed legs
　　　　　　　　　　　　　　　　were instead
　　　　　Crow wings affording me the chance
　　　　　To cruise the region at top speed
　　　　　And see if our friend waits to be freed
　　　　　From a snare perhaps, that someone spread—
　　　　　Our friend whose step is so spirited.
Her love for us is too warm to have cooled as you have said."
　　　　　Whereupon the crow set sail
And from a distance discerned the rash gazelle
　　　　　Teased by toils that kept her lying down;
Came back and told the others where she had been thrown;
For there was no point in an explanation
　　　　　Of what had made her pitiable,
Wasting time till chances of rescue had flown.
　　　　　He was no pedantic schoolteaching fool;
　　　　　He had too much good sense for one;
　　　　　So hastened and when he'd told them all,
　　　　　His news was pondered by the three.
　　　　　Then, although two replied immediately
　　　　　That they would speed as the crow flies,
　　　　　To their comrade now a hunter's prize,
The crow said the tortoise must remain; that with her anatomy
And pace, she'd arrive in time for the death of the gazelle.
　　　　　So, sooner than it takes to tell,
The two set off to try to rescue her—
　　　　　The lovable and faithful hind,
　　　　　Their nimble little mountain friend.
　　　　　Obsessed with haste but at the rear,
　　　　　The poor tortoise dotted the scene behind,
Deploring her stunted legs—with justification—
　　　　　And house she must wear to her destination.
　　　　　Nibblegnaw had a name that fitted the person,
　　　　　For he gnawed the snare in two; and picture his
　　　　　　　　　　　　　　　　delight.
The hunter came and stormed, "Robbed of what was my
　　　　　　　　　　　　　　　　right?"

Nibblegnaw saw a hole and was instantly hid,
The crow flew to a tree, and woods screened the gazelle.
      The hunter, by this time half mad,
      At loss of reward he'd thought infallible,
Saw the tortoise, felt mounting anger fade,
      And said, "Should I lose heart? My loss is acute
But I have at hand a substitute,"
And thrust it in his bag—the tortoise, sacrificed for her aid
To the rest, if the crow had not been fleet
      And warned the gazelle who hastened from her
                        retreat,
Feigned injury and was limping in plain sight.
      The man threw down his bag to make him light,
That had held him back; with the result that Nibblegnaw
Cut the knots of the pouch and the tortoise got away.
      He'd rescued two, furthermore,
Both of whom the hunter had planned to devour.

The story is one of Pilpay's which I have remade,
On which with Apollo's leave I could let my fancies run;
Indeed if you desired, it never would be done—
      Like Iliads or Odysseys, I'm afraid.
Nibblegnaw was the hero who dealt the decisive blow,
Although of the four, each was a rescuer.
House-aback-tortoise roused affection in the crow
      To play the part of messenger
After serving as scout—the first role he had played.
The gazelle drew the hunter off, in pursuit of whom he delayed
Till Nibblegnaw could let the tortoise get away;
      So each of the four friends played a part
      And contrived to serve in a special way.
Which deserved the prize? If my word has weight, I would say
                        the heart.

XVI

THE WOODS AND THE WOODMAN

A woodcutter had split or perhaps had mislaid
The ax-handle to which he had fitted the blade.
Replacing it meant that the man was delayed
And the forest was spared from which wood was conveyed.
    A suppliant then, as his manner made plain,
    The man asked the woods to afford him again
    A branch, just one which he would take
    For one more haft which he would make
And he would fell trees in a place farther on,
Permitting oaks and pines to flourish where they'd grown,
Since everyone admired their vast height and fair form.
This was a service the woods did without alarm,
Followed by deep regret, since with his ax helved as before,
    The hard wretch slashed to the core,
    The very trees that had staunched his grief,
    Felling trunks he could barely span
    Although they groaned as their sap ran—
    Martyred to benefit a thief.

Ingrates are typical of our world everywhere—
Downright turncoats against him who made them his care.
I tire of laboring the point. Show me the kindly wood
    That has not known ingratitude
    And could not tell what I'm telling you.
Irony, alas, for one to argue long and hard.
    Ingratitude and violence too,
    Are evils nothing can retard.

XVII

THE FOX, THE WOLF, AND THE HORSE

A fox still fairly young, though one with an old head,
Saw a horse, the very first that he had chanced to see,
And summoned a wolf—an outright fool. "Quick," he said;
  "A marvel is grazing where we played.
He is superb; he threw me in an ecstasy."
—"Stronger than we?" With a scornful laugh the wolf went on,
  "Picture him, if you will, for me."
The fox said, "I'd be delighted to if ever shown
How artists work. I'd portray him willingly for you
  And enjoy your joy in what I'd done.
Come, though. Who knows? Perhaps—one can't be sure—
  Fortune may find for starved stomachs a cure."
They went, and the horse, without curiosity
About such visitors, was cropping the grass steadily
Since loose, and was going to dash from the field
When the fox began, "My lord, your two servants are here
To ask if you would permit your name to be revealed."
Born with some sort of brain in his skull—well concealed—
The horse said, "Read it, sirs, the whole thing is clear
On the underside of my hoof where the shoe has been nailed."
The fox made the excuse that his training was poor
And said to the horse, "Since I had parents with no funds to spare,
I could not go to school and am an unlettered boor,
But the wolf is highborn and can read words anywhere."
  Bemused by what the horse had said,
  The wolf came up. Praise had gone to his head
And cost him four teeth. A shod hoof; jaw thrust too near;
A kicked fool and "I'm off," from the cleverer—
  Who galloped away as the fool bled;
And the fox said, "Brother, he has proved satisfactorily
  A point we admit theoretically—
Steel-engraved it on your jaw conspicuously:
Be on your guard lest novelty mean tragedy."

[303]

XVIII

THE FOX AND THE TURKEYS

Baiting a fox who'd spring in air,
Some turkeys had perched in a tree, their citadel.
The furred foe was trotting up near and circling far,
    Scanning each feathered sentinel;
Then snarled, "How now! I, set at naught by turkeycocks!
Shallow gobblers defy an experienced fox!
Never, by all the gods, no"; and caught them as will appear.
The moon glared so white that his every move was clear;
The birds could see as plainly as if it were noon,
Yet he was used to vigils despite a brilliant moon,
With tricks in his bag to offset any plight.
His forepaws trod air as he made his body light;
He'd feign that death had cut him short, then in a flash would rise;
    Harlequin in each new disguise
    Was not so varied a multitude.
He'd willow out his tail like flame that sinks and flies;
    His effort knew no interlude;
He did so well not a turkey could close its eyes.
As he trotted to and fro, each overweary bird
    Would stare till its scared eyes blurred.
The poor things held to the perch so dizzily
That one by one the flock fell; each was borne from the tree
To Master Fox's lair; he took nearly half of them home,
Indeed, had endless turkeys for his use.

Defeat is a thing which constant fear can induce.
    Beg for trouble and it will come.

XIX

THE APE

Now in Paris there happens to be
An ape for whom folk found a mate.
Aping some husbands known to me,
He beat her, and she, disconsolate,
Poor thing, with beaten bones and broken heart, died in
the end.
Their distraught son would burst out—
Lamenting what no one could mend:
The beater laughed—she was not about—
Some new love having replaced her,
Beaten by him also, we infer,
Since he haunts the tavern and comes home in his cups.

Avoid the imitative mind—anything forced
Done by authors or jackanapes—
Though authors as apes are the worst.

XX

THE SCYTHIAN PHILOSOPHER

Once a philosopher famed for austerity,
Left Scythia that he might taste luxury
And sailed to Greece where he met in his wanderings
A sage like the one Vergil has made memorable—
Who seemed a king or god, remote from mundane things,
Since like the gods he was at peace and all seemed well.
Now a garden enabled his life to expand
And the Scythian found him pruning hook in hand
Lopping here and there what looked unprofitable.
He sundered and slendered, curtailing this and that,
Careful that not a dead twig be spared;
Then for care to excess, Nature paid a sure reward.

[305]

"But are you not inconsiderate?"
The Scythian inquired. He said, "Is it good
To denude a tree of twigs and leave it scarcely one?
Lay down your pruning hook; your onslaught is too rude.
　　　　Permit Time to do what needs to be done:
Dead wood will soon be adrift on the Styx' dark flood."
The sage said, "Remove sere boughs and when they are gone,
　　　　One has benefited what remain."
The Scythian returned to his bleak shore,
Seized his own pruning hook, was at work hour on hour,
Enjoining upon any in the vicinity
　　　　That they work—the whole community.
He sheared off whatever was beautiful,
Indiscriminately trimmed and cut down,
　　　　Persevering in reduction
　　　　Beneath new moons and full
Till none of his trees could bear.

　　　　　　　　In this Scythian
　　　　We have the injudicious man
　　　　Or so-called Stoic, who would restrain
His best emotions along with the depraved—
　　　　Renouncing each innocent thing that he craved.
As for me, such perverted logic is my bane.
Don't smother the fire in my heart which makes life dear;
Do not snuff me out yet. I'm not laid on my bier.

XXI

THE ELEPHANT AND JUPITER'S MONKEY

Once both the elephant and the rhinoceros
Claimed priority when the two would appear,
So resolved to fight the thing out face to face,
And named a certain day; then rumor caught the ear
　　　　That Jupiter's messenger
With his official rod would presently be there—
A monkey known as Will, at least in fairy lore.
　　　　Now the elephant thought an ambassador

Would approach him as a flatterer,
For pride was the animal's snare
And dominated him more and more.
He awaited good Will, who appeared to postpone
The presenting of state documents;
Although before he had gone
He chanced to present his compliments.
The elephant had hoped for words of an official tone,
Whereas the monkey offered none.
The gods had been equable as usual,
In fact had not yet heard about the quarrel.
Why should it disturb anyone
What a fly—or an elephant—had done?
So the elephant himself referred to the duel that loomed
And said, "Cousin Jove will see from his throne any day
A fight between two monsters who have been groomed
For a really terrific display."
—"Combat?" the monkey asked, haughtier than before—
To which the other said, "Sir! You've not heard of my complaint!
The rhinoceros would displace the elephant.
Elephantis and Rhinocera are at war.
You are aware of our realms, known to everyone."
Courtier Will said, "It is in truth rather rare
When Heaven's dome echoes with triviality."
Forced to assume humility,
The shamed beast inquired, "What errand lured you to our
sphere?"
—"Two ants could not part a straw evenly:
We have all things in our care. As for what you've brought
to my ear,
We've not heard that you and a fellow creature were at odds:
Great and small are the same in the eyes of the gods."

XXII

THE FOOL AND THE SAGE

Here a fool stoned a sage. To the boor who was rude
The sage said, "My friend, you have stoned me thoroughly;
For your far too hard work, take a guinea from me;
Though for all that you did I've paid less than I should.
They say that a workman ought to be paid:
Now there goes a man better situated;
Best aim stones at him and be paid perhaps more."
Lured by hope of reward for his bad behavior,
      Our fool stoned the other citizen,
But this time got no gold for the service done.
Armed grooms came running, laid hold of our man,
      Drubbed him, and left him half dead of his pain.

    Kings have about them every sort of fool
    Who can make them laugh at your expense
    But in curbing fools is it desirable
    To cudgel them, if your self-defense
    Is not powerful? Set them on a stranger
    Whose logic is of a sort which will linger.

XXIII

THE ENGLISH FOX

To Madame Harvey

Tender heart, strong good sense, interacting as one,
And countless qualities besides, have been your dower—
Nobility in short, with miraculous power
      Of swaying mankind and getting things done.
You are candid, daring, with the gift of intimacy,
Even though Jove rage and times are tempestuous,
Until thought soars in praise of one so magnanimous

[308]

However you disclaim it all in modesty;
Who dislike display and are irked by eulogy,
So I'm matter-of-fact and brief; but I confess
        I am weaving garlands of friendliness
        For the land of your nativity,
Which you love. The English mind is a thorough one,
Effecting what temperament urges be done,
Pursuing things to their source with tireless diligence,
Till the sciences expand in consequence.
I would say (by no means as a courtier)
That the British have more penetration than the rest;
        As your hound if experts were to compare,
        Has a keener nose than France's best,
Your fox has better brains, a fact now demonstrated
        By one whom danger instigated
        To manage to deserve his name.
He invented a trick, indeed, that had never before been tried.
The rogue had been tracked down, had almost lost the game
To the keen-nosed pack that gave tongue on every side;
        But a gibbet stood there
        From which vermin hung head down—
Badgers, foxes, owls, and such as made blood their fare—
Warning the passerby not to do as they had done
And their colleague, at bay, hung himself with the dead;
As we picture Hannibal cornered by Roman commands,
By generals thrown off the scent—outsmarted by a wiser
                        head—
Till the old fox had managed to slip from their hands.

        Here leaders who had got the clue,
Surrounded the fox as he dangled like an effigy.
They began to bay, but since unpermissibly
The master felt, he silenced the crass ado,
Without suspecting the trick, or what a fool he had been,
And said, "Some nearby den has saved my paladin;
Dogs do not yelp round bones that portend no recompense,
        Like yonder decent citizens.
The scamp will be back afterwhile!" And he was, hapless one,
        While the whole pack bayed in unison
About the gallows from which he had hung himself head down.

[309]

Since the ruse had worked, he had dared to use the same,
Once more, assuming that he would escape the trap:
But this time the fox laid his bones in death's lap.
Take his plight to heart and vary your stratagem!
No hunter would think of a trick quite so good
If he instead of the fox were pursued,
However shrewd he was. When has mentality
Been lacking in any true Englishman?
   Though I do not say that apathy
   May not have betrayed one now and then.

Just a word, not more, for fear you tire
   Of much that I could wish were said.
   Praise labored till one's surfeited
   Is uncongenial to my lyre.
   Seldom that any song or verse
Can flatter a really initiate ear
Or penetrate where foreign tongues are understood.
   You have heard your prince declare
   That one touch of love is better far
   Than fourfold praise in unctuous mood.
Be moved to accept late verses which I dedicate
   To you as my Muse ends her address,
   Although I'm blushing, I confess,
   For words which are inadequate.
   Even so, be pleased to lend your ear
   To the homage I embody here
Of her who's brought to Britain, a deity drawn
   From fair Cythera's hemisphere.
   Our Duchess of Mazarin, let me explain,
Is the goddess of Love to whom I refer.

XXIV

THE JUDGE, THE HOSPITALER, AND THE HERMIT

Zealous to aid mankind, each of the three was a saint
Fired by the same wise aim, marked by the same restraint,
Though each took his own individual course,

For all roads lead to Rome. Each persevered alone
Toward a goal to which many another had gone.
Depressed that lawsuits bled poor folk without remorse
And that among the costs, a judge must be well paid,
One of the saints proposed to obviate such strain
And chose to be a judge yet forgo what he might gain
Since helpless man must keep the laws which he has made
Till half his life is spent in the courts of chancery;
Half, I said? Three-fourths; the remaining quarter too.
So the magistrate resolved to see what he could do
To counteract that phase of heartless hypocrisy;
But the second, who toiled that the ill be made whole,
I admire most of all; ending pain as our goal
Is the merciful work that seems saintliest;
Yet the ill then as now, let no ministrant rest,
Visiting on the man who came to bear them aid,
Sour looks, rash petitions, unending abuse:
"It's only for friends that his efforts are made—
        To us he gives an excuse."
Still, such ingratitude was but a featherweight
Compared with the judge's case. He found as magistrate,
        Every verdict discredited
        Since not one that he hazarded
        Was admittedly equable.
So constant ingratitude's smart sped the arbiter
To the saint at the hospital, keen to confer;
Each worn down by complaints heart can scarcely endure,
Both reduced to renouncing what they had thought good,
Bound they'd bury regret in the depths of the wood.
By a brook where the rocks made retirement secure,
Safe from rushing winds, with verdure overhead,
They found a third saint and asked how best proceed.
He answered, "Seek within, a decision worthy the name—
        In your mind; why that of another man?
Ask yourself and thus take the best course that you can.
I think the Almighty would have it our foremost aim.
Have you found yourself? Not where the world drove you mad;
Only if ever, where quiet was to be had—
Not elsewhere by any species of stratagem.
        Stir the pool: is what you see there you?

[311]

Worry—you cannot think when that is what you do;
   The soul is then a murky place—
Crystalline before troubled by man's ambition.
Dear friends," said the saint, "don't make a commotion
   And then you can recognize your face.
We must each find seclusion when seeking the source,"
   And the hermit ceased. He was terse.
They believed him and took his advice in due course.

Don't infer that I mean that work is a curse.
Laws are an aid; the poor need care; and when our health is bad,
We call physicians in. All need men who know the laws.
Thank God, the world is full of them and always was.
Wealth and honors are things which folk wish that they had,
But bind another's wounds and one has healed his own.
O ministers, judges, and you near the throne,
   Who deal with the world of fact,
You are the hampered whom misfortune has attacked,
However powerful, whom good fortune corrupts.
Though you look at friends, it's as if your eyes were gone.
Then if there is a chance to think and be alone,
   Some flatterer interrupts.

I'd make the lesson plain—or wish I could—
And hope that it may serve year after year
As my gift to kings—to all the wise and good.
   Where better end my work than here?

APPENDIX TO THE FABLES

THE SUN AND THE FROGS [1]

The daughters of the marsh owed the sun, their master,
    Thanks for a home and for all he had done:
War, poverty, and such familiar disaster
Had not cursed the haunts of the batrachian;
So the creatures throve and soon they were everywhere.
These frogs or queens of the swamp, to speak with care
    (For what does it cost to use, when all is said,
    A name that is honorable?)
Now the frogs dared to disparage their only aid
    And had grown detestable.
Rashness, pride, and ingratitude had repaid
    Kindness from their one good friend;
Yet not an hour in which they did not offend!
    No one could sleep for what they said;
        If one trusted every slur,
        They would assuredly
        Have aroused everybody
        Against the sun, their rescuer,
Since they said, "The sun's fire will smite and all be dead
    Unless immediately led
    To humble the omnipotent
    At his least quiver of unrest."
        The deputies' loud chant
        Resounded from the east to the west:
        One would infer from the sound,
        That the world went round
        Anything that a frog said

[1] Louis XIV (the sun) considered that Holland had been liberated by Henry IV and Louis XIII, therefore looked upon the Dutch as ingrates by reason of their cabal against French interests in 1672, the date of this fable.

Whom one of the four swamps bred.
They pestered the air
Hour on hour, though each one
Should have smothered despair
And refrained from contention.
Alas for the poor fools' health
If wrath foments the sun's fire.
The aquatic commonwealth
Will regret its rashness, too late to retire.

THE LEAGUE OF RATS [1]

For years a mouse feared a cat
Who'd lurk in a passage all day when it could.
What foresight would avail? Thinking advice might be good,
The mouse went next door to an eminent rat
Surrounded by luxury
In a haunt of the aristocracy:
'Twas said he had said wherever he'd been,
He'd never dreaded a cat nabob
Teeth, paws, or claws of tom or tab.
The braggart said, "Dear Madam Silverskin,
Now frankly, I confess,
While I could not myself end the cause of your distress,
I shall summon the rats who live near here
And ere long I shall lead your cat by the ear."
The scared mouse curtsied her deference
And the rat called a conference
With all speed, where he chose to hold audience—
The buttery better say,
Which scores of rats traversed, feasting with insouciance.
A-shiver in his dismay,
The fine friend could scarcely make plain what he'd
convey.
"Tell us," one rat besought, "what has happened to you today?"
He said, "This is the cause of my disquietude.

[1] The League (rats), assembled by the Emperor of Austria; the mouse, Holland; Louis (the cat) crossed the Rhine in 1672 and the rats fled.

We must rescue a mouse and immediately;
   For her adversary,
  Raminograb, makes mice his special food.
   When this Beelzebub of cats
Has vanquished the mice, he will turn to the rats."
Each said, "True. Up! To arms. Rush to our friends' defense!"
The sterner got on with the business of the day—
   Buckling armor upon the back,
Thrusting rations of cheese in the haversack,
And then went forth to win or throw their lives away,
   Smiling as though at dainties spread,
   With a tread as gay as valorous.
   The cat more alert meanwhile, than they,
  Already held the mouse by the head.
   The cavaliers were breathless
   To crush their dear friends' enemy
   Till he who could be remorseless,
Marched forth with a growl to meet the embattled enemy.
   Since sagacity, responsive to stress,
   Knew enough not to delay,
The entire league abandoned attempts to aggress
   And prudently slipped away—
   Convinced of a rat-hole's worth.
Any rat who went out, gave Old Rough a wide berth!

DAPHNIS AND ALCIMADURA

IN THE MANNER OF THEOCRITUS

To Madame de la Mesangère [1]

  Charming inheritor
Of the qualities of a mother whom myriads admire,
Yourself besieged by those who but see you to adore,
And others ignited by Love's fire,
  Let me in prefacing this verse,

[1] Madame de la Sablière's daughter, a young widow at the time the fable was written, courted by the Comte de Nocé, whose suit was favored by Madame de la Sablière. Marriage followed in 1690, five years after the fable was published.

Try to share one compliment with two
And dedicate an incense of which Parnassus was the source
Which the secrets of my trade would now distill for you.
   I've much to say and yet aspire
   To say it briefly lest you tire,
   Economizing voice and lyre
Before old age and lack of time have quenched my fire.
I'll not do more than praise your tender-heartedness,
Your exalted thoughts, your charm and your wit,
Since none compare, whatever their advantages,
Except her mind with which your own is interknit.
   Curb thorns which might prick one who'd seek
   His roses, if Love's lips some day
   Should dare to lightly brush your cheek.
   He'll say and better, what I've tried to say—
Also punish those who turn deaf ears and won't obey
   When he commands—as will appear.

   Letting her fancy play,
The fairest of the fair once challenged Love to war.
   Alcimadura's the name she bore.
The proud wild girl held aloof or would dart off to the woods
Or would dance on the green or on meadows in flower,
   And defied any law but her moods.
She pleased herself, and to be sure was beautiful,
   But as hardened as intractable.
The captivating thing, despite her stony air,
Was truly treasure-trove could one have conquered her!
Now Daphnis was highborn and of consummate grace,
But loved her to his hurt. No pretty commonplace,
No glance toward where he fared, no word, not even one,
Since the maiden he would win looked on him with disdain,
   He longed that death might interfere,
   Then hoped that his love might yet appear,
   And inquired for her who gave him pain—
Ignored, alas, as by a hurricane.
   No one indeed came forth to hear,
From the fatal home where the ingrate was decked by friends
Who had gathered to honor her natal day
   As her loveliness lent what beauty may

To treasure the rosebed, arbor, or emerald meadows lend.
The youth cried, "I had hoped to expire before your eyes,
        But as an offender whom you despise,
I need not wonder that you refuse each plea as in the past—
This time to watch me die—my somberest request and last.
Yet at my death my father will do as asked by me,
        And lay at your feet my earthly goods,
        Once viewed unappreciatively.
I have bequeathed you meadows and adjoining woods,
        My sheep and dog, their guardian.
        As for the rest, this shall be done:
        My friends shall rear you a fane
        Where folk may worship now and then,
And substitute for any faded flower, a fragrant one.
Close to the shrine, I shall have them set a stone
        And carve these words along the curve:
"Daphnis died of love for her. Passerby, respect distress
And pause and say, 'A lover was victim here of heartlessness—
        Of Alcimadura who would not swerve.' "
With his last word, he was aware of mortal hurt—
Minded to persevere but death had cut him short.
The ingrate then fared forth in state as was her way;
They begged her linger at least decorously dumb,
And perhaps shed tears for Daphnis' martyrdom.
Venus' child was a fool, she felt, whom she need not obey.
That evening as she derided Cupid and his law
And was dancing with friends about the god's similitude,
The statue fell with a crash and crushed the nymph like straw.

        Whereupon out of a cloud,
These words re-echoed throughout the neighborhood:
"Let all folk revere love; death has subdued the proud."
Meanwhile they saw descending toward the Styx, the astonished
                                        shade
Of Daphnis—a-tremble to be overtaken by her by whom he
                                        had been stirred.
All Erebus was aware as the comely murderess prayed,
Entreating forgiveness of the shepherd, who no more deigned
                                        to have heard,
Than Ajax, Ulysses; or Dido, Aeneas who had not stayed.

[319]

INDEXES

INDEX OF TITLES AND FIRST LINES

(English)

INDEX OF ORIGINAL TITLES AND FIRST LINES

(French)